§§§§
§§§§

ANTHROPOLOGY AND EARLY LAW

ANTHROPOLOGY AND EARLY LAW

EDITED BY LAWRENCE KRADER

SELECTED FROM THE WRITINGS OF

Paul Vinogradoff · *Frederic W. Maitland*

Frederick Pollock · *Maxime Kovalevsky*

Rudolf Huebner · *Frederic Seebohm*

BASIC BOOKS, INC. · New York, London

CONTENTS

Introduction   3
    Lawrence Krader

§§ **PART I LAW AND CUSTOM**
§§
1. Custom and Law   19
    Paul Vinogradoff

2. The Old English Customary Laws   31
    Frederick Pollock

§§ **PART II KINSHIP AND LAW**
§§
3. The Organization of Kinship   57
    Paul Vinogradoff

4. The Cymric Evidence   75
    Frederic Seebohm

5. Beowulf   100
    Frederic Seebohm

§§ **PART III LAW OF HOUSEHOLD AND**
§§ **FAMILY**
6. The Joint Family   117
    Paul Vinogradoff

7. Germanic Law of the Family and Marriage   129
    Rudolf Huebner

8. The Modern Russian Family   148
    Maxime Kovalevsky

v

§§
§§ **PART IV   SUCCESSION, INHERITANCE, AND DESCENT**

9.   Inheritance and Descent   173

Frederick Pollock and Frederic W. Maitland

§§
§§ **PART V   LAW, PERSON, AND CORPORATION**

10.   Man, Right, and Association   237

Rudolf Huebner

11.   Corporation and Person   300

Frederick Pollock and Frederic W. Maitland

Biographical Notes   337
Index   339

§§§§
§§§§

ANTHROPOLOGY AND EARLY LAW

INTRODUCTION

Lawrence Krader

The Relations of Anthropology and Law in Historical Jurisprudence

During the nineteenth century a field of study was developed in England which has maintained a powerful presence in both anthropology and the law. This is historical jurisprudence, which traces current practices and institutions of the law back to their antecedents in bygone eras.

The students of this field at the end of the nineteenth century in England include, in the first instance, Frederic W. Maitland, Paul Vinogradoff, and Frederick Pollock, and certain of their colleagues on the European continent, such as Rudolf Huebner. Their intellectual forebear was Henry Maine, who gave their field of research its direction and method. However, Maitland, Vinogradoff, and Pollock followed Maine not blindly, but selectively and critically, and this was true of their attitude among themselves. Selections from their writings and Huebner's, together with those of Frederic Seebohm and Maxime Kovalevsky, their contemporaries of similar bent, have been combined in this book. These writers cannot properly be called a school, although they were united by their subject matter and their way of approaching it. They were divided by their more general aims and by their mental set—particularly in their critical ability. Maitland and Vinogradoff are notable for the high degree of their critical faculty, Seebohm and Kovalevsky less so. They enriched the fields of anthropology and law, while at the same time they were creatures of their era. This is not a bad thing, however, for many of their problems were valid ones even though interest in some of them is lessened today, particularly in regard to the historical unity of European culture and its institutions. This unity provided the frame for their studies, and they were able to affirm it through the law; their conclusions have generally stood up very well.

Anthropologists should read Maitland, Vinogradoff, and their colleagues because the law is a part of society. These legal historians made sound analyses of social problems, and hence they are valuable as methodologists. They contribute good accounts of societies, and of social institutions, and hence are valuable as ethnographers. They illuminate the history of anthropology and of the law, and many concepts and terms, such as agnation, cognation, corporation, were early shared between comparative jurisprudence and social anthropology; here are their primary usages. The number of terms which have been used in many circles with varying denotations were fixed in their legal and anthropological meanings by these writers. Their contributions have influenced anthropological terminology in such matters as patriarchy and matriarchy, and they were influenced in turn by anthropological usages of that time.[1]

The purpose of their approach to jurisprudence was to account for social development by understanding the origins, similarities, and differences in legal development; their method directly relates the study of the law to the study of society, and further to the history of both. This was assured partly by the recognition, usually implicit, particularly in comparative jurisprudence, that the law is but one set of rules in a given society among many other sets of rules by which men arrange their affairs. We will return to this thought.[2]

The historical study of the law opposes the idea that the law is a self-contained system which proceeds analytically—that is, by perfecting its own internal devices—and independently of the society around it.[3] It must be recognized that full-time professionalism in the law of Western society has indeed created its own spirit. In consequence, rules governing the behavior of professionals, and those who come in contact with them, are to a high degree self-generating and self-regulating. Law men are jealous of their status as masters of their field and reject the impulsive and nonprofessional actions of strangers to their field. This view is shared with that of professionals in general and is one of the defining attributes of professionalism. But those who have studied the law as a historical tradition have shown that it developed out of a past when the law was not practiced by professionals trained for that purpose, and when the law rules were enmeshed in all kinds of other rules, such as moral and religious rules, or work rules. But the work of the law got done. Further, even in the simplest and least professionalized legal systems, determinations of precedents, that is, of the relevance and force of past legal practices, are essayed, judgments are made within the limits of these determinations, and practices to organize action on these judgments are handed down. Moreover, the judges themselves are judged and their practices accepted, amended, or rejected.

We will not attempt a complete definition of the law, but we can propose a set of common denominators on this subject: (1) The law is identifiable as such in all societies. (2) Certain legal tasks are shared by societies with and without professionals in the law. (a) In both kinds of societies the law has procedures for determining, on the submission of an individual who claims he has suffered a wrong, whether a wrong has in fact been committed, whether it can be righted, and by what means. (b) The law everywhere contains procedures for resolving social disputes. (c) The law contains means of determining whether the society at large should take an interest in trouble cases or whether these are of interest only to the individuals concerned, their immediate kin, neighbors, colleagues, and friends. (We will have occasion in the chapters which follow to consider whether a murder is a public affair, that is, the concern of the society at large through its duly constituted authorities, or a private affair.) (d) Among all peoples the law includes procedures for its own internal regulation and administration. Even in cases of nonliterate and nonprofessional law, there is the notion of rules of evidence, for example, a means of determining whether a piece of evidence is valid and has been validated in a given instance.

The Study of Legal Institutions of the Indo-European Speaking Peoples

These common denominators of the law are to be found at work in past ages of European history. The specialists in early European law show the workings of the law in Western society before the day of professionalism and specialism. We will see from their writings that the law rules, both in substance and procedure (the rules governing the application of their substance), were only later unraveled and organized in a separate social institution which administered them. Thus men of law acted just as, for instance, priests in their churches and master-craftsmen in their guilds, in administering their profession in its relations to the laity, and the internal rules whereby they were governed in relation to themselves. The process of unraveling was not easy, because the scope of the law (and of the church) had the entire society as its province; the guilds and other medieval corporations were limited to running their own affairs. The law later came to reflect this double standard: in its substance it covers (like the church) many aspects of the entire society, while in its rules of internal self-government it tends to act like a closed corporation, much as the guilds. It was the historical students of the law who first became aware, and who in turn made the other scholarly professionals aware, of this earlier state of things. However, the relations between rules of law, morals, work, etc., while now separated in professional practice, are just as close, and the respective fields as mutually dependent, as before. One of the principal contributions of anthropology and of historical jurisprudence has been to show how the different institutions of society, that is, the law, family, economy, religion, etc., are interrelated, how they shape and determine each other, whether professionally organized or not.

The comparative study of culture was jointly worked out in the nineteenth century by specialists in jurisprudence and anthropology, to their common profit. Comparative and historical jurisprudence, as investigated by the authors of this book, dealt with a genetically related body of cultures, the Indo-European, which gave unity to their findings and methods. This approach contrasted with comparative legal studies elsewhere, such as those of A. H. Post and Joseph Kohler, who gathered comparisons of the law of any and all societies. Maitland, Vinogradoff, and their colleagues came closer to dealing with unities of culture and of cultural history, and hence closer to the canon of culture as developed in anthropology, than did Post or Kohler. Studying a civilization as a whole provides the only valid cultural and historical context for a particular observation. This is a central factor in controlling the meaning of the observed fact or datum. It has been established since the beginning of the nineteenth century (although not at once) that the Greek, Latin and Romance, Armenian, Germanic, Celtic, Slavic, Albanian, Baltic, Iranic, Sanskrit and Indic languages and language groups are related by common origin, however their subsequent relationships has become obscured. The proposed linguistic unity on genetic grounds raises the question of a unity of culture among these peoples, which the students of comparative law explored in their own way. Thus, if the Latin and Sanskrit languages are eventually related, then the ancient Roman Law of the Twelve Tables and Sanskrit Laws of Manu should be explored for possible relationship. In addition to specific legal institutions there are other, related social issues to be explored. The customary practices of farmers of different nations in regulating fields and pastures, practices which may be of considerable antiquity, can possibly be shown to have a common origin. So can practices regarding marriage arrangements, descent, and inheritance—the area of utmost conservatism in the law today; here canon or church-derived law is still influential, even in atheist, agnostic, or free-thinking communities. These are common subjects of anthropology and the law.

Maine's field was the Indo-European legal and speech community as a whole, while his followers cut out for study this or that folk-legal tradition within it: Celtic, Germanic-Saxon, Roman, Slavic, etc. They were mainly concerned with giving depth and breadth to their own legal traditions. The generation after Maine—that is, Maitland, Vinogradoff, Pollock, Seebohm —were inclined to let go the study of Orientalism, in this case the Hindu and Sanskrit traditions. They focused their attention on the Roman, Celtic, and Germanic roots of English law and culture, and in the course of doing so they studied the economy and society of ancient and medieval European cultures as well as their laws.

Their effort was parallel to that of James Frazer, who was, if we want to insist on denominative appellations, more properly an anthropologist, studying as he did in his *Golden Bough* the primitive among us. Modern Western civilization, according to this notion, has its roots in ancient barbarism, and he traced the folkways of Europe, reaching back to the eras prior to Christianism and literacy. He came upon customs alive in his day, and even today, whose history is vast and long; he touched the theme of the unity and continuity of European culture. And so did Vinogradoff, Maitland, and the others in their way.

The Custom, Folk, and Law

The law, in historical and comparative jurisprudence, derives from custom, which is the life of the folk. Maine, Maitland, and Vinogradoff advocated research into what the people say and do about conflicts between neighbors over boundaries, between brothers over an inheritance, between parties over terms of an agreement or contract and its fulfillment, or between judge and accused in a criminal case over what constitutes valid evidence.

The great name in historical and comparative jurisprudence at the beginning of the nineteenth century is F. C. von Savigny in Germany, who wrote on Roman law in the Middle Ages, and who further studied international private law and right of ownership, always in the context of their historical antecedents. As Vinogradoff put it, Savigny, Maine, and their spiritual descendants reacted against the radical rationalism of the French Revolution and the Napoleonic period. Their interest in the study of archaic custom, however, was not romantic but shared with the Romantic movement of that period a conviction that that which is of the folk is right. However, unlike most of the poetic Romantics, such as Wordsworth, Byron, and Shelley in England, or Pushkin in Russia, who were liberal and even radical in their political convictions, Savigny and Maine were politically conservative, each in his epoch and country. The law, they argued, is determined by historical antecedents and by rational psychology.

Vinogradoff himself, far from being a conservative, protested against the tsarist regime in the 1870's and 1880's and had to transplant himself to England. There is no evidence that Maitland shared Vinogradoff's views on political change, but he was sympathetic to the man, and so was Maitland's brother-in-law, H. A. L. Fischer, historian and philosopher. These men shared another stand of thought with anthropologists of their era. Maine in particular was convinced of the evolutionary process in culture. The law proceeded from personal judgments and commands based upon personal status to contract—that is, to stages in which customary rules were fixed and codified more objectively and impersonally. These views were shared by Seebohm and Kovalevsky. However, Maitland did not agree with the doctrine that all humanity followed a single line of cultural evolution. According to a view popular in his time, property right evolved from collective to individual, and mankind in general from collectivity to individuality. Maitland argued that the earliest forms of property (as far as he had come upon them in his studies) were individual and not collective.

Otto Gierke is another writer whose work provided a foundation for the English group. Gierke had this in common with Maine, that he sought the historical base for modern institutions. He brought out the relationship of the medieval association to the modern corporation.[4]

The postulates shared by Maine and those who appear in this book were these: (1) The law has evolved from implicit and loose rules to explicit and fixed rules. (2) The law derives from folk custom and is not the invention of men of the law. (3) The law is embedded in society and is a means to understanding the society in which it is found. (4) The study of society is a means to understanding the law of the society.

Anthropology and Early Law

The term "early law" as used here corresponds to the principal area of research of Maitland, Vinogradoff, and the others, who dealt primarily with the law and society of ancient and medieval times in European civilization, when cultures were not too different from the subject of ethnology of that time. The law was in the early time closely related to folk legal custom. Maitland and the other writers argue from the premise that, as societies evolved, their law became an ever more specialized instrument in the hands of ever more specialized legal persons.

Law and Anthropology

Looking beyond the men whose writings are gathered in these pages, no one is more closely concerned with the theme of this book than Emile Durkheim. For him the law had a special place in the study of society. He was concerned in his *Division of Labor in Society* with how societies are maintained and perpetuate themselves: that is, with social solidarity, its sources and meaning. There are, moreover, different kinds of social solidarity, simple and complex. For the classification of the different societies according to this schema, a visible symbol is needed. Such a symbol is the law: not laws of society as formulated by social scientists, but as juridical rules and legislation. The law is nothing else, wrote Durkheim, than the organization of social life; it has stability and precision in a greater degree than is found in those aspects of social life where the law in its technical sense does not obtain and is not found. All essential varieties of social solidarity are reflected in the law. But social relations are also regulated by custom, albeit, to be sure, not with such great precision. Moreover, custom is not always in accord with the law, particularly as to the rigor of application of the law. Nevertheless, Durkheim regarded custom normally to be the basis of the law. But, he went on, the law has precision, importance, and continuity, thus differing from social relations deriving from custom, which conveys but diffuse regulations, lacking in importance and continuity. He concluded that in the law, *sensu stricto,* are produced those types of social solidarity which are essential; they are the only ones we need to know in regard to the regulation of social solidarity.

The function of the law in the strict sense as the regulating element in social solidarity was overstated by Durkheim. On the contrary, the self-governing associations, including religious orders and guilds, do not form part of the legal system but have nevertheless made essential contributions to social solidarity. In historical fact they have made possible greater legal precision. Together all these regulating sets, plus others, form the body of rules governing and perpetuating the solidarity of society. But if the law is equated with all these rules, then we are merely saying that regulations produce regulations which are essential. This is true but circular, and adds little to our understanding of the forces of social solidarity. Durkheim's statements should be modified, for there are areas of social relations outside the law which have precision, importance, and continuity.

A. R. Radcliffe-Brown, a modern British social anthropologist, regarded the law as a form of organized social sanction, which operates to effect social control. He followed Durkheim in the theoretical view of organized social sanctions, including the law, as developments out of diffuse social sanctions, the latter being nonspecific and hence difficult to classify.[5] Radcliffe-Brown held that the field of the law is identical with organized legal sanctions, and further that certain simpler societies are without law. The behavior which the law elsewhere covers is covered in the less complex societies by custom and convention. Further, he proposed that law, custom, and convention are all supported by social sanctions. The position which he adopted is not contradicted by the view expounded in this book. Our present concern is with behavior shared by professionals in Western law and those who act in an identifiably similar manner as nonprofessionals in other social contexts, and not with legal institutions as such.[6] The idea of a universal type of legal behavior system is at the same time sympathetic with the approach of historical jurisprudence, and is contrasted with that of the analytic school by Radcliffe-Brown and by us.

Vinogradoff and Huebner, whose work the former introduced in its English translation, directly related law and custom, as did Maitland and Pollock. In the matter of theory, Huebner's contribution is of the greatest importance to the law, anthropology, to social science generally, and to the philosophy of man (see Chapter 7). Huebner shows that the ancient Germanic family did not accept a newborn infant directly into its membership. It had to be formally accepted in a ritual act. As a result of this acceptance ritual, which could also be denied the infant, it received a status, that of a human being; it was not disregarded and left to die without further ado, a fate accorded to infrahuman things, without identity, which the society did not identify and with which humanity had no identification. Further, the infant was by right, and at the moment of ritual acceptance, potentially a person and actually on the way to becoming one. The ideas of status, identity, right, and person are central to all current discussion of human affairs. While they were not given definitive treatment in Huebner, nevertheless the materials he gathered are germane and useful to us today.

It lies outside the scope of this book to demonstrate how, in the view of some legal thinkers, social analysis may be applied in the law (the Americans W. N. Hohfeld and Roscoe Pound were leaders of this movement). The study of actual cases may suggest other modes of relating law and society.

The Book and the Writers

Our plan is to divide the work into five parts. In each part, whole chapters or essays from the authors cited have been included. Only Pollock's and Maitland's *History of English Law* and Huebner's *History of German Law* have been excerpted (at length) because of special problems in their presentation; these writers did not develop whole subjects as unities in themselves but presented them through their respective books on the historical development of the law. If Vinogradoff dominates, and has the preponderance in total number of pages in the book, it is no less than his due, for his eminence in the joint field of anthropology and early law should be recognized.

We have said the men whose writings are collected here did not constitute a school of thought. Nevertheless, they had much in common, enough to suggest a unity of subject, its development, and their approach to it. Aside from the dialectic of their accord and disagreement as a normal activity among scholars, they are bound by time and space: the last half of the nineteenth century and beginning of the twentieth in England. At least this is true of Maitland, Pollock, Seebohm, and Vinogradoff. To this group we have added Huebner and Kovalevsky because their work was directly relevant to that of the first four, in fact made so by the activity of Maitland and the others.

Maine belonged to the preceding generation, in the middle of the last century. He brought Kovalevsky to Oxford to deliver the Ilchester lectures on Russian peasant customs. The text of those lectures, one of which is included in this book, was dedicated to Maine. Pollock and Vinogradoff carried on at Oxford the teaching of comparative and historical jurisprudence which Maine had introduced. It was Maitland who provided the central link in the next generation. He was instrumental in bringing Vinogradoff to England. He joined his name with that of Pollock in bringing out the *History of English Law;* at the same time, it must be noted, that the book was fundamentally Maitland's.

Seebohm expresses in many of his publications his debt to Maine, Maitland, and Vinogradoff; and the latter, particularly Vinogradoff, although rating but moderately the sum total of his contribution, in turn express their debt to his research. Although Seebohm was not a fully committed professional in these matters, nevertheless he has a high mark for his research and not a modest one, for it is both significant and to the point, although he is uncritical in his use of sources and in the conclusions he draws from them.

These writers chiefly conceived of society in the restricted sense of a body of legal, social, economic, political, and ecclesiastic institutions and their activity in the social processes of legislation, contractual agreement, and above all of acquisition, holding, and alienation of real property. More rarely did they relate these institutions and processes to broader concerns and trends of the cultures they studied: freedom, communalism, individuation, socialism (although Maitland had written on freedom as a philosophico-literary subject[7]); least of all did they attempt to relate these matters to technical and material culture.

Seebohm sided with Fustel de Coulanges,[8] in reaction against the Germanists (in the terminology then current) such as G. L. von Maurer,[9] who saw in the ancient Germans' customs the sources of freedom and democracy. The so-called Germanist school had its source in the idealization of an earlier epoch. Fustel for his part came under the criticism of Durkheim; the latter opposed the theory of social development by imposition from above and from without the culture, which he saw partly in Fustel and partly in those associated with his view. The specific issue was that of Roman-Mediterranean influence on the rise of civilization in northern Europe as opposed to development from within, together with the relative merits of the different stages of civilization in the different epochs in both geographic areas. We cannot pursue this point but can only indicate that it was a controversial (and not fruitful) issue of a bygone period to which Vinogradoff and his colleagues also related. Comparative jurisprudence is a soft view of the law, for several reasons. (1) It is a scholarly approach, removed from the harsh realities of daily practice, in which are involved the wrongs, the sufferings, the injustice and justice of real, living people: comparative jurisprudence necessarily involves a long view of human affairs. (2) The scholars represented in the present collection concerned themselves with societies of the past—which reinforces the first point. (3) Just as important as the first two points, their common approach dealt with the substance of the law of societies which were not highly professionalized, in which the men of the law were not distant from the rest of society, or yet fully formed into a professional, and in this sense corporate, body, with conscious adherence, rules of self-perpetuation, rules of membership, etc. They stood outside and even opposed to the law as a fixed body of rules, to men of law as a fixed body, and to the law as a hard school, for they were aware of a time and state when it was not. The study of comparative jurisprudence is a humane discipline and joins with a part of anthropology in this common domain.

NOTES

[1] Matriarchy and patriarchy had been discussed by earlier anthropologists who came to this field from the law, among them J. F. McLennan (*Primitive Marriage*, Edinburgh, 1865; see also his *Studies in Ancient History*, Vols. I and II, 1876) and J. J. Bachofen (*Das Mutterrecht*, Stuttgart, 1861). These terms are often loosely applied but, in brief, both designate forms of authority within the family, and possibly, but not necessarily, within other social institutions such as the village or the tribe. They are not, however, forms of family, village, or tribal organization. Both McLennan and Bachofen were simple evolutionists; their use of sources of information was naïve, even for its day. They are not of interest to the present work because there is very little of the law as such to be found in their writings. Finally, they lacked the control of their material which is to be gained only by reference to its context.

Bachofen distinguished between the family and the form of authority which it comprised. However, he went further and considered that the family was founded on father-right (patriarchate) or mother-right (matriarchate); moreover, the entire culture is borne upon this or that form of family rule, from which it takes its characteristic form. Finally, he maintained the matriarchate is the beginning of all development, out of which a higher spiritual order later, the patriarchate, emerges. Savigny's influence on Bachofen is evident in Bachofen's interest in the folk and in cultural development.

[2] E. A. Hoebel in his *Primitive Law* (Cambridge, Mass.: Harvard University Press, 1954), p. 15, proposes the following: "Substantively, law consists of a specially demarked set of social norms that are maintained through the application of 'legal' sanctions. The entire operating system of sanctioning norms is what constitutes a system of social control. Law as a process is an aspect of the total system of social control. . . ."

[3] H. L. A. Hart in his introduction to John Austin's *The Province of Jurisprudence Determined* (New York: Noonday Press, 1954) raises two questions in connection with the analytical formalist approach to the law. The first is whether it is a defining characteristic of a *legal system* that it should provide for sanctions. The second question is whether, apart from the necessity of a provision for sanctions, it is possible to define (*n.b.: not* derive) the notion of a *legal system purely in terms of structure,* and so without reference to any specific human need which the system must attempt to satisfy! The first italics in the citation are Professor Hart's, the second are mine. The point is not whether anyone has actually adopted the viewpoint that the law is a self-contained system. Austin, a legal thinker of the early nineteenth century in England, was moving in this direction. But the view noted above is not Austin's; it is Hart's reformulation, which carried Austin's view a bit further, in order to express it in its most daring and purest way. This view of the law, then, is counterposed to the view of the students of historical and comparative jurisprudence.

Put another way, the relation between the nature and the sources of the law is at issue. It is the nature of the law to provide rules of a certain kind for human relations of a certain kind. The historical approach to the law traces these rules back to their antecedents, which become the source of the law, or at least one of its principal sources. The analytical school, as Hart indicated, derives (*n.b.: not* defines) the law from its contemporary functions; that is, given the nature of human nature and its needs, the legal system answers (some of) them: needs such as the security of the person from violence, or exclusive possession of one's private goods.

The law, wrote Hart, has been dominated by the Austinian view, not the historical approach. Society as an internal factor influencing the development of the law has since then entered another way: by the Supreme Court reading the election returns; by judges and other court officers recognizing how economic deprivation and cultural deprivation generally influence delinquency and crime.

⁴ Otto Gierke, *Das deutsche Genossenschaftsrecht* (*German Law of Association*), 1868–81. His work was translated in part, with a critical introduction and notes, by Maitland, who published his excerpt, *Political Theories of the Middle Age*, in 1900. Ernest Barker, English political philosopher, whose work is not unrelated to that of Maitland, edited and translated with an introduction and critical apparatus another part of Gierke under the title *Natural Law and the Theory of Society*, 1934. The period covered in Barker's translated excerpt is 1500–1800.

⁵ A. R. Radcliffe-Brown, "Primitive Law" and "Social Sanction," *Encyclopaedia of the Social Sciences* (New York: Macmillan, 1933), Vols. IX and XIII. Reprinted in his *Structure and Function in Primitive Society* (London: Cohen and West, 1952).

⁶ On the difference between legal institutions and legal behavior see also K. N. Llewellyn and E. A. Hoebel, *The Cheyenne Way: Conflict and Case Law in Primitive Jurisprudence* (Norman, Okla.: University of Oklahoma Press, 1941).

⁷ H. E. Bell, *Maitland: A Critical Examination and Assessment* (London: Adam and Charles Black, 1965), is a sympathetic life of the man and an acute review of his work. He is shown to rank among those historians and legal scholars in England whose contributions have been of the highest order of competence and brilliance.

⁸ N. D. Fustel de Coulanges, French medieval and classical historian of the nineteenth century. See his *The Ancient City*, tr. W. Small (Boston, 1901); also his *Origin of Property in Land*, tr. M. Ashley (London, 1892).

⁹ G. L. von Maurer, German historian and statesman of the nineteenth century. See his *Geschichte der Dorfverfassung in Deutschland* (*History of Village Constitution in Germany*), 2 vols., 1865–66; also his *Geschichte der Fronhöfe, der Bauernhöfe und der Hofverfassung in Deutschland* (*History of Corvée Farming, Peasant Farming and Farm Constitution in Germany*), 4 vols., 1862–63.

Part I

Law and Custom

Chapter I is a selection from the writings of Paul Vinogradoff, whose argument for the customary source of law serves
as the best guide to our theme. According to Vinogradoff, law,
legislation, explicit rules of society and the state all originate in
custom. They are not imposed—better, ought not be imposed—
from above, but rise from below, from the society which comes
to recognize them. Laws as entered in the books then are related
to the customs of the people, but somewhat changed in legislation,
such that the people come to recognize their legal reformulation.
The process of restating custom as law is universal; it is found in
primitive tribes as well as in states whose legislative institutions
are explicitly established.

The society of Vinogradoff's closest concern was the English,
whose past was relevant to its then contemporary (late nineteenth,
early twentieth century) laws. Thus Vinogradoff studied the law
and society of ancient Rome, of the medieval Celtic ancestors of
the Gaels and Welsh, and of the medieval Saxons. Moreover, he
examined Roman law in terms of its popular roots, and for the
same reasons. Vinogradoff not only related the law and anthropology of his day but went a step further. He left excellent records
of early societies which should become a part of anthropological
literature.

Frederick Pollock, in treating customary law, calls attention
to a matter of interest to modern anthropology, particularly to

students of folk and peasant societies and communities: the traditional land laws of England. He divides land into four categories: folk-land, that which was held by the nation or folks as a whole; common land, held by a community; family or individual holdings; and book-land, that which was held subject to a piece of writing, a legal instrument, or book. Much of his commentary is just, but Vinogradoff has pointed out that folk-land did not comprise land held in common by the entire folk, but land that was subject to folk right, as opposed to book-land, which was subject to law as derived but already separated from folk right.*

This consideration, however, does not destroy Pollock's fourfold classification of land. Book-land and folk-land are indeed defined according to the basis in right for determining a holding. The remaining two categories of land are defined in terms of the nature of the holdings and of the landholders. Thus common land is held as communal and the family land as family or individual property.

In the notes Pollock appended to the chapter, which are not included in this selection, he discusses practices of communal land management among ancient Germans. He points out that the society was already stratified . . . or, as Tacitus put it, separated into ranks of varying dignities, when this system was in force. Nevertheless, each community acted in concert, dividing the entire land of the township and making periodic allotments and reallotments, giving more to those of higher rank, less to those of lower. Thus, within the village commune, and according to communal action, those of higher rank were held in richer and those of lower rank in relatively poorer condition. In this commune, rank and wealth were closely linked together.

L. K.

---

* Vinogradoff, *Collected Papers,* Vol. I (London: Oxford, 1928), *Folkland,* pp. 91–111.

§§ 1

CUSTOM AND LAW

Paul Vinogradoff

We are accustomed nowadays to the enactment of laws by the State; and we regard legislation—the deliberate elaboration of legal rules—as one of the principal functions of the State. It does not, however, require much learning in order to perceive that such conscious and direct legislation is of comparatively recent growth; it is the attribute of a definitely organized State, the result of a fairly advanced political civilization. In rudimentary unions, in so-called barbaric tribes, even in feudal societies, rules of conduct are usually established, not by direct and general commands, but by the gradual consolidation of opinions and habits. The historical development of law starts with custom. Rules are not imposed from above by legislative authorities but rise from below, from the society which comes to recognize them. The best opportunities for observing the formation and application of custom are presented when primitive societies are living their life before the eyes and under the control of more advanced nations, as, e.g., in British India, or among the tribes of the Indonesian Archipelago ruled by the Dutch. Some of the heterogeneous population of the Roman Empire were in a similar condition, and the same may be said of most of the peoples of Mediaeval Europe confronted

From Paul Vinogradoff, *Custom and Right* (Oslo: Instituttet för Sammenlignende Kulturforskning, 1925), Ch. 2.

by the Universal Church which had inherited the remnants of antique civilization. This latter case, that of the European barbarians, is especially interesting for us because it reflects the origins of legal institutions of our own society.

The Jurisconsults of Imperial Rome, bent on formulating a coherent doctrine of legal obligation, derived customary rules (*consuetudines*) from the same source as laws (*leges*), namely from the will of the people; Salvius Julianus taught that in the case of law such will was said to be manifested by express consent to an enactment, while custom was established by tacit consent as implied by the facts of actual usage. We need not attach too much importance to the theoretical assumption that the will of the people is the ultimate source of law in all its forms. What is really significant is the stress laid on habits (*mores*) as the psychological explanation of customary law. The reference to *mores* is a recurrent one in the language of Roman writers, Varro, Cicero, Quintilian. We come across it even in technical terms: we hear of a *deductio quae moribus fit* in the case of formal eviction conducted by agreement between the parties in a dispute as to land. The main points are the unofficial formation of such a rule of conduct, its recurrent manifestation by concrete facts, and its explanation by a moral submission of the mind. The doctrine was meant, evidently, to apply to Roman citizens in general, but it was particularly adapted to the juridical life of the autonomous communities included in the Empire: its practical significance was felt chiefly in the acceptance by Roman authorities of peculiar rules of local origin. Mitteis' great work on *Reichsrecht und Volksrecht* contains ample materials for the study of this form of juridical life in the Eastern provinces of the Empire. The practice of the tribunals which had to apply the law had obviously great importance in the recognition of custom, and a saying of Ulpian calls attention to the part played by judicial decisions in disputed cases for the continuance of custom. If it is admitted that custom stands by the side of enacted law, the question arises as to the relative value of the two sources. A rescript of Constantine addressed to a Governor of Africa lays down the requirement that custom should not be in contradiction with law or with reason. The superiority of law over custom was insisted upon in order to enable the representatives of Imperial unity in the province to overrule, if necessary, popular customs. This does not militate against the acceptance of provincial or local divergences of a kind which did not move the central authority to assert its superior power.

As for reasonableness, the notion is a wide one and could be used for different purposes by those who controlled the administration of justice in the provinces. The *ratio*—the leading idea of a particular institution—lease or sale, for example—may be meant; or the general principles prevailing in Roman law—e.g. the decisive role assigned to free consent in transactions; or the reasonableness of plain common sense as against eccentric or unfair solutions. The glossators used to cite as an example of the latter variety the rule obtaining in Bologna, according to which a carrier was not responsible for any mishap that might have befallen a cask of wine or a bale of goods consigned to his care, if the owner of the merchandise touched the load with his hand. This customary rule must have been suggested by the wish to draw a clear line between the liabilities of the owner and of the carrier by forbidding the former even to lay a finger on the load once the carrier had taken charge of it. Yet by some commentators the rule was deemed preposterous and unreasonable.

The test of unreasonableness could only be made effective by the intervention of superior authority, and it is evidently in view of such intervention by way of judicial decision that Constantine had mentioned it in his rescript to a provincial governor. In an earlier case Septimus Severus and Caracalla permitted the inhabitants of a town on the Dniestr (Akerman) to let a bad custom stand in respect of former applications of it, but not to allow any recurrence of it in the future.

Similar problems presented themselves to the hierarchy of Western Christendom in the period when a compact body of Canon Law grew up as a result of the action of Councils and Popes. What position was to be assigned to the national and regional customs obtaining in the various countries in distinction from the legal rules decreed by legitimate authority for the Catholic Church? A considerable latitude was conceded to old-established customs of ecclesiastical institutions—bishoprics, chapters, monasteries—and also to special views of the laity as to limits of secular and ecclesiastical jurisdictions, in cases of

investitures, intestate succession, marriage, legitimacy, etc. At
the same time the supreme authority of the Roman curia had to
be maintained in fundamental questions. The history of the
relations between temporal and spiritual power is full of incidents
arising from these conflicting tendencies, and it is not my object
to review these dramatic struggles. I must, however, call attention
to one or two characteristic facts drawn from the literary developments which accompanied such disputes in practice. It is hardly
accidental that the first great codifier of Canon Law, Gratian,
writing at a critical moment in the history of the struggle of the
Papacy for power, went back to the doctrine laid down in Constantine's rescript, and, while assigning considerable importance
to ancient custom, laid stress on the superiority of law as stated
and confirmed by Papal authority. It is also well worthy of notice
that in the XIII century, which may be called the century of the
triumphant ascendancy of the Church, the Popes relaxed, as it
were, the strict discipline of juridical unity and allowed a wider
margin to customs, primarily, of course, provincial and local
customs. One of the Decretals of Gregory IX proclaims the
validity of custom even when derogatory of the law, when the
former is established by ancient practice and is not contrary to
reason. Boniface VIII's Decretal *In Sexto* is particularly explicit;
it refers pointedly to the fact that although the Pope bears all
the general precepts of law *scrinio pectoris sui,* he is not necessarily cognizant of local peculiarities and must be supposed to have
conceded all customs which he has not expressly forbidden. It is
evident that the wisdom of the Roman Curia prevented it from
embarking on a dangerous campaign against provincial peculiarities, as this would have brought it into unnecessary and un-
profitable conflicts with national and local traditions. The
Decretals of Gregory IX were contemporary with the famous
revolts of the English magnates against the introduction of the
Canon Law rule as to legitimation by subsequent marriage.

Although this problem of the relation between law and custom
occupies most space and attracts most attention in the writings
of the Canonists and Legists, the positive conditions which call
customary rules into existence are also beginning to be defined
and discussed. The conception is gaining ground that the binding
force of custom has to be derived from popular conviction that

matters—say, succession or contract—should be treated in a certain way. This is the root of the requirement as to *opinio necessitatis*. The submission to the customary rule in a concrete case, for example as to the equal partition of chattels among the children of the deceased, or the attribution of some particular goods, e.g. trinkets, to certain persons, such as daughters, is the result of the previous opinion of the persons concerned, as members of a group, that this is equitable and right. If such a common opinion does not exist, there can be no valid customary rule.

The requirements of long usage and of reasonableness were maintained and further developed by Canonists. The former were not understood in the sense of practices established at a time of which memory does not run, but rather treated in connection with rules of prescription: the terms of ten and twenty years are often referred to. More interesting is the interpretation given to the requirement of reasonableness. The prevailing idea was suggested by the teaching on the law of nature, as formulated e.g. by Thomas Aquinas. This law has its roots in reason, and is implanted by God in human beings to serve as guidance in their conduct. It is the highest manifestation of law in the world apart from rules directly revealed in Scripture; it serves even to distinguish among the latter, between universal commandments and ceremonial precepts or decrees fitted to the special needs of the Hebrew people. In the hands of the professional Canonists this leading idea is worked out in the sense that customs should be deemed unreasonable if they are in contradiction with general rules derived from the law of nature and from equity or if they promote vice and thereby endanger salvation. It is not easy to see what else could have been meant by the contrast between custom and general law.

When the creation of custom is ascribed to conviction or opinion, the question as to the nature and limits of the group in which such an opinion is prevalent arises as a matter of course. It is not the views of separate individuals or chance crowds that can be accepted as decisive in settling a rule which is to be recognized and followed by all. If there is to be common conviction and common actions, what is the community by which the rule is established? The Canonists reckon with various communities of this kind—with colleges and chapters, with cities, provinces, nations, the catholic body of the Church. As Gierke has shown, Canonist doctrine regarded all corporate bodies as institutions "arranged" for the purpose of carrying out various tasks of secular or spiritual intercourse. As such they had no real existence apart from the State or the Church that had called them into being or accepted them when contrived by individuals.

The range of observation was greatly enlarged by the entrance on the scene of the autonomous groups of barbaric and feudal communities—kingdoms, manors, boroughs, townships, counties, tribes, etc. These political and social bodies were obliged to take up the examination of concrete problems of customary law from that very side of opinion or conviction which remained so obscure in canonistic literature. The writers who attempted to treat systematically of customary law—Beaumanoir, Eike von Repgow, Bracton—were not a match for the glossators and Canonists in respect of theoretical deductions, but they arranged and explained the positive rules in a way which makes it possible for us to discover several leading ideas in their exposition, and the abundant materials gathered in custumals, pleadings and decisions corroborate and extend these conclusions.

Investigations were conducted as to the existence and exact bearing of customary rules. The powerful centralization produced in England by the Norman conquest led to the formation of a common doctrine of the Royal courts which came to be accepted as "common law" and was derived from judicial decisions used as precedents. This doctrine represents the juridical influence of the military class and has been a powerful factor in modifying in all directions the older traditions. Even in England, however, peculiar customs were recognized in certain localities and had often to be ascertained by the courts. The most extensive concession of this kind was made to Kent, where the ancient usages connected with gavelkind tenure were recorded towards the end of the XIII century, according to tradition, at an eyre of Sir John Berwick in 1293. Local usages of towns, manors and even families were often admitted as regards succession, services and rents, and in such cases their contents and duration were ascertained by inquests of juries called for the purpose. In this way some traces of more ancient custom of Anglo-Saxon, Danish or Norse origin were preserved in the rules governing the status of

340 K855a
C.1

socagers and sokemen. But the principal storehouse of customary law distinct from common law is to be found in manorial practice. In France, owing to the disruption of the country into a number of autonomous and almost independent regions, law took a different course. In the central region around Paris, in Normandy, Brittany, Picardy, Anjou, Poitou, Maine, Touraine, Languedoc, Guyenne, Burgundy, etc., special customs arose; in each region the customs of the military class are not so overwhelmingly predominant as in England. As a result the traditions of the free, rent-paying classes of the *roturiers* preserve a much greater vitality and sometimes come to influence the arrangements of the military class. They are ascertained in many cases by verdicts of inquests similar to the English juries, though not formed with the same regularity. The *enquête par turbe* gave evidence as one body; it was usually composed of advocates, merchants, substantial farmers, or house-owners called up by office or by the parish as experts in customary law. The ultimate decision, as in England, rested with the judges. The action of the judicial element in settling customary rules is well exemplified by a book like that of Beaumanoir, who treats of the custom of Beauvaisis from the point of view of his experience as a judge in the bailliage of Clermont.

The popular character of customary law is more marked in Germany. The country was divided into a great number of more or less autonomous political formations—not only provinces, tribal regions (*Stämme*) and territorial principalities of varying size, but into military groups under feudal law (*Lehnrechte*), serjeanties under special service customs (*Dienstrechte*), rural districts under peasant customs (*Bauernrechte*), towns under borough customs (*Stadtrechte*), etc. All these varieties developed customary rules of their own, and the task of ascertaining their contents was one of the most important features of German juridical life. This was effected in two different ways—by appointing as assessors in the Courts men well cognizant of the convictions and usages of the various circles: these were the *Schöffen* (*scabini*), the denomination being attributed more especially to the representatives of the free men who did not lay claim to nobility of birth (*schöffenbar freie*). It was to them that people looked for the declaration of the law of the land (*Landrecht*);

lesser freemen, e.g. the *Bargilden* and even *Landsassen* of Saxony, were also governed in most of their relations by *"Landlaw."*

The second method consisted in obtaining pronouncements on matters of customary law from specially appointed inquests. The persons called upon to make such pronouncements might be the same as the *Schöffen* employed in administering justice, but there were also occasions when questions were addressed to a wider circle of experts. In any case a pronouncement of this kind (*Weisthum*) was regarded as embodying a verdict based on the sense of right of the community. The collections of German and Danish *Weisthümer* present invaluable materials for the history of legal and economic arrangements in rural Germany.

The situation in the Scandinavian countries is even more interesting. Thanks to the incomplete sway of feudalism and to the compact native population, not intermixed to the same extent with the Romanesque elements as was the case in the South and in the West, Swedish, Norwegian, and to a lesser extent Danish law has remained for a long time based on this ancient customary tradition. If we take the Swedish provincial laws as an example we find that they go back professedly to oral popular tradition preserved in the centuries immediately preceding their fixation in writing by means of a regular system of declarations made by elected experts—*laghmen*—in the presence and with the approval of popular assemblies. The *Westgötalag,* the *Östgötalag,* and the *Uplandslag* have preserved the memory of leading "speakers" of this kind—Lumber, Aikill, Vigers—and they refer to a continuous tradition of pronouncement from the IX to the XIII century. Such a system is undoubtedly the result of the preponderance in a differentiated society of leading landowners exercising a great deal of authority in all political, economic, and legal affairs. The *laghman* appears as a professional expert and cannot be described as a representative of ancient democracy. Nevertheless his pronouncements were regarded not as products of his superior intellect and skill, but as revelations of national lore. The institution of the "lawspeaker" must undoubtedly be regarded as a striking instance of a process of law growth which derived its authority not from an outside sovereignty imposed on the people, but from the concentration of popular ideas and practices into definite pronouncements by spokesmen entitled to voice the convictions of the people.

Let us examine some of the substantive features of this law conditioned by the peculiarities of its formation. A comparative survey of Western European customs discloses, as it seems to me, three main factors: business practice, tradition, and reflective formulation. In speaking of business practice I have in view the various usages arising from non-litigious intercourse between members of a community. It is evident that customs regulating marriage, succession, the discipline of children, the status of women in the family, the management of fields, woods, pastures, etc. grew up not as cunning devices, but as convenient arrangements between people brought together by circumstances. Before being enforced as legal rules such arrangements passed through the stage of usage and habit. Sometimes we catch a glimpse of the actual transition from one stage to the other. The composition for a murdered relative was originally offered and accepted as a varying peace compromise, depending on the forces in conflict, the actual risks, the state of mind of the parties. Eventually definite tariffs are worked out requiring definite amounts to be claimed by various relations in accordance with the social status of the slain.

The right of the youngest son to inherit his father's homestead grew out of the practice of letting elder brothers set up on their own account before the death of the father with such outfit as they could get according to the means of the family and to the accepted notions of the country-side.

Social habits and conventions acted as intermediate links between arrangements of a more or less fluctuating nature and customs crystallized as legal rules. Mediaeval commercial law was commonly declared and applied by juries of experts composed partly of foreigners—Germans, Flemings. This process has been going on in modern times and may be noticed to some extent even now. The Law Merchant was until the second half of the XVIII century a body of customs developed in business intercourse apart from Common Law. In our days the Stock Exchange is regulated by practices formed within the circle of its members in transacting business.

Let us turn back to the epoch when the customary law was not an exception but the principal form of juridical life. The sources insist again and again on the necessity of long duration, of "inveterate" habit, but this requirement must not be taken too strictly; many customary rules did not appeal for their recognition to more than a continuous usage during some twenty or forty years. But these are barriers drawn for the sake of evidence in courts. In reality many customs have continued for centuries in a world little disturbed by brisk intercourse and widespread commerce. In fact, one of the most curious features of the situation consists in the survival of rules and habits whose roots are embedded in unfathomable antiquity and which emerge sometimes from the depth of popular life after having disappeared for long years from the surface of legal administration. Julius Ficker has made a laborious study of such traditional currents in Germanic custom. His attempts at tracing the paths by which inheritance and kinship have become differentiated among the Germanic tribes cannot be said to have achieved uniform success: they suffer from a pedantic striving to assign a definite place to every detail in accordance with a favourite theory that similarities in treatment are to be explained as ramifications of a common stock. Obvious considerations as to the influence of other ethnological factors than the Germanic race are brushed aside after a few casual remarks; ancient records are not studied with the necessary critical attention. Yet Ficker's point of view has enabled him to throw light on some important facts. His best suggestions concern the value of late Spanish and Portuguese customary records (*Fueros*) for the reconstruction of legal customs carried over by the Goths on their wanderings from the shores of the Baltic into the Pyrenean peninsula. The blood feud had been officially abolished in the *Lex Wisigothorum,* and capital punishment for murder had been introduced; yet the feud reappears in full vigour in the *Fueros* on the old lines of revenge and composition. An ancient arrangement of Kinship is revealed by the terminology of collateral relationship based on counting brotherhoods of cousins who appear in the side lines as first brothers (*Hermanos primos* or simply *primos, Hermanos secondos, Hermanos tercios*) and similar numbers are assigned to the uncles on both sides (*Tio primo, Tio secondo*). In connection with this nomenclature duties and rights are assigned to collaterals along the line of contemporary generations, not of common descent. It would seem as if at a certain stage kindreds were arranged around the kernel of the family household in concentric circles of contemporaries with duties as to mutual support and defence, and corresponding claims to part of the inheritance. So far as the Spanish example is concerned Ficker's deductions are based on good evidence and are very instructive. But are we to infer with him that a similar numbering of brotherhoods in Iceland must be explained by descent from a common stock and not by the working of the same principle of alliances between contemporaries? This ranging of kinsmen by generations finds many illustrations in the life of primitive tribes—Malays, American Indians, etc.

A counterpoise to this conservatism of ancient law is presented by the necessity of adaptation to varying circumstances and surroundings. It is sufficient to compare, for instance, the consecutive versions of a regional law, in order to perceive the gradual changes in the juridical treatment of social problems. These changes are undoubtedly achieved to a great extent by the working of the factor of business intercourse already noticed. But the most important share belongs in this respect to the reflective thought of the judges who had to decide disputed points in the course of actual trial. Very characteristic instances of such a revision and modification of customary rules may be gathered from the records of Swedish law or in early common law in England. As Maitland has shown, that law was undergoing a radical transformation towards 1200 A.D., since the judicial reforms of Henry II. All the topics of family law, for example, the property rights of the wife, courtesy of England, free bench, wardship, etc., are being subjected to revision from the point of view of Norman feudalism and on many occasions contradictions and fluctuations are to be observed in the views of judges reflected in Glanvill's and Bracton's accounts. The fact that in England we have before us a body of juridical custom rising to the dignity of common law marks a difference in degree and not in kind. The jurisdiction of the Chatelet and of Parliament in Paris modified the Coutume de Paris in the same way as the jurisdiction of the Bench in Westminster, of the King's Council, and of Parliament shaped the feudal and socage customs of England.

The growth of customary law is certainly analogous to the social processes which originate language and folklore. Each particular statement may have been the result of some personal initiative or effort, but the aggregate appears as a product of the life of the people; tradition and imitation play a not less important part in it than actual invention.

§§ 2

THE OLD ENGLISH
CUSTOMARY LAWS

Frederick Pollock

It has been said that the most hopeful way to understand the present structure of our land laws may be to pick out separately the various elements which are now mingled in the mass. Let us begin with that which is the oldest, the most popular, and still in some respects the most persistent—I mean the customary Germanic law which our ancestors brought with them from the mainland on their first settlement in this country, and developed after their own fashion, with little foreign interference or influence for good or for ill, until the reign of Edward the Confessor. Whatever else may be said of the early English land system, as preserved to us in Anglo-Saxon records and interpreted by modern scholars, it certainly had not the merit of simplicity. The modern law, though far from simple, is definite, and in the main uniform. Copyhold lands are subject to peculiar incidents and modes of alienation, and certain ancient varieties of tenure survive as local customs of inheritance. But with these exceptions, the substance of the law is the same for every piece of land in England. Before the Conquest there was no more one and the same law for every parcel of land than there was one and the same law for every

From Frederick Pollock, *The Land Laws* (London: Macmillan, 1883), Ch. 2.

man. Land, like men, was impressed with different legal qualities
and conditions, though its condition was not unchangeable. Separate property in land was well known; full and free private ownership, as we now understand it, was an innovation, and for a long
time exceptional, though its constant tendency was to encroach
on the earlier forms of tenure.

There were no less than four distinct species of landed property.
First and apart from all the rest there was the *folk-land*, the land
which belonged to no person or particular community, but to the
nation. It answers exactly, in name and in kind, to the *ager
publicus* of the Romans, and is supposed to have consisted
originally of the land which remained over after sufficient allotments had been made to all the freemen of the invading host on
the first settlement of the tribe. The folk-lands of the several
kingdoms and principalities founded by the Teutonic invaders
became the folk-land of the English when England was brought
under one rule. Portions of the folk-land might be, and frequently
were, turned into private property by grant from the sovereign
power; or, without altering the ultimate public property in the
land, the possession and enjoyment of it might be, and constantly
were, let out to individuals. In the shires exposed to invasion this
was the means both of rewarding past services in war, and
securing the aid of the holders for the defence of the country in
the future. Then there was the *common land* held as separate
property, not by single owners, but by communities, something
like the lands of colleges and other corporations at the present
day, and as land is still held by village communities in India and
the eastern Slavonic countries of Europe. The enjoyment of these
common lands was like that of the folk-land on a smaller scale:
that is, the property remained in the corporate society, as we
may call it in modern language, while the use was allotted by the
common authority of the society among its members. But from
a very early time considerable parts of these allotments became
permanent, and assumed the nature of private property. When
Tacitus described the institutions of the Germans of his time (and
all modern research has only gone to confirm his account, which
was once treated as a romance), each man's homestead was
already his own, or perhaps we should rather say each family's.
The land thus marked off from the common stock appears to have

been described as *yrfe-land* or *erf-land,* heir-land (in modern High German, *erbland*)—that is, land passing by descent. In old times it could not be disposed of by the holder, but a custom gradually arose of alienating it by will, and perhaps by purchase, within the limits of the family. Freedom of alienation became greater as the bonds of the village community or township and of the family were loosened. The order of the steps would be of this kind: First, no alienation, but only inheritance; then alienation within the family, but with the consent of the possible heirs as well as the community; lastly the consent of the community would become a mere form. Where a lord of the manor had acquired the powers of the community, he probably acquired among them the veto on alienation which in historical times he certainly possessed. In this later shape also the restriction became a formality, but not an empty one. The lord's consent could not be refused if the accustomed dues and fines were paid, but the dues and fines remained as a source of profit. The holder of heir-land, in his relation to the community, must have gone through nearly the same phases as the copyholder in relation to the lord of the manor, except that there never was a time when he was not secure in his holding; and this exception may turn out less important than it seems when we come to consider the origin and early history of copyholds. Probably the power of alienation differed in different parts of the country according to local custom. We do not know exactly how things stood when the old English forms of free ownership were swallowed up by the feudal doctrine of tenure. It does not appear, however, that the consent of the family ever became needless or merely formal, or that alienation to strangers was allowed. Lastly, there was *bócland,* or book-land, the land held in several property under the express terms of a written instrument, or book as it was then called. Such grants could be made in the first instance only by the king with the consent of his Witan. This tenure was of comparatively late introduction, and came in under the influence of the Church, and in favour of grants to religious houses.

Here we have at last something that comes up to full ownership, as we now understand it; but it is worth noting that when it does occur, it is not really of home growth. It is taken over from ecclesiastical, in other words from Roman habits of mind. There were no limits to the power of disposal enjoyed by the owner of book-land, save those which might be laid upon him by the terms of the grant itself. He could without any further leave or consent grant it in his lifetime, as he had received it, by *book,* or dispose of it by his will. Book-land, with its full separate ownership, being an innovation, though an early one, it is clear that all book-land must have been created out of folk-land, common land, or heir-land. As to common land, there is no reason to think that communities as such had any power of alienating their lands, either by book or otherwise, or ever attempted to do so. Moreover, one object of a grant of book-land was commonly the spiritual benefit of the grantor, to be derived from the prayers of the religious house which took an immediate or ultimate interest. And this motive could not well exist in the case of a community. Still less, one would think, had the king any right to deal with the common lands of particular communities. Nevertheless, we find a certain number of charters granting rights over common land, and sometimes apparently portions of the common land itself. It is tempting to suppose that the land, wood, or meadow described as *common* in both Latin and English is really nothing else than a parcel of the folk-land. But this seems untenable, because in that case the expression would be much more frequent, and for other reasons. Perhaps we may suppose that in these cases the grantees already held the land as an allotment of either folk-land or common land. They may well have had by custom some sort of right to a renewal of the allotment to themselves or their descendants. If this were so, the effect of the grant would be to confirm the customary title in perpetuity, and to release the land from most of the public dues and services to which land other than book-land was subject. The release of these burdens would require a regular grant from the king, with the consent of the Witan, just as much as the severance of a new portion from the folk-land. This, however, is given only as a conjecture. We know very little about the way in which common land was actually dealt with before the Conquest, and its relation to folk-land is particularly obscure. Next as to heir-land, we cannot say with our present means of knowledge that it was never turned into book-land; but it could not have been lawfully done without the consent of every one who could possibly inherit. Such dealings were from time to time attempted and objected to.

There is not any evidence that they were ever openly undertaken, or could take effect by any recognised means. Of encroachments and irregular dealings we do not speak for the present. Only folk-land, then, remains; and thus it appears that the ultimate legal origin of book-land must, as a rule, have been a grant made out of the folk-land. Ample records of such grants are preserved, and are, in fact, our chief means of knowledge as to the relation of book-land to folk-land. The grant could be effectually made, as above said, only by the king with the consent of the Witan, and also of his superior king, if he acknowledged any (for our records begin in a time when there were still many kings and under-kings of many tribes and kindreds of the English). Not only this consent was required for grants in perpetuity to private persons, but if the king wished to appropriate any part of the folk-land as his own heritage, a grant to himself had to be made out with the express sanction of his counsellors, in just the same form as if it had been to any other person. The notion that all public property was the king's, and that the king on the other hand could not hold property like a private person, came in after the Conquest. Yet we find somewhat earlier that when a man is forjudged of life and lands for cowardice in battle, as the lands held by him of a private lord go to that lord, so any book-land he may have does not become folk-land again, but is forfeit to the king. In practice, however, it is hardly doubtful that from a very early time much of the increase of book-land at the expense of folk-land took place in irregular ways. It may often have been under colour of an occupation which was rightful in its origin, but as often, perhaps, by mere encroachment. The king and other great men had certain rights over the waste folk-land, and rights of use tended then, as much as they do now, to grow into claims of property in the hands of the strongest. It fared with the folk-land of the kingdom very much as it fared some centuries later, for similar reasons, with the common lands of the village or township which had become a manor. As early as the eighth century grants were made recklessly out of folk-land in the north of England to persons who professed the religious character merely to have the grant without the burden of the ordinary secular dues and services. Whether book-land also increased at the expense of heir-land is not so clear; though it seems likely enough that men of substance attempted to dispose of part of their heir-land as book-land, to pious uses or otherwise. It is certain that grants and wills of land described by the donors as book-land were not uncommonly disputed by their families, and that an ordinance of the Witan was thought needful to enforce even express prohibitions against alienation out of the family contained in the original "book." The interests that were created in book-land by the original grants varied a good deal in their nature and duration. It is not known how far they were regulated by any fixed laws or usages. Sometimes a free and absolute power of disposal was conferred by the terms of the "book" on the person to whom the grant was made. Sometimes a special case of descent was prescribed, so that the disposition was analogous to a modern entail, or alienation was allowed only within the family.

It is doubtful, however, whether the will of the grantor was in such cases strictly observed in practice. A very common form was to grant an interest for one or more lives in succession, say to Oswine or Æthelwulf and to two heirs whomsoever he shall choose after his own time, with an ultimate gift to a religious house.

Such was in its main outlines the Old-English system of land tenure. But we must not suppose that all or most of the actual occupiers and tillers of the soil held by any of these titles. If we did, we should fall into the same mistake as a foreigner, who in our own time should imagine from reading modern English lawbooks that the whole or the greater part of the present occupiers are freeholders. There was indeed nothing, or next to nothing, resembling even distantly in form our modern leases for years and other inferior tenancies. Nor was there, as there has been ever since the fourteenth century, any distinct class of labourers working on other people's land and paid by money wages. Nevertheless, a great part of the cultivation of the land was undertaken by people who occupied it by the agreement or permission of the superior owner, and paid for its use in money, in kind, or in labour, not uncommonly in all three. Land thus held was known as *lǽn-land,* and the tenant was said to hold it (literally to sit on it) upon *lǽn.* The word, it is almost needless to add, is our modern *loan.* The lands of bishoprics and religious houses, insofar as they were not tilled by serfs belonging to the house and under its direct management, were dealt with in this manner; and we may well think that religious corporations had the chief hand in introducing læns, as they certainly had some centuries later with regard to leases of the modern type. The condition of the tenants of læn-land was various. The smallest of them were little better than cottiers; the largest may have been no worse than substantial farmers. Now and then they obtained a more permanent estate by grant from the owner, or as we should now say acquired the freehold. We have examples of a tenant of læn-land receiving a grant of his tenement by book, to hold it for book-land as fully as he did for læn-land; and it appears to have been a well-known practice for lords to make such grants to deserving tenants.

This kind of tenancy was at first of minor importance. Towards the date of the Conquest, however, a great proportion of the actual occupiers must have held their lands on læn. In a certain sense it is even true to say that læn-land ultimately supplanted everything else, and that no other kind of landed property is recognised by the strict theory of modern English law. Historically, the growth of læn-land, and the changes thereupon consequent, are intimately connected with the personal relation of lord and man, of which, therefore, something must be said. It was familiar in England long before the Conquest, and constantly tended to assume greater importance in the constitution of society. At first it was confined to the small body of personal followers attached to the leaders of the Germanic tribes. At that time it was personal and nothing more, and there was no loss of rank or dignity on the follower's part. The chief's or king's companions must be free, and might be noble, and their service was an honour. The modern European orders of nobility and knighthood owe to this aspect of the institution the greater part of their titles, their system, and their ceremonial; and European monarchies owe to it nearly all the pomp that surrounds them, and much of the sentiment on which their continuance depends. For many generations before the Norman Conquest, as distinctions of rank and substance between freemen increased, the old community of equals had been virtually replaced by a ruling class with a humbler and less wealthy multitude in dependence on them. For some time this state of things had become associated with the tenure of land to a considerable extent, and had thus prepared the way for the feudal and manorial system. Feudalism is the complete association of territorial with personal dependence. The tenant is not only an occupier who pays the owner in money or in kind for the use of the land; he owes him personal service and allegiance. The lord himself may be in like manner bound to an over-lord, and he again to another above him, until we come to someone who holds of no lord, and who, in the developed feudal theory, must be an absolutely sovereign prince. Old-English land law never reached this stage, but it was tending towards it so fast that the Conquest may be said to have only hastened its transformation.

As far as the personal relation is concerned, we find it established in the earliest times of which we have any trustworthy account. Every man was expected either to be of substance enough to answer all payments he might become liable for, whether to private suitors as damages or composition or to the public as fines, or to be dependent on a lord who could answer for him. Much as in English society of a far later time we find "masterless men" to be a name of thieves, vagrants, and peace-breakers, we find before the Conquest that no honest man can be without a lord unless he is a lord himself. In the first half of the tenth century this is fixed as a positive rule, and the lordless man must find a lord at his peril. If he or his kindred for him fail to do this, he becomes outlawed, and may be dealt with as a robber. The men who had risen to the condition of being lords and protectors of the smaller freemen were naturally great or relatively great landowners. Their ancestors, we may suppose, had been distinguished by birth or exploits among their fellows, English or Danish, even before their settlement in this land. Enjoying at first a kind of undefined primacy among their equals, they gradually assumed a position of command. From the first, we may be pretty sure, their possessions were notably greater than those of common men, and gave them a corresponding influence on all public occasions. Each of them imitated the king to the best of his power by surrounding himself with a band of personal followers. And the sorts of men likely to seek the personal service of a lord, or become dependent on him, were increased by several causes. The natural growth of population is one of these, for the land allotted in the first instance to the freemen of the conquering host would in a few generations be a too scanty means of livelihood for their descendants. Men with no secured possessions of their own were driven to find a place in dependence on those who had land and goods to spare. Another large class of free dependents were those who had property, but were not strong enough to guard it in times of trouble. These commended themselves to a lord for protection, and with themselves their land. There were likewise the manumitted serfs, a class which became considerable in the tenth and eleventh centuries, manumission being encouraged by the Church and reckoned a pious work. Neither were the old motives wanting which in the time of Tacitus had led the young men of the German peoples to cast in their lot with kings and chiefs. Adventurers in search of warlike renown or booty, exiles driven from their home by civil strife, or flying the vengeance of a slain man's kindred, craftsmen skilled in the arts which supplied the luxuries and recreations of life, such as then they were; all these still contributed to swell the number of dependents, as they had once chiefly formed it. So far the connection with land tenure appears as accidental. The companion may or may not be a landholder; and if he is, the lord to whom he is personally attached may or may not be his superior in respect of the land. On the other hand we do not know, and have no right to assume, that the man who occupied another's land on læn was necessarily his personal dependent. In course of time, however, and by steps of which the beginning may lie farther back than the earliest of our documents, the dependent becomes a tenant, and at last dependency and tenancy become in legal theory co-extensive. According to the tenant's degree of personal rank, the inchoate tenancy takes a different complexion. The personal aid and service rendered in war to the king and the earls by their more distinguished followers comes to be looked on as the equivalent of the benefits received by them. Even before the Conquest there are traces of duties and relations hardly distinguishable from the true military tenures of a later age. The free landowners owing military service to the nation are becoming tenants holding their lands by military service of the king.

Among the smaller folk things happened somewhat differently. Their hereditary holdings were subject to the order and regulation of the township out of whose common land the holdings had in the first instance been allotted. Probably the business of the township was for the most part swayed by a few leading members even when its constitution was nearest the primitive type. The passage from this aristocracy of natural selection to the petty monarchy wielded in after-times by the lord of the manor may have taken place in various ways, and most likely did, according to circumstances, take place in all of them. In some townships a chief house might become richer and more prosperous than the others, until its head possessed a commanding influence, and the poorer members were glad to become his dependents. But the man who had thriven and become a lord in his own township would be sought as a protector, sooner or later, by strangers also. There were times of warfare between kingdom and kingdom, and later of Danish harrying and general disorder, in which old bounds and usages were overridden, and the bonds of society loosened. There were times of distress, too, when freemen were ready to "bow their heads for meat" to any one who would support them, insomuch that the neediest of them were driven to become not merely dependents but serfs. Thus the dominion of the stronger landholders, once set on foot, was increased by the submission of many sorts of people, now singly, now collectively. Whole townships, it is likely enough, resolved to seek a lord while they yet held together as organised communities. On the other hand, it is no less likely that the dependents of a great man, gathered together at first from all the country round, without any fellowship among them but that of a common subjection, formed communities modelled on the old free townships of which they or their fathers had been members. Grants of public jurisdiction and revenues from the king completed the strength and pre-eminence of the lords. The township was turned into a manor, and its hereditary freemen into the lord's tenants. The common land came to be looked on as the lord's land, and the old popular courts which dealt with local affairs as the lord's courts. He was no longer first among equals, but a ruler over inferiors. This process, repeated all over the country, had long before the Conquest made England into a land of great estates, cultivated partly by personally free dependents and partly by serfs. But it had not altogether supplanted the smaller free tenancies, and the old communal ownership and tillage was still widely prevalent, though the community might have over it a lord claiming dues and services.

We may now ask what became of these divisions of land tenure as they existed before the Conquest, and what traces they have left on the modern law. These traces will appear on examination to be far deeper and more lasting than is commonly known. The inquiry, therefore, is something more than a piece of minute antiquarian curiosity. First we may dispose of book-land. I have tried to show that its importance as a normal and constant element in the Old-English land system has hitherto been overrated. If this is right, we may the more easily understand the certain fact that we hear next to nothing of book-land after the Conquest. Many of the great estates, probably most, were confiscated on account of the owner's resistance to William. There must have been many cases, however, notably those of religious houses, where the substance and enjoyment of possession remained undisturbed. In these cases the form was none the less superseded by the new Anglo-Norman theory of tenure and the corresponding forms which it introduced. The Norman charter, which in strictness was only evidence of the corporal act of investiture, took the place of the English "book"; and where no real services were performed by the landholder, nominal ones were invented to save the credit of the theory. Religious persons were supposed to hold their lands on condition of performing divine services[1] which would assure the spiritual benefit of the grantor and his heirs, as the lay tenants held theirs by rendering to the lord the temporal and tangible benefits of military or agricultural aid. And the lands of ecclesiastical corporations are to this day said to be held by the tenure of *frank almoigne* or free alms, though the explanation which originally supported the fiction of a tenure has disappeared since the Reformation. Such lands now represent book-land, so far as anything can represent it in our modern system. There is no doubt that at least some of them are in fact ancient book-land which has been held without a break in title since it was first granted by some West-Saxon or Mercian king with the witness and consent of his Witan. Of course no new book-land was created after the Conquest. Not only the forms of legal docu-

---

[1] Services, that is, not specifically defined or demandable. In some cases the services were definite, and then the tenure was "by divine service," strictly so called, in opposition to *frank almoigne*.

ments were changed, but the creation of book-land in the old sense and in the old fashion was impossible. It was created, as we have seen, out of folk-land. But there was now no folk-land to make it of.

This brings us to the second question. What became of the folk-land? The answer to this is both short and certain. It became the king's land. The king not only dealt with the land which had been the nation's without the counsel or consent of the Witan or anyone else, but treated it as if it were in all respects his private inheritance. For several centuries the distinction between property held and administered by the king in right of the Crown and on behalf of the nation, and property belonging to him as an individual, was utterly effaced. After the Conquest the folk-land which had not been granted away for book-land, and remained in the king's hands as its public administrator, was thrown into one mass with what had come to the Crown by forfeitures and confiscations, and the whole was registered in Domesday as *Terra Regis*. And whatever parts of this are described as having belonged to the Crown in the time of King Edward must be either unallotted folk-land, or land which had been allotted to the king or come to him by forfeiture to hold as book-land in his private right, and had not been alienated by him since.

Next we take up the common land. As to this there is no doubt that much of it went on being occupied and used in the old fashion down to our own time. Indeed historical records about it are scanty, and the modern survival of practices which can be explained only by a general system of common ownership is the best evidence we have that the system really existed in the past, a circumstance which ought to make us careful in other cases how we draw negative inferences from the dearth of positive evidence in early times. The lands which in modern times have remained subject to communal regulation are variously known as commonable, open, or intermixed fields, and very frequently as Lammas lands. In the last few generations the progress of enclosure and partition has been rapid, and the amount of these lands has been notably diminished even within living memory. It will be convenient, however, to speak in the present tense of the facts which less than forty years ago were put on record by careful and competent observers as then actually existing. Another generation earlier, about the beginning of this century, more than half the land of some English counties was under one or another variety of these usages. They differ in detail, but the general type is that from seedtime to harvest the land is divided among several occupiers, tilling each his own portion, and after the harvest (that is, on or about old Lammas day, or the 12th of August in the reformed calendar, whence the name of Lammas lands) it is thrown open for pasturage, sometimes to the same persons who have occupied them in severalty, sometimes to a larger class. The occupiers for tillage are generally bound to a customary rotation of crops and fallow, which of itself is such as to point to days of very primitive farming.[2] Many commonable hay-fields are also found which are thrown open earlier in the year, as soon as the hay-harvest is over. It is significant that these usages are stated to be most prevalent in those parts of the country where the soil is most fertile, and the land was therefore taken into cultivation at a very early time. The subdivision of the allotments for several cultivation is extremely minute, so that even a considerable owner of land of this kind will have it all in little parcels of at most a couple of acres each. It is found that where this system prevails the farmers are collected in agricultural villages, whereas in the parts where complete severalty of ownership is the rule we find scattered and independent homesteads. One cannot overlook the historical significance of such a fact; the conclusion is almost irresistible that the village in these cases represents the original township or community to which the land belonged as its *ager publicus* on a small scale, just as the folk-land belonged to the whole kingdom. It is no less fit to be noted that the country of open and common fields is also the country of small copyholds.

Another fact of some importance is that, although in the modern legal theory a parish or township is not capable of holding lands, yet lands belonging to a parish, and administered by the churchwardens in aid of its other sources of revenue, are frequently met with; so frequently, indeed, that the difficulties of legal title resulting from this state of things were brought to the attention of Parliament within the present century, and in one of

---

[2] The regular course is wheat, oats or beans, and fallow. A four-course rotation is also met with, and exceptionally the bare alternation of crop and fallow.

the Poor Law statutes the churchwardens and overseers of any parish to which land belongs were incidentally made a body corporate for the purpose of dealing with it. Sometimes these parish lands are within the modern boundaries, but by no means always. For example, the parish of Sampford Spiney in South Devon lately held a piece of land in the parish of Tamerton, as much as twelve miles away. Such outlying lands can hardly be supposed to have belonged to the township in ancient times; more probably they represent mediaeval gifts to pious uses. It would now be impossible, unless in specially favourable conditions which may sometimes exist, to trace the history of these parish properties with any certainty. In the case I have mentioned nothing whatever is known about it, all early records of the parish having been lost by neglect. In some cases the use of the property for parish purposes is known to go back to the time of the Reformation or earlier. This, however, is still consistent with a gift or appropriation long since the Conquest. But the fact of gifts being made to the parish at all shows that for the popular mind it retained its existence as a kind of corporate body, though the law refused to acknowledge it. And at last Parliament, as we have just seen, had to bring the law round again to the popular view.

The village greens which still exist in many parts of the country may fairly be regarded as a remnant of old unappropriated common land. Here the modern legal theory simply reverses the order of the facts. These bits of ground used by the inhabitants for recreation are in most cases ground which never really belonged to any several owner. Not having been allotted by the township when the township was a reality, and having escaped wholly or in part from the encroachment of the lord or his agents, they remain open for common enjoyment. But the theory of the law-books is that they belonged to the lord, and that in early times he granted rights of enjoyment over it, or allowed them to grow up by way of custom. And though of late years judges have more than once admitted from the bench the historical futility of this theory, it is now hardly possible to break with it altogether for legal purposes. We now speak of a custom for the inhabitants of a parish to dance or to play lawful games at seasonable times on such and such a piece of land, the land being imagined to belong to some person whose ordinary rights over it as owner are limited by the customary use of strangers. This is really fiction and nothing else in the majority of cases; but the fiction is inveterate.

Rights of common have a similar history, though both the facts and the legal treatment of them are more complex. The simpler case of the village green may help us to a clear understanding of the legal nature of a common. According to the doctrine of the books a common is the waste of a manor. It may happen that the wastes of two or more manors adjoin, and sometimes the common, or moor, or whatever it may be called, is a royal forest —that is, a hunting preserve created since the Conquest. The presence of trees, I need hardly say, is not required to make a forest in this sense. The great mark of it is the absence of enclosures. Dartmoor is a forest, and (but for modern plantations) trees grow on it only in a few sheltered hollows. These cases offer peculiarities of their own which to the lawyer are extremely curious. But just now we will confine ourselves to the more ordinary case of a common lying wholly within the bounds of a single manor. The waste of the manor, then, is in the modern legal theory so much of the lord's land as his predecessors have not found it worth while either to take into cultivation on their own account or to let out to tenants. Those predecessors have at some remote time granted to their tenants various privileges over this unoccupied land; the liberty of pasture, or of taking sand and gravel, or cutting underwood, and such like matters convenient for the use and enjoyment of their cultivated holdings. These liberties have ripened by long continuance into rights which the lord can no longer withhold. All the rights of the commoners are thus conceived as having been carved, as it were, out of the original full and absolute dominion of some imaginary predecessor of the existing lord. It is allowed, indeed, that in the one case of common pasture the tenant's right might be in some measure independent of the lord's will, being annexed by law to his tenement if there was nothing to exclude it. This is the doctrine of "common appendant." But the general theory was as I have stated. We have great reason to say again, as we said in the particular case of the village green, that this theory reverses the facts. We cannot say it, however, without some qualifications. A great many of the manors now or formerly existing represent ancient communities in which, little by little, the authority of the community was engrossed by the most considerable man in it, until he became the lord, and the other landholders became his dependents. But a manor might also be formed without going through the earlier stages at all. Free dependents and emancipated serfs might gather round a lord until they formed a community comparable in size to the old free township. Under such conditions we should expect usages to spring up imitated from those of the older communities, and modelled as far as possible on them; but these usages would in such a case really owe their force to the permission and consent of the lord, as they were feigned to do by the theory of the lawyers in the case where the lord was only an overgrown member of the township. Thus we have a possible class of cases in which the theory to some extent answers to the real facts. I say only to some extent; for even in these cases, whether they were few or many (and I am not disposed to think they were many), the usages were not invented by the tenants or the lord, but were framed on the customs already established elsewhere. On the whole, then, we may say that rights of common and all similar rights are derived either from the ancient use and enjoyment of undivided common land under the customary regulations imposed by the township to which the land belonged, or from use and enjoyment really granted by lords to their inferior tenants in imitation of the ancient customs. The old common land, then, is represented on the one hand by such remnants of the common system of cultivation as now exist in England, or lately existed; on the other hand, by rights of common and the like. In the one set of usages we have the regulation by the community of the allotment and tillage of its cultivable land; in the other the enjoyment of the unallotted and untilled land by its members for pasture and other advantages in aid of their several allotments.

Lastly, what became of the land held by individuals as their inheritance, not by the exceptional privilege of a "book" or charter, but according to the varying custom of the country, and probably without any written evidence of title at all? It is impossible for us now to get any direct proof about this; but for my own part I believe that such land went on being held by the old customs for centuries after the Conquest, and is to a great extent represented by copyholds; a form of tenure which is now fast disappearing, and may be extinct in another generation or two, but on which a large proportion of English land was held down to the present century. We are told in all the books dealing with the history of our land laws or land tenure, from Sir Edward Coke downwards, that the copyholders of the modern and later mediaeval English system grew out of the villein of earlier times. The statement is certainly true in some sense; but it is capable of so many that it is important to determine which of them we mean to adopt. The meaning of the proposition depends on the meaning of its terms. The first of them is clear enough. We all know, or may easily know whenever we please, what is meant by a copyholder. A copyholder is a tenant of a manor who is said to hold his tenement "at the will of the lord according to the custom of the manor." This means that the tenant's rights are nominally dependent on the will of the lord; but the lord is bound to exercise his will according to the custom, so that the tenant is really as safe as if he were an absolute owner. The lord's petty monarchy over the manor, whatever it may have been formerly, is now a strictly constitutional one. The tenant's title, however, is evidenced not by deeds in his own possession, but by the records of the lord's court, which show the admission of successive tenants by the lord or his steward. For this reason the tenant is said to hold "by copy of court roll." He is generally debarred from some of the rights of an absolute owner, such as cutting timber and opening mines, and has to pay fines on alienation; and often, besides these, the curious and vexatious fine in kind called a heriot on a succession. These payments represent a price paid for the lord's consent to admit a purchaser or accept the deceased tenant's heir; which once, no doubt, was arbitrary— in other words, the most the lord could get. In the modern law the money payments have become fixed, but the heriot of the best beast, or sometimes the best chattel of any kind, may still in many cases be demanded. Also there are money rents payable to the lord which once were of substantial value, and often can be made out to have been the full letting value of the land in the thirteenth or fourteenth century. Thus much for a general notion, rough but sufficient for our immediate purpose, of the nature of copyhold tenure.

But as to the other term of the proposition, what do we mean by a villein? As far as the word goes, it is the Latin *villanus,* which in itself means nothing more than an inhabitant of a vill or township. At the time of the Conquest, and long after, the *villanus* was a personally free tenant holding land under a lord, and owing to that lord certain rents and agricultural services. The rents were sometimes in farm produce, but sometimes (and in course of time generally) in money payments representing its commuted average value. Nor were these *villani* properly so called even the lowest class of free tenants. There were others, described by various names, whose services were more burdensome, and the lowest of these must have been little better off than true serfs. It is not always easy to draw the line between the free and the unfree tillers of the soil. But there is not the least doubt that a large number of serfs existed. The proper Latin name for a man in this condition was *servus* or *nativus.* Probably most of them were descendants of the British population who had been spared in the English Conquest. At all events, they were personally in their lords' ownership, and were at their mercy in everything short of life and limb. Whatever they held of land or goods was held only by the lord's permission and might be recalled at his will. We know that before the Conquest freemen were not uncommonly driven by want to become bondsmen. But sometimes they stopped short of this degradation, and accepted land to be held on servile and precarious terms, but without giving up their personal freedom, or their rights of property in their movable goods. We know that similar terms were after the Norman Conquest forced on many Englishmen who had been hostile to the Normans without actually bearing arms against them; and we may suspect that similar arrangements had centuries before been made, especially in the western parts, between the conquering Englishman and the conquered Welshman. There are abundant possible historical sources of precarious tenures intermediate between full security and that bare holding on sufferance which hardly ever exists in practice; and however troublesome these are to the lawyer when he meets with them, we really ought to be surprised, if at all, that there are not more of them. Only the tendency of usage to become fixed has saved us from a great deal more trouble of this kind. On the whole, we find, at and

after the time of the Conquest, three distinct types of actual
occupiers of the soil.

There are the freemen, holding more or less land on terms of
more or less burdensome service, and called by sundry names
accordingly, but on fixed terms in every case. There are the
bondsmen, who are in a lord's hand and can call nothing their
own, whose holdings are precarious, and who are taxed at the
lord's will. And there are the degraded freemen (whether the
remnant of a conquered race, or decayed members of the ruling
one), who are not personally enslaved, but whose holdings are of
a servile and precarious kind. Moreover, the holdings retained
the character once fixed upon them; so that by successive changes
of ownership it might and did happen that the same man would
hold some land by free and other by bondsman's service, and the
nature of the services did not affect his personal condition. On
the other hand, a serf might deal as a freeman with any one
except his lord, and might, if he could, hold free land, under the
risk of the lord reclaiming him. The test of a servile holding was
liability to be taxed at the will of the lord. Its other incidents were
in practice fixed by usage even at the time of the Conquest, and
in many cases the holders acquired some kind of inchoate
hereditary right.

If we bear in mind these distinctions, it is not very difficult to
form a reasonable conception of the early history of copyholds.
Positive proof we can hardly expect, as there is a great gap in our
authorities for a century and more after Domesday, and we have
hardly any detailed records in the shape of court rolls and
accounts for another century after that. Unfortunately the whole
subject has in modern times been confused by the ambiguous use
of words. The meaning of the old *villanus,* which was at first no
less honourable a name than our yeoman, became degraded after
the Conquest, and both in Latin, and in the French form *villein,*
it was used to stand for *nativus,* with which it properly had nothing to do. The old customary tenure by labour-rents was still
called villenage, and thus the customary tenants and the serfs
became completely mixed up in the apprehension of modern text-
writers. Mediaeval lawyers, no doubt, strove to be accurate with
this awkward nomenclature. When they meant *nativus,* they spoke
in express terms of a "villein by blood." They were careful to

distinguish the old or privileged villenage, which was really a free though more or less onerous tenure, from the villenage of base and uncertain tenure, and again to distinguish the service due in respect of the land from the personal condition of the holder. But in later times these things were overlooked, and the result was the popular account of copyholds: namely that (in Blackstone's language) "copyholders are in truth no other than villeins, who by a long series of immemorial encroachments on the lord have at last established a customary right to those estates which before were held absolutely at the lord's will:" villeins being understood as villeins by blood or *nativi*. It would be nearer the truth to say that by a long series of encroachments and fictions the lords, and lawyers acting in the interest of the lords, got people to believe that the lord's will was the origin of those ancient customary rights which before were absolute.

When we have once shaken off the false theory of Blackstone (I say of Blackstone, for I cannot find that anybody stated it so positively before him), the nature of existing copyhold customs is really enough by itself to carry conviction of their great antiquity. Of this kind is the custom of "borough-English," or, as it is more expressively called in some parts, "cradle-holding," by which the course of descent is neither to the eldest son as at common law, nor to all equally as in the old tenure of gavelkind which still subsists in Kent, but to the youngest son exclusively. Such a rule of descent is very difficult to account for. But the difficulty we now have in understanding it is some proof that it comes down from a forgotten condition of society; and the fact that it was so deeply rooted as to survive the Norman Conquest seems to show that it was ancient then. Similar customs are found in various parts of Europe, and in some cases have been kept up in modern times in spite of the modern law taking no account of them. Probably the explanation is that there was a time when each son of a family as he came of age was entitled to an allotment out of common land. Thus the sons in turn parted off from the family and were provided for, and the homestead was left for the youngest. Such a state of things is actually recorded in the old Welsh laws. It might be inferred that the custom as found in England is of Welsh origin, and is in fact a primitive usage which has survived not only the Norman but the English

Conquest. In that case, however, we should expect to find it prevalent not in the south and centre, but in the west and southwest of England.

Whatever account may be given of particular customs, we need have no fear in saying that the modern copyholders are the historical successors of the old English free landholders who had inheritable titles according to local custom, evidenced not by writing but by the witness of the neighbours, and paid dues and services originally to the State or community, and afterwards to a lord. If the copyholders now seem too few to fill so large a place in the history, we have to remember that the amount of land held on this tenure has for a long time been fast diminishing. Late in the sixteenth century one-third of the land in England was still copyhold. The archaic incidents of the tenure being found in modern practice inconvenient to everybody concerned with the land, and productive of far more vexation to the tenant than advantage to the lord, the manorial rights have in later times been constantly extinguished by agreement, and of late years under the powers of requiring enfranchisement on proper terms given by the Copyhold Acts of both lords and tenants. In various parts of the country there are customary estates of the nature of copyhold, but in which the tenant's position is still insecure. He holds for one or more lives, or sometimes for a short term of years; and renewal, though it is the rule, is not a matter of established right. This tenure is common in the western counties, and may fairly be thought to represent the terms on which the conquered Welsh population were allowed by the English settlers to retain their lands. In Cornwall there are or were certain "conventionary tenants" holding by a title renewable at intervals of seven years, the tenant paying a fine on renewal. As the old customs of Brittany present analogies to this tenure not only in substance but in name, it is all but certain that the Cornish custom is older than the English settlement. The same may be said of the peculiar mining customs of Cornwall and parts of Derbyshire, which entitle adventurers to work mines under any man's waste land if he does not work them himself, paying to the owner the customary dues and royalties. In Cornwall this is called "tin-bounding," from the setting out of the working by bounds which is the adventurer's first step towards establishing his claim.

The like custom existed in the mining districts of Devon as long as tin-streaming was there practised.

The detailed pursuit of special and local customs, however, much more the attempt to trace their history and affinities, would lead us too far. Enough has been said to show that customs older than the Norman Conquest, and perhaps older than the English Conquest, have been far more persistent, and have left far deeper marks in the modern structure of the law, than is generally understood. We must pass on to the feudal period of English land tenure, and trace the effects of the feudal doctrines and policy which for so long overlaid the ancient customs without destroying them.

Part II

Kinship and Law

Custom and kinship are common concerns of anthropology and jurisprudence. Vinogradoff argued that custom is the source of law and that to find the customs from which the law derives one must study the kinship organization of early societies. This makes for a neat equation—too neat. However, the differentiation of societies into (1) those organized under the rule of a state with institutions for making laws (ministries, legislatures) and enforcing them (law courts, police) and (2) those without such specific and defined institutions may make clearer the reason for paying attention to custom and kinship. The functions taken over by legislatures and law courts may usually be traced to customary procedures for settling disputes, punishing crimes, and establishing rules of behavior by which points of dispute and criminal acts will be recognized. The organized group of kinship at times performs much the same function in primitive societies as the state does in those societies that have a more powerful and formal mode of political organization.

Vinogradoff was interested in tracing English law to one of its sources in Germanic and Celtic law, and beyond. In particular, he takes up the institution of the *wergeld,* or blood fine, paid in compensation for certain crimes, such as murder. Instead of punishing a murderer by imprisonment or death, the Anglo-Saxon society imposed a fine in wealth, such as cattle, upon the murderer and his kin, to be paid to the victim's surviving kin. The wergeld was a carefully defined institution, and the kin group from which it was collected and to which it was paid, the amount of the payment, and the severity of the crime were carefully defined as well.

In Chapters 4 and 5, Frederic Seebohm's treatment of the medieval Welsh and Anglo-Saxon law from the viewpoint of historical and literary sources is introduced. At issue is the nature of Welsh social life. For Seebohm the Welsh term *gwely* denoted a unit of a tribe which was formed of related *gwelys*. But did the Welsh know that their *gwelys* had any relation to one another, that they were parts of a tribe, which in turn was part of a tribal system? Seebohm's generalization—that the medieval Welsh *must have* lived in a tribal condition since they were related by blood ties and had no king—must be set aside, for it is only a speculation derived from a stereotyped notion.

These passages from Seebohm's work exemplify anthropological research at both its best and its worst. At best Seebohm's insights are acute, his scholarship vast. He gives us much knowledge of the medieval Welsh system of landholding and of the Anglo-Saxon blood feud and blood money. But it is important to recognize that he went too far and generalized his evidence according to preconceived theory. Much of the work of Vinogradoff and later writers on the wergeld (blood fine) takes the form of a dialogue with Seebohm and serves to delimit his concepts. This process is specifically notable with regard to the blood payment of the killing of a man. Seebohm's chapter on *Beowulf* is modest and more factual. In it he reconstructs the social, economic, and political life of the early Northmen from the evidence afforded by the great epic. He observes a parallel—between the Germanic (Norse) *gesith* and the Welsh *gwely*—which is probably founded in historical fact. His account of the blood feud and blood fine is a convincing extraction of social and legal evidence from a literary source. (Many other authors, such as J. G. Frazer in *The Golden Bough,* have similarly used literary works for anthropological analysis.)

The action of *Beowulf* takes place in the sixth century A.D. or earlier. Its theme is the defeat of a dragon, Grendel, by a royal hero, Beowulf, who thereby saves the kingly house of the Danes; Beowulf himself is later killed by another dragon. The poem contains supernatural as well as legal-factual matter, and both are of ethnographic interest; the Anglo-Saxons believed in dragons and feared them, but were not daunted, and in fact they told in *Beowulf* how a mortal man overcame them. This is just as interesting to anthropologists as the fact that one of the means these people had of righting a wrong was levying a blood fine.

L. K.

§§ 3

THE ORGANIZATION OF KINSHIP

Paul Vinogradoff

The most profound difference between modern and ancient organization consists in the fact that modern society starts from individuals and adjusts itself primarily to the claims of the individual, whereas ancient society starts from groups and subordinates individual interests to the claims of these groups. There are two general reasons for this state of things. To begin with, there is the weakness and insecurity of the single man in barbaric surroundings, which drives him to seek companionship and to place himself under protection at any price. It is only by close union that tribesmen can survive in the difficult struggle for life against outsiders. A single man would be a lost man. In the words of Robertson Smith, "It is only by mutual help, by avoiding intestine quarrels and subordinating individual interests to those of the kin, that, in the hard conditions of desert life, and in a state of constant war with outsiders, a tribe can hope to hold its own. To get the full benefit of this mutual support, the group or *hayy* must not only fight together, but as far as possible move together."

From Paul Vinogradoff, *Outlines of Historical Jurisprudence,* Vol. I (London: Clarendon Press, 1920), Tribal Law, Ch. 8. By permission of Clarendon Press, Oxford.

There is also a second reason which may not perhaps be so clearly perceived by those who deal with these matters. In modern society the State has assumed the monopoly of political co-ordination. It is the State which rules, makes laws, and eventually enforces them by coercion. Such a State, as a wide and more or less abstract union, did not exist in ancient times. The commonwealth was not centered in one sovereign body towering immeasurably about single individuals and meting out to every one his portion of right. Therefore the necessary political elements, which are never absent from any human society, were distributed among formations which we regard now from the point of view of private law: churches, local bodies, kindreds.

The organization of kinship for purposes of defence and mutual help is naturally dependent on the manner in which relationship is constituted in primitive societies. Of the three possible methods of treating relation, the agnatic, the cognatic, and the totem system—we have to reckon in the case of the Aryan nations only with the first two. The totemic classification does not manifest itself, because the nations in question became known to us in the fairly advanced stage of development connected with separate households.

There is also a marked tendency towards agnatism which admits of a more compact and effective organization of the group under the household rule of a patriarch or of a substitute selected from his male relatives.

In order to see the process actually at work in historical circumstances, let us glance at the way in which this agnatic principle has been developed by some of the Aryan races.

Among the *Hindus,* agnatic relationship was certainly the prevailing one: and it should always be borne in mind in dealing with the Aryans in general that, as far back as we can look, we find the predominance of the patriarchal family. We need not necessarily conclude that the patriarchal family was a primordial institution. But apart from the question of absolutely primeval origins, it is incontestable that within that section of Aryan history which is known to us by actual evidence, agnatism arising out of the patriarchal family is certainly the social starting-point of kinship. Thus, according to Gautama, "*Sapindas* (blood relations within sex degrees), *Sagotras* (relations bearing a common

family name), or those connected by descent from the same
Rishi (*vaidika gotra*), and the wife shall share (the estate) of a
person deceased without (male) issue (or an appointed daughter)." Cognates are indicated by the term *Bandhu.*

Greek and Roman antiquities provide well-known examples of
the action of agnatism. The *genos* (*patra*) is as old as Greece
itself: in these associations the patriarchal principle is clearly
fundamental. Aristotle says: "The family is the association estab-
ished by nature for the supply of man's everyday wants, and the
members of it are called by Charondas 'companions of the cup-
board' [*homesipuous*], and by Epimenides the Cretan 'companions of the manger' [*homokapous*]. But when several families
are united and the association aims at something more than the
supply of daily needs, then comes into existence the village. And
the most natural form of the village appears to be that of a
colony from the family composed of the children and the grandchildren who are said to be 'suckled with the same milk'
[*homogalaktos*]."

The period of the Eupatrids in Athens may serve as an example. The ancient constitution of that city before Cleisthenes
was entirely based on a federation of phratries and *genē.* All these
alliances were essentially agnatic; they possessed the usual characteristic features—they started from the household around a
hearth fire, though the unit of association was frequently enlarged
by adoption; but it was always thought that the adopted sons
stepped entirely into the position of those naturally born. The
marriage of the heiress (*epiklēros*) with the nearest agnate in
Greece, the succession and guardianship of agnates in Rome, are
striking expressions of the prevalence of relationship through
males in the social organization of the classical world.

In the case of the Teutons the *sword side* has a natural and
marked precedence over the *spindle side* in all matters concerning
defence and ownership of land. Among Scandinavian folk the
Frostathing law may serve as an example. The customary law of
tribes settled around Trondhjem in Norway treats wergeld from the
agnatic point of view. All those who take the principal parts of the
composition, the *baugar,* are agnates of various degrees; relationship through women is relegated to a subordinate position as the

nefgildi. A woman takes a *baug* only exceptionally, when she is the only daughter and heiress of a slain man (*baugrygr*).

By the side of the principal ties of relationship which start from a patriarchal household and spread out in the ramifications of agnatism, the Aryan nations recognize in a lesser degree the value of relationship through women. There arises a dualism of relationship—on the side of the father (the *spear*) and on the side of the mother (the *spindle*). If we proceed one generation higher, we have to reckon with an alliance of four families in the ascending line, because the descent from four grandparents converges in the case of every individual. If we go further back again to the great-grandfathers and great-grandmothers, we may get *eight lines* of converging descent, etc. The Frisians were actually organized on the basis of certain definite bodies of relationship called the *Klüfte* (corresponding to the four grandparents) and the *Fechten* (corresponding to the eight great-grandparents).[1]

The Germanic conception of the *Sippe* (*sibja*—Goth.) came to be applied to relationship on both sides—through males and through females, although there are clear traces of an earlier arrangement on strictly agnatic principles.

The stream of feeling of union naturally diminishes with the remoteness of the degree of kinship. The further two persons are apart from each other in generation and household, the less powerful will be the bond of union between them: and we must therefore expect that in all systems of relationship it will be necessary to recognize certain concentric circles within which the rights and duties of the relations are more or less intense. On the evidence of actual facts, this is certainly true; we may observe everywhere this characteristic formation of circles.

A conspicuous example is to be found in Greek criminal procedure—the survival of the right of *accusation by the kindred*. Homicide was, in the view of ancient Greek law, chiefly a private

---

[1]
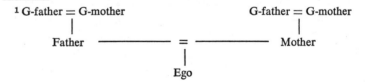

wrong: or perhaps it would be more accurate to say that it was a public wrong which was inflicted not on the city, but on a clan. Hence came the rule of Greek criminal law that, when a man was slain, the accusation against the slayer should come from the relatives of the man killed. The principle is very definitely formulated in a law of Dracon of 621 B.C. The fragment was transcribed after the overthrow of the Four Hundred about 409 B.C., and thanks to this transcription we have an authentic record of the early law as to homicide: a law, it is to be remembered, which preceded the Solonian by one generation. The principal prosecutors are members of the *amchisteia,* a circle of close relationship.[2]

"The lead in a prosecution of the slayer in the market-place shall be taken by all relations nearer than the degree of cousinship, and cousins and children of cousins, and sons-in-law and fathers-in-law and members of the phratry shall join in the prosecution. And if there be a question as to conciliation, then, if there be a father or brother or sons, they shall all join in allowing the conciliation, and if any one of them opposes it, he shall prevail."

Thus the initial accusation had to be made in the market by relations within the degree of first cousins once removed, and it is very important to note that in the next stage this wider kindred merges in the *phratry,* the extension of the *genos:* so that ultimately these kindreds are conceived as big households federated in phratries. The next provision of the law is that, while the kindred can claim the execution of the offender, they are also empowered to enter into a compromise with him. But the decision as to conciliation must be unanimous on the part of the narrower family circle, and even one single dissentient voice is an effective bar to the whole proceeding. If there are no direct

---

[2] The *amchisteia* in the fifth and fourth centuries comprised the collaterals up to the degree of first cousins once removed or, possibly, of second cousins (corresponding to the Latin *sobrini*), both on the male and on the female side. In the case of succession we meet the same extension of the narrow household circle into the *amchisteia,* comprising relations *mechri anepsiotētos,* that is, up to first cousins once removed, but in this case the claims of relations through females (sisters, aunts and cousins) are admitted, although the male side is preferred. In view of the constitution of the *patra* or *genos* it can hardly be doubted that the fourth century rule was an extension of an earlier agnatic arrangement.

relatives, then the decision devolves solely on the phratry, ten members of which are empowered to declare for composition if they think proper.

In this particular instance we are dealing with an advanced civilization: Athens about 621 B.C. had become not only very civilized, but to a great extent commercialized; the Greeks looked at relationship more or less from a point of view resembling our own; and yet the dependence of the individual on the kindred is strongly expressed. Among other races which developed much more slowly, we find the same idea of concentric circles of relationship more definitely connected with the growth of the households. A notable example appears among the Celts in the Irish *Fine*.[3] The principle of organization does not merely estimate

[3] *Gelfine*—own household descendants of the same father: brothers, nephews, sons, grandsons.

Derbfine—certain kin: descendants of the same grandfathers: uncles, first cousins, first cousins' sons.

Iarfine—further kin: descendants of great-grandfathers: great-uncles, second cousins and their sons.

Indfine—end of kin: fourth degree—third cousins.

Derbfine	*Iarfine*	*Indfine*
Certain	Subsequent	Final
	3rd degree	
son of 1st cousin	son of 2nd cousin	son of 3rd cousin
	2nd degree	
1st cousin Mac bráthar athar	2nd cousin	3rd cousin
	1st degree	
paternal uncle Bráthir athar	grand-uncle	great-grand-uncle
grand-father	great-grand-father	great-great-grand-father

Gelfine					*Derbfine*	*Iarfine*	*Indfine*
4th degree,	3rd degree,	2nd degree,	1st degree,				
great-great-grand-son	great-grand-son	grand-son	son	father	Sen-athair	Sen-sen-athair	great-grand-father
Indúa	Iarmúa	Úa	Mac	Athair			

Dóini, outsiders to the family, form a fifth class.

the degree of proximity, but leads to a computation ascending to the heads of definite households.

The conclusion to be drawn from all these examples is that even in cases when the blood tie is recognized, relations are organized according to households, so that cognatism appears as the result of an alliance between patriarchally organized families. This is the essence of the *stirpes or parentelae,* as they were called in mediaeval times. The *stirps* consisted of descendants of one particular household: it could be the house of the father or mother,[4] but it could also be the house of an uncle, as the representative of a connection through the grandfather, or that of a great-uncle—the descendant of a great-grandfather.

In its wider extension relationship becomes kinship. When organized into a group, it acts as a union for the purposes of self-defence and other vital social requirements. Let us notice the material distinction between a kindred and a clan. The latter embraces only agnatic relations: it is based on the idea of the ever-expanding household, and agnation is the fundamental principle which creates and maintains it. In the kindred, on the other hand, cognation is admitted as a concurrent conception. But while it is both useful and necessary to observe these differences in terminology, which express very different notions and give rise to very different kinds of rights, it is not to be supposed that because clans come into existence, the kindred in the wider sense becomes impossible, or *vice versa.* It is necessary to emphasize this fact, because the contrast of the two principles has given rise to some misconceptions in the treatment of the subject. After studying social formations merely from the point of view of the clan, and realizing the fundamental difference between the principles of clan and kindred, many writers have supposed that the two things are to some extent mutually exclusive. Fustel de Coulanges, for instance, entirely disregards cognatic ties in the construction of the Roman and Greek family. On the other hand, even so authoritative a historian as Maitland declared that as soon as men recognize the wide circle of cognatic relationship, we had better cease to speak of clans. In reality it is erroneous

---

[4] The alliance between the household of the father and that of the mother is clearly expressed in Old Norwegian Law, as *fadherm* and *modherni.*

to make the terms mutually exclusive in this rigid manner; for on examining the evidence we find that in innumerable cases the two formations overlap, as it were, and combine in all kinds of compromises suggested by utility. In many cases, though we find a very pronounced recognition of the clan principle, another powerful influence is also asserting itself: the necessity for alliances in self-defence makes it desirable to call in other clans or kindreds into association with the principal group. In this way around a kernel of agnatic relationship supplementary cognatic alliances are formed. On the other hand, it is easy to realize that in course of time, as the individual becomes more and more emancipated and the State grows stronger, the strict principle of clan organization begins to fade. In proportion as it declines, individual relationship takes the place of the household bond. It is along such lines of transition that the history of social institutions is found to proceed.

Let us look at the clan as the more consistent manifestation of agnatic kinship. All the members of the clan traced their pedigree from one original household and all regarded themselves as having a share by right in the territory held by the collective body of the clan. Thus there is a lively personal consciousness of the principle of combination between representatives of all kinds of social grades and occupations. The intensity of the feeling for the clan was best shown when attempts were made to disband this kind of organization. Scott provides us in *Rob Roy* with a vivid account of the circumstances under which the clan McGregor was outlawed and subjected to protracted persecution.

What were the leading features in the normal organization and management of a clan? They have been made familiar to us in literary form by Walter Scott. In some of his descriptions of Scotch life he has provided remarkable pictures of these arrangements, and his account is highly valuable not only for its intrinsic vigour and interest, but for the accuracy of the information it contains. In *Waverley,* for example, he gives us a picture of the clan of Fergus MacIvor, in 1745, and it should be remembered that this is not merely an imaginative description, but one which would have applied with perfect appropriateness to any of the great clans of Scottish history—the MacDonalds, Gordons, Mackintoshs, etc. In Chapter XX we are told that during the rising of 1745 a chieftain invited an English officer to a banquet. At the head of the table sat the chief and his visitor; then the elders of the chief's tribe, wadsetters and tacksmen, as they were called, who occupied portions of the estates as mortgagers or lessees, sat next in rank; lower down their sons and nephews and foster-brothers; then the officers of the chief's household, according to their order, and lowest of all, the tenants who actually cultivated the land. Outside this group—on the green—was a multitude of Highlanders of a yet inferior description, who nevertheless were entitled to take part in the meal. "These stout idle kinsmen of mine," explained the chieftain, "account my estate as held in trust for their support, and I must find them beef and ale, while the rogues do nothing but practise the broad sword, or wander about the hills shooting, fishing, hunting, drinking and making love to the lasses of the strath."

We need not dwell further on these expressions of corporate life, for their meaning is fairly well realized in England. Let us consider in greater detail the internal organization of these social unions. No better evidence can be adduced for this purpose than that of Welsh documents. The strong ties of the *wyrion* or kindred are produced by the actual growth of households through many generations. In the Denbigh Extent, the Black Book of St. David's, the Record of Carnarvon, and similar documents, we can watch the progress of the clan organization from stage to stage. Let us take one simple and characteristic example of a Welsh clan-unit. It is the *lectum* or stock of a certain Rand Vaghan ap Asser. Its beginnings may be tabulated as on page 66.

Such groups often represent something like sixty persons, counting only males. There is a definitely organized system of defence which includes the male members of the clan down to the seventh degree. The clan was by no means an amorphous and ill-organized mass. It is governed by certain strict rules of relationship, which form two inner circles: a narrower, limited to second cousins or to the fourth generation, and a wider which stretches to the seventh and to the ninth generation.

The first and most obvious purpose of the clan organization is to provide an adequate defence for its members. This necessity expresses itself in the blood-feud, one of the most primordial

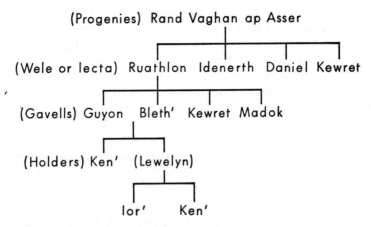

institutions of society: it represents the vengeance taken by the body of kinsmen for a wrong inflicted on one of their number. Though its origin goes very far back in history, it is not confined merely to primitive communities: we can find notable examples of it in comparatively late society. For instance, this is how Domesday Book describes its occurrence in a Welsh district: "If a Welshman slays another, the relations of the deceased assemble and harry the slayer and his relatives, and set their houses on fire until the corpse of the dead man is buried the next day about noon. Of the loot the king recovers one-third and they get the rest in peace." Certain police considerations are beginning to assert themselves as regards the exercise of natural right, but they culminate in a claim to a third of the booty and limitation of the harrying in point of time.

The blood-feud generally resolves into a system of *composition* or material compensation for the injury inflicted. It is easy to understand that in primitive societies, when a wrong done to a single individual might lead to retribution by a whole group of kindred, there was a constant danger of private war, which would be exceedingly injurious to society at large unless checked by *arbitration*. The incipient State did all it could to render conciliation acceptable to individual disputants, and it did not always have a very easy task. The desire for personal vengeance was very strong: and we must not suppose that because at a very early stage we find elaborate tariffs of payments for various wrongs, the principle of reconciliation was established beyond cavil. The practice is described in a graphic manner by Miklosich as regards Southern Slavs:

The humiliating position which the guilty person assumes in the presence of the injured party, and which is indeed the main feature of the ceremony, is supposed to tame the savage mood of the avenger and to incline him to forgiveness. The same object is thought to be achieved by the bringing forward of innocent and helpless infants. The kerchiefs, *mouchoirs,* which Vialla describes as lying in the cradles of these infants, are presents, the acceptance of which is the first indication that the injured party is willing to forgive. It is probable, however, that this interpretation rests on a misunderstanding, for according to J. G. Kohl each of the children is presented with a little cloth by the injured man as being his god-child. The murderous weapon hanging round the neck of the guilty person denotes that he is entirely in the power of the injured person. Vialla and Kohl state that the weapon is deliberately broken. The associations of god-parents and of chosen brothers are intended to confirm the friendship of the tribes. The presence of many members of both tribes gives the act of atonement the necessary publicity. The part played by the priest in the transaction in no way transforms it into a religious or ecclesiastical ceremony; his presence is to be explained sufficiently by the fact that the assembly needs the aid of some one able to write. So much for the rites of atonement in Montenegro and the neighbouring territories.

The corresponding ceremony among the Albanians so closely resembles that usual among the Montenegrins that an influence must undoubtedly have been exercised by one nation over the other. The fact that the Montenegrin ceremony differs in certain respects from that of other Slav nations, and that it is precisely in these respects that it coincides with the Albanian rites, would lead one to suppose that the influence came from the Albanians. Moreover, the Albanian act seems clearer. The priest adjures the injured person in the name of the Cross, the Book, and the innocent Blood. . . .

In many cases there were among the people a strong feeling against "composition" and a marked reluctance to adopt it in practice. As an example of the disgust with which compensation was often regarded, we may take the famous story of the cursed treasure as told in the Edda and in Germanic Sagas.

Three gods, Odin, Hoenir and Loki, start on one of their usual wanderings round the world, and put up at the house of a certain Hreidmar. They sleep there, and in the morning go out to the stream which runs by the house and see an otter catching fish in the stream. They kill it, but it turns out to be the son of the owner of the house who had taken that shape for the purpose of fishing. The surviving kinsmen ought to take revenge, but prefer to accept gold as compensation. This gold is obtained from a dwarf, Andvari, who curses any one into whose possession his treasure, and especially a magic ring of his, may come.

Evidently the practice of taking gold in compensation for blood was repulsive to the primitive mind. At the same time, there is the testimony of whole systems of law to show that the composition for injuries came to be treated in a perfectly business-like fashion and that individuals and wrongs to individuals were actually paid for in carefully estimated sums of cash. Let me quote an interesting fragment from the Anglo-Saxon laws.[5]

(1) *Twelfhyndes mannes wer is twelf hund scyllinga.*

The wergeld of a 1200-man is twelve hundred shillings.

(1, 1) *Twyhyndes mannes wer is twa hund scill'.*

The wergeld of a 200-man is two hundred shillings.

(2) *Gif man ofslægen weordhe, gylde hine man swa he geboren sy.*

If a man is slain, let the measure of compensation be according to his birth.

(3) *And riht is, dhæt se slaga, sidhdhan he weres beweddod hæbbe, finde dhærto wærborh, be tham dhe dhærto gebyrige: dhæt is æt twelfhyndum were gebyriadh twelf men to werborge, VIII fæderenmægdhe and IIII medrenmægdhe.*

And it is right that the slayer, when he has given a gage as to the wergeld, should also find the pledges required by it: that is, for the wergeld of a 1200-man twelve men shall be pledges, eight from the father's line and four from the mother's line.

---

[5] The Old English þ has been rendered by *th* and ð by *dh*.

(4) *Dhonne thæt gedon sy, dhonne rære man cyninges munde, dhæt is dhæt hy ealle gemænum handum of ægdhere mægdhe on anum wæpne dham semende syllan, dhæt cyninges mund stande.*

When that has been done, let the king's peace be established between them: that is, let them all of both lines of descent give sign by joining hands upon one weapon before an arbitrator that the king's peace is established.

(4, I) *Of dham dæge on XXI nihtan gylde man CXX scill' to healsfange æt twelfhyndum were.*

For 21 nights after that day let there be a payment of 120 shillings as a *Halsfang* from the wergeld of a 1200-man.

(5) *Healsfang gebyredh bearnum, brodhrum and fæderan; ne gebyredh nanum mæge dhæt feodh . . . bute dham dhe sy binnan cneowe.*

Halsfang falls to children, brothers and father's brothers: and that payment falls to no other kin save those who are "within the knee."

(6) *Of dham dæge, dhe dhæt healsfang agolden sy, on XXI nihtan gylde man dha manbote; dhæs on XXI nihtan dhæt fyhtewite; dhæs on XXI nihtan dhæs weres dhæt frumgyld; and swa fordh thæt fulgolden sy on dham fyrste, dhe witan geræden.*

For 21 nights from the day when the *Halsfang* has been paid, let the manbot be paid: then for 21 nights the *fyhtewite* (*id est forisfactura pugne*); then for 21 nights the frumgild (*id est prima redditio*) of the same wergeld; and so forth until full payment shall be made up to the time decreed by the *witan*.

(6, I) *Sidhdhan man mot mid lufe ofgan, gif man hwile . . . fulle freondrædne habban.*

Thereafter the slayer may abide in love, if he desire to have full fellowship with his friends.

(7) *Eal man sceal æt cyrliscum were be thære mædhe don, dhe him to gebyredh, swa we be twelfhyndum tealdan.*

The same things shall be observed touching the wergeld of a ceorl, according to the sum that befits him, even as we have written concerning a 1200-man.

There are two points to be particularly noted: (1) the marked preponderance of the agnatic element, the influence of the male relations of the father. These kinsmen claim two-thirds of the compensation of the *frumgild* portion of the *magbót,* and also stand security for the payment of two-thirds. They are therefore assumed to be interested in the affair twice as strongly as the kin on the mother's side. (2) The nearest relatives of the deceased come in only for a share, and not a very large share, of the compensation: they take altogether one-tenth, the *Halsfang,* and possibly some portion of the *frumgild.* Two-tenths go to the lord and the king, while the kindred at large take no less than seven-tenths, although, probably, the closer circle of relations shared in this portion. If so, its members would take only as members of the general body of the kindred.

An interesting situation created by the conflict between traditions of kinship organization and settlement on individualistic lines is presented by Icelandic law. Their collection, the *Grágás,* makes a most elaborate statement as to the shares of wergeld (*nidgjold*) to be received and paid by relatives of various degrees in case of manslaughter, when the slayer has been outlawed and has left the country. The payments are arranged in three sections, of which the first—to near relations—is particularly called *baugar,* in accordance with Norwegian terminology; but the general heading of the chapter treating of this subject, *baugatal,* and the mention of all the *baugar* in the sequel, indicates that all the fractions of the wergeld of 120 *öre* enumerated in it were *baugar* in a wider sense. The limit of kinship is drawn in this statement at the degree of fourth cousins (*thridhia brödhra ens vegna*). This is not an isolated calculation of relationship. Icelandic "poor law" builds up its system of assistance to destitute people on a combination between income and relationship, and the latter is limited in the same way as in *baugatal,* namely, by the degree of fourth cousins. This establishes the fact that we have to deal with actual conditions, and not with mere reminiscences of Norwegian custom. In the twelfth century, at any rate, kindreds had grown into sufficiently extensive and ramified groups to admit of a reckoning of rights and duties stretching to the degree of fourth cousins, issued in the direct line from a common ancestor who may have lived some 150 years before. The tracing of descent from an *atavus* (great-great-great-grandfather) was a possible contingency, even if the original settlers of the *Landnama* are to be considered as single individuals: although in many cases brothers and cousins of various degrees had migrated together. However this may be, emigrants from a country where kinship was as strongly developed as it was in Norway, kept up the conception, and it naturally gave rise to a new crop of rules based on relationship in the new home. I have to insist on these points of detail in order to guard against the extreme view that *baugatal* is unreal, and could not possibly be applied in practice in Iceland. It presents, of course, a kind of diagram or scheme, which covers all sorts of possible ramifications, and for this very reason must have been constantly modified in practice. But it would be rather reckless to reject such a deliberate statement of legal custom, which, besides, is entirely in agreement with similar rules in all varieties of barbaric law, and with statements in other parts of the *Grágás*. The fact that the Sagas do not allude in detail to the repartition of payment between the members of kindreds can certainly not invalidate the definite statement of the law-book: such minute questions did not interest the story-tellers or their public, while the fact that those who helped in the feud were rewarded by shares in fines is not infrequently noticed in the Sagas. As we know of many instances of increased payments (e.g. triple wergelds in Njála), we have to bear in mind that the official standards of payment and distribution were supplemented in many cases by voluntary agreements in which both the amount and the repartition must have greatly varied.

One problem remains, however: how is the statement of the *baugatal* to be reconciled or combined with the directions of the chapter immediately preceding it—the *vigslódi* (consequences of homicide) of the *Grágás?* The fine mentioned in the chapter is, however, specifically distinguished from the *baugar* and the supplementary payments of the *nidgjold*. It is a uniform fine of 48 öre, called *Rettr,* and is payable in cases of manslaughter, rape, wounding and assault. For its application in cases of homicide we get a definite formula in the *Stadharhálsbók* version of the Law. The accuser claims, besides, the property of the slayer. This procedure takes place only in cases of outlawry, but outlawry is the starting-point for the application of all *vigslódi* rules. They are intended to regulate the claim of the nearest heir of the deceased, and are independent of the actual prosecution of the feud or suit,[6] as well as of the *nidgjold*. This fact in itself shows that we have to deal here with personal rights not covered by feud and composition. For this reason women take shares according to *vigslódi*, while they are excluded in *baugatal*.

On the whole, there can be no doubt that, although Icelandic conditions favoured scattered settlements and individualistic enterprise, the support of kinsmen was one of the most effective means of protection against aggression and violence. There are no traces of a clan system, but the Scandinavian kindred, the *aet*, is in full vigour, and its influence increases as generations follow one another in wider ramifications. The *thridhia brödhra* (fourth cousins) cannot be considered as a necessary element of every kindred, but their mention remains characteristic, even though it only marks a possible and occasional limit.

By a remarkable coincidence the same features are to be observed in the social organization of Celtic peoples. With the Celts of North Wales, the kin was organized much more stringently than among the Anglo-Saxons or Scandinavians. It was in fact a clan, but the fundamental provisions concerning the payment of composition are the same. The system observed among these Celtic tribes is recorded, for instance, in the version of the Venedotian Code; it estimates the shares of agnatic relations, or rather of the father's kindred, at twice as much as those of the mother's.

The first third (of the *galanas*) falls on the murderer, and the mother and father and brothers and sisters with him, for those persons would receive with him a third of the galanas if paid to them, therefore let them pay so with him . . . (one-third of it on the mother and father, one-third on brothers and sisters, and one-third on the murderer . . . males paying two parts and females one).

The remaining two-thirds fall on the kindred (two parts of it

---

6 *Bötr allar om vigsaear ligo arftaco menn hvart sem theirero kazlar edha konor hvergi er söc söcir edha huergi adhile ed.* (Whosoever institutes the suit or is leader.) It is improbable that this sentence should be referred exclusively to the time before the rule of 944 which forbade women to prosecute in slaying suits.

on the kindred of the father and one part on the kindred of the mother).

The kindred for this purpose is confined within the seventh generation:

1. Brother   = *braut.*
2. 1st cousin   = *keuenderu.*
3. 2nd cousin   = *keuerderu.*
4. 3rd cousin   = *keyuyn.*
5. 4th cousin   = *gorcheyuen.*
6. 5th cousin   = *gorchau.*
7. Son of 5th cousin = *mab gorchau.*

Feud and composition are by no means the only expression of kindred solidarity in ancient law. Some notion as to the extent of mutual support may be gathered for instance from a passage from the law of the Salian Franks (*c.* 60 A.D.) which deals with the case of a man who has renounced his kindred—a case which may have occurred frequently, for it is easy to understand that, as individualistic conceptions began to assert themselves, a man might not wish to make himself responsible for the deeds of his kindred, and, *vice versa,* the kindred might not desire the presence among its members of particularly untrustworthy individuals. The ceremony of renunciation took the symbolic form of breaking sticks over the head of the man who quitted the kindred (*qui se de parentela tollere vult*). He renounced his claims to inheritance and oath-help, and all other forms of solidarity with the kindred. After this renunciation by him, his former kinsmen could not claim either inheritance or composition in respect of this person.

In this ceremony one of the most important features is the renunciation of oath-help. This was a most fundamental institution of tribal communities. We have seen that when disputes take the form of an actual feud, the kindred support the individual in the prosecution of his claim by force. In the same way, when the issue has to be decided not by violent means, but by the award of a regularly constituted court, a modified form of the struggle is usual: the claimant comes before the tribunal surrounded by his kindred, who take the responsibility of supporting him very much as in actual battle. They swear in support of his contention. This is the result of the view that collisions occur not between individuals, but between societies: and if one member of a kindred or clan has to come forth as accuser or accused, he appears in conjunction with his natural helpers, and the legal issue proceeds on the lines of assertion and compurgation in cases when there was a reasonable probability of the assertion being true. On the other hand, if appearances were strongly against a contention, the court usually awarded ordeal. Much depended, of course, on the manner in which the burden of proof was assigned by the tribunal.

It is impossible here to consider the practice of compurgation in all its details: the important point for us to note is that here in court, as well as on the field of battle, kindreds were pitted against each other as unions.

There are a certain number of other functions and duties which arise as incidental to the main activities of the kindred organization. We find, for example, that the kin assume responsibility for the guardianship of minors. We are not told exactly who the guardians were, nor on what principle they were appointed to the office. It is a constant disadvantage of ancient evidence that it leaves us in the dark as to everyday occurrences, which are supposed to be known to everybody and therefore do not need to be recorded. It seems clear, however, that in early times the kin, besides providing individual guardians, exercised the same general functions of guardianship as are definitely assigned to the State by later law.

Again, as has already been mentioned, the kindred took and gave securities in connection with weddings, and it has been noted how provision is made that when a woman passes to the house of her husband, certain bonds are kept up which ensure her remaining in touch with her own kindred.

In some instances the kin undertook the maintenance of destitute people. This appears, for example, in Iceland, where tribal arrangements were necessarily individualized, and the tribal principle resolved itself very largely into a succession of claims and duties. In India, on the other hand, the weight of supporting needy members was thrown on the kindreds as groups, and on their natural subdivisions.

§§ 4

THE CYMRIC EVIDENCE

Frederic Seebohm

The Unit of Cymric Tribal Society

[I will now] give a brief summary of the results of the evidence contained in the volume on the *Tribal System in Wales,* adding at the same time such further details as may be useful in helping us to realize the methods by which tribal custom worked itself out in practice.

The chief fact revealed by the examination of the Extents and Surveys of different parts of Wales made after the English conquest, taken together with the Cymric Codes, was that the unit of society and of land-occupation under Cymric tribal custom was not the individual, and not the immediate family, but the group of kindred known as the *"Wele"* or *"Gwely."*

Such and such a Villata or District is described in the surveys as in the occupation of the gwelys of so and so, the Latin word used for *gwely* being *lectus* or bed.

The form of society thus revealed was *patriarchal* in the sense that the common ancestor (generally conceived to be the great-grandfather) during his life, and even after his death, was regarded as the head of the *gwely* or group of his descendants for three generations. In his name as its head this family group

From Frederic Seebohm, *Tribal Custom in Anglo-Saxon Law* (London: Longmans, Green, 1902), Ch. 2.

occupied land and had grazing rights over certain districts, sometimes alone, more often in common with other family groups.

As to what is meant by land ownership in the full modern sense, the question may not have arisen, or it might have come in gradually sooner or later, as agriculture came more and more into prominence. What property, strictly speaking, the tribesmen owned consisted mainly of herds of cattle.

Naturally, therefore, what rights over land they may have had were mainly rights of occupation and grazing in certain districts for their herds. Their agriculture was secondary, and consisted of the right to plough up such portions of the waste or common pasture as year by year might be required for their corn crop. All that need be said at this moment about their agriculture is that it was an open field husbandry, the result of the co-ploughing of a common plough-team normally of 8 oxen, the joint contribution of several tribesmen.

Returning to the gwely, we find that when a child was born into it, whether boy or girl, it was formally acknowledged by the kindred. It remained "at the father's platter" to a certain age (generally 14), and then the father ceased to be responsible. The boy at 14 became the "man and kin" of the chieftain of the family group, or it might be of the higher kindred embracing several of the gwelys. From that moment the boy obtained by "kin and descent" a tribesman's right of maintenance. That is to say, he received from the chieftain his *da,* probably in the form of an allotment of cattle,[1] and with it the right to join in the co-ploughing of the waste. He became thus a tribesman on his own hook,

---

[1] Prof. Rhys informs me that *da* in Carnarvonshire local dialect still means "cattle," while in other parts of Wales it has the wider meaning of "goods."

The allotment of cattle involved grazing rights, and often separate homesteads. Accordingly in the Denbigh Extent we find that so and so "*habet domum*" or "*non habet domum.*"

This dependence for maintenance of the boy upon the higher chieftain is indirectly confirmed by the Extents, which mention among the chieftain's rights the "fosterage of youths" etc.

That the chieftain who gives the *da* was the "chief of kindred" and not a mere territorial lord is shown by the fact that when a stranger family have lived in the land till they have formed a kindred by intermarriage with Cymraes, all the members of the family become "man and kin" to the chief of kindred of the new kindred.

apart from his father. So that the unit of society was not simply the family in the modern sense of a parent and his children, but the wider kindred of the gwely or the group of related gwelys headed by the chieftain who provided the *da*.

The Constitution and Working of the Gwely

Now, as the gwely was the unit of land-occupation, it is worth while to try to realize a little further what it was and how it worked.

Viewed in its simplest and perhaps original form, it was a family group of four generations, the landed rights of which were vested in the great-grandfather as its chieftain.

The tribesmen, his descendants, had only rights of maintenance. By right of "kin and descent" they had received their *da* from the chieftain. The flocks and herds of the chieftain were the common stock out of which the *da* had been given, and there is reason to believe that under earlier custom, on the death of a tribesman, his *da* went back into the common stock of the chieftain.

At the date of the codes it did so when the tribesman died *without issue*. But in the codes a *peculium* of private property of which the *da* was the kernel is recognized and allowed to descend to a tribesman's children instead of falling into the common stock.

When the great-grandfather died, the chieftainship, with the landed rights and the herds, was divided between his sons, who as brothers thus became chiefs of sub-gwelys. But the original gwely did not then break up, because there would be a right of division *per capita* when the brothers were dead between first cousins, and when the first cousins were dead between second cousins.

The division between brothers was probably originally made only between those sons of the parent who were living at his death. Like the sons of the surviving brothers, the sons of a deceased brother must be content with their *da* till all the brothers were dead, and in the division between first cousins they would take their share *per capita* along with the rest.

But at the time of the codes, by what Continental examples lead us to regard as an innovation, the orphaned nephews were allowed in the division to succeed at once, side by side with their uncles, to the share and position which their father would have taken had he survived.

Even after this innovation, if a brother had died *without issue,* his brothers as brothers did not at once succeed as co-heirs. The share fell into the common stock till a division, and then went to all the co-inheritors *per capita,* so that cousins, and it might be even second cousins, took their shares in it.

The introduction of succession by representation to a deceased father's property and privilege was, as we shall see in Continental cases, a step taken in the direction of individual ownership. It complicated the matter of the division or devolution of the chieftainship in the gwely, but it is a point of interest in connection with the Continental evidence.

A clear understanding of the constitution and working of the gwely, as a typical family group, is so important to this inquiry that it is worth while to place before the reader the passages in codes upon which, taken together with the surveys, the foregoing description of it rests.

The following is the clause in the Venedotian Code describing what took place in the gwely, under the heading "The Law of Brothers for Land":

Thus, brothers are to share land between them: four *erws* to every *tyddyn* [homestead]. Bleddyn, son of Cynvyn, altered it to twelve erws to the *uchelwr,* and eight to the *aillt,* and four to the *godaeog;* yet, nevertheless, it is most usual that four erws be in the tyddyn. . . .

If there be no buildings on the land, the youngest son is to divide all the patrimony (*trew y tat*), and the eldest is to choose, and each in seniority choose unto the youngest.

If there be buildings the youngest brother but one is to divide the tyddyns, for in that case he is the meter; and the youngest to have his choice of the tyddyns; and after that he is to divide all the patrimony; and by seniority they are to choose unto the youngest; and that division is to continue during the lives of the brothers.

And after the brothers are dead, the first cousins are to equalise if they will it; and thus they are to do: the heir of the youngest brother is to equalise, and the heir of the eldest brother is to choose, and so by seniority unto the youngest; and that distribution is to continue between them during their lives.

And if second cousins should dislike the distribution which took place between their parents, they also may co-equate in the same manner as the first cousins; and after that division no one is either to distribute or to co-equate. *Tir gwelyauc* is to be treated as we have above stated.

In the Dimetian Code the same rules of division are stated as follows:

When brothers share their patrimony (*tref-eu-tat*) between them, the youngest is to have the principal tyddyn, and all the buildings of his father, and eight erws of land, his boiler, his fuel hatchet, and his coulter, because a father cannot give those three to any but the youngest son, and though they should be pledged they never become forfeited. Then let every brother take a home-stead (*eissydyn*) with eight erws of land, and the youngest son is to share, and they are to choose in succession from the eldest to the youngest.

Three times shall the same patrimony be shared between three grades of a kindred, first between brothers, the second time between cousins, the third time between second cousins, after that there is no propriate share of land. . . .

After there shall have been a sharing of land acquiesced in by co-inheritors, no one of them has a claim on the share of the other, he having issue, except for a sub-share *when the time for that shall arrive.* Yet whosoever shall not have any issue of his body, *his co-inheritors, within the three degrees of kin from the stock, are to be his heirs.*

Only by adhering very closely to these texts can the gwely be understood. They seem at first sight to refer to the tyddyns or homesteads, but, as we have seen, the landed rights of grazing in the villatae in which the gwelys were located were included also.

It would obviously be a fair critical question to ask, what happened when the second cousins at last broke up the gwely of their grandfather and divided the land, or let us say the home-steads and the tribal rights of grazing on the land, for the last time equally *per capita*? There might be twenty or thirty of such second cousins. Did the original gwely split up into twenty or thirty new gwelys? Let us try to realise what happened by carefully following the text, in the light of the Denbigh Survey.

Let us take a hypothetical case in which the gwely of X is described by the surveyor as holding an undivided share of the rights of pasture, etc., in a particular villata or in several villatae; and assume that, according to the record, the internal divisions of the gwely followed the family division of the descendants of X, as in the following table. Then, applying the rules of the clauses as to *tir gwelyauc,* let us see how it would work out in the hypothetical case stated.

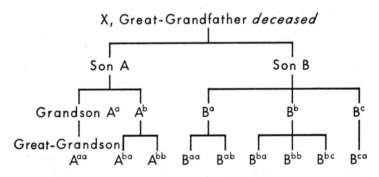

Now let us suppose that X (the great-grandfather, from whom the gwely is called the gwely of X) is dead. While his sons A and B are alive they share equally in the grazing and other rights. When A is dead and so long as B is alive no change is made except that A's two sons share equally their father's right to which, in the phrase of the codes, they have "ascended." B at length dies. There are five grandsons, first cousins, who have a right to share in the rights of the gwely of X *per capita.* There is now therefore a rearrangement after which A's sons share and hold jointly only two fifths while B's three sons hold jointly three fifths. Equality *per capita* among grandsons has now been effected. But the gwely goes on. It cannot be broken up because in another generation the great-grandsons may require a fresh division.

Next let us see what happens when all the grandsons are dead and the final division *per capita* takes place. There are nine great-grandsons. Is the gwely of X now to be divided into nine new gwelys? Certainly not. The grandsons of A are entitled to three ninths only, and this they divide *per capita,* being first cousins; one family takes one third and the other two thirds. The portion which has fallen to them of family rights in the gwely of X has become a separate gwely, called either the gwely of A or, as we sometimes find in the Denbigh Survey, the "gwely of the grandsons of A"—"*gwely weiryon A.*" The other portion has become either the gwely of B or the gwely of the grandsons of B—"*gwely weiryon B.*"

The grandsons of B, being first cousins, have of course redivided their six ninths equally *per capita,* and the internal rights of the gwely of the grandsons of B are

B^a's two children have $\frac{2}{6}$ths   ⎫
B^b's three children have $\frac{3}{6}$ths ⎬ of $\frac{6}{9}$ths.
B^c's one son has $\frac{1}{6}$th   ⎭

They cannot break up the gwely of "the grandsons of B" because they are not second cousins. But when all of them are dead, their children will be second cousins and may do so, and then three new gwelys will be formed in the same way as above, and so on for ever. The process is continuous and always within the same rules of *tir gwelyauc.*

This seems to be the state of things as regards succession within the gwely resulting from the rules laid down in the Codes and found at work by the surveyors of the Lordship of the Honour of Denbigh. But we must remember that, apart from these rights of succession, each tribesman on becoming a tribesman had been the recipient of his *da,* and so had had cattle of his own all along in the common herd.

Finally, the position of females in the gwely should not pass without recognition. They are not mentioned in the statements of landed rights because, provision having been made for their maintenance independently of their father, they were assumed, whilst claiming their *gwaddol* or portion, to take this with them, on marriage, out of the gwely. They ought to be married into another gwely, within which their sons in due course would receive inheritance and landed rights by paternity. Only on failure of this could their sons claim landed rights by maternity in their mother's original gwely.

The Liability of the Wider Kindred
for Galanas in Case of Homicide

Such being the gwely, we pass on to the wider kindred, embracing the descendants of seven (and for some purposes nine) generations from a common ancestor.

We find from the Cymric Codes that the members of the wider kindred had common responsibilities in case of a homicide causing a blood feud between kindreds. A murder *within* this wider kindred was regarded as a family matter. The murderer was too near of blood to be slain. No atonement could be made for so unnatural a crime. There was no blood fine or *galanas* within the kindred. The murderer must be exiled. But a murder of a member of one kindred by the member of another, inasmuch as, if unatoned for, it would under tribal custom have produced a blood feud between the two kindreds, was the proper subject for the substituted payment of the blood fine or galanas. The galanas was thus a payment from one kindred to another in lieu of the blood feud. But its amount was divided in payment on one side and in distribution on the other, in varying proportion according to nearness of relationship to the murderer or the murdered person as the case might be. And in these payments and receipts all the individual tribesmen within the kindred who had received their *da* must take their share if needful.

The question who had to pay and who had to receive was moreover complicated further by the fact that it involved maternal relations as well as paternal relations. It has been very properly pointed out that, however it might be as regards money payments, it is difficult to conceive how the liability of maternal relations could be worked in the case of actual blood feud and fighting. A man might have to fight for his maternal relations against his paternal relations, or the reverse. In such a case what must he do? How should he act? He might be in an impossible position.

Light upon this point and others may be obtained, perhaps, when the evidence of *Beowulf* is analysed. This evidence will show that a man may have good cause under tribal custom not to join in some feuds. And further it will remind us that feuds often arose in contravention of tribal usage, breaking the peace which in theory the link of marriage ought to have secured.

In the meantime it would seem possible that the custom of a tribe might, for anything we know, forbid marriage *within* the near relationships of the gwely, and *beyond* the limits of the wider kindred. In such a case, paternal and maternal relations might all be within the kindred, so that properly speaking a quarrel between them could not become the subject of a feud.

In such matters it is obvious that a good deal must depend upon the view taken of marriage itself at the particular stage of evolution in which the society might be. And it may as well be said at once that we should be quite wrong were we to regard marriage from the Roman point of view, *i.e.* as a transfer of the woman out of the *potestas* of her parents into the *potestas* of the husband. The Cymric example, to begin with, was quite different. The marriage of sisters to tribesmen from whom their sons could inherit tribal rights was a duty cast upon the kinsmen to the gwely.[2] It was thus an arrangement between two gwelys—a link between them—but no transfer. If a wife were slain, her galanas or death fine did not go to the husband and his family; it went to her kindred. If a wife should commit murder, it was the wife's family and not the husband's on which rested the payment of galanas for her crime. If the husband were killed the wife took one third of the saraad or fine for insult and wounding, but she took no part of the galanas of her husband.[3]

These points are in a sense unexpected. They belong to a stage of social life as far removed from Roman rules, or modern ones, as they are from the stage in which a wife was either purchased outright or stolen. And yet we shall find them in principle more or less clearly repeated in the varying customs of some of the tribes whose laws we are about to examine.

---

[2] If the sister was married to an *alltud* and her son killed a person, two thirds of the galanas fell on the mother's kindred but there was no liability beyond the gwely or second cousins.

[3] On separation, husband and wife divided the cattle and most other things equally.

The Fiscal Unit for the Purpose of
Food-Rents to the Chieftains

The structure of tribal society in Wales is one thing. The practical working of its rules is another. Until we can, to some extent, realize its methods and see how its results could be worked out in everyday life, it must remain to some extent vague and mysterious. The nearer we get to its core, the greater its value as an instrument in further research.

We cannot, therefore, afford to disregard any hints that the Codes and surveys may give us, attention to which would help us to realise its methods or ways of working.

The Denbigh Extent, as already said, enables us to realise that, on the English conquest, the lordship of Denbigh was divided into grazing districts which had become the units of tribal food-rents, and which were adopted for purposes of future taxation. These districts were called by the scribes *villatae,* and were occupied by gwelys of tribesmen and sometimes also by gwelys of non-tribesmen. Their homesteads or huts were occupied in severalty. Their grazing rights were undivided common rights, and within each gwely the rights of families and individuals were also undivided common rights.

Further, the Denbigh Extent shows how easy it was to shift the whole body of tribesmen of this or that gwely, with its herds, from one district to another, according to convenience or the needs of population, without disturbing the complex rights within the gwely. The families and individuals carried their rights, *inter se,* with them wherever they and their herds might go, and were liable to pay the dues required from whatever villata for the time being might be occupied by them.

Even the homesteads of the tribesmen seem to have been temporary, in the light of the description given by Giraldus Cambrensis. They could carry their hearth-stones with them wherever they went, so that the result seems to be that the groups of kindreds could always have been easily shifted about, as they were in fact after the English conquest, from one district or villata to another. The geographical divisions thus became the permanent fiscal units in tribal arrangements. Both in the surveys and in the Codes we find the villata or district, and not the family group, the fixed unit for tribal food-rents to the chieftain, and for taxation after the English conquest.

The surveys so far agree with the Codes. The villata of the surveys was the taxable unit, and in some cases still paid the tunc pound (or 20s.) in lieu of the chieftain's food-rents. In other cases escheats and other causes had varied the amount. In the Codes of South Wales the unit for the tunc pound was the *tref*, and in the Venedotian Code of North Wales the *maenol* of four trefs.

Now, as in the surveys the family groups or gwelys were located so as to occupy sometimes several villatae, and sometimes undivided shares in villatae along with others, so, if we may take the villata of the surveys as equivalent to the tref or maenol of the Codes, we must expect to find that the kindreds of tribesmen at the period of the Codes were scattered in the same way over the trefs and maenols. And, as the maenol was a group of trefs, the tref is the unit of tribal occupation as to which a clear understanding is most necessary. In this, however, we may be, after all, only partly successful.

The word *tref*, though generally used for a homestead or hamlet, seems from its other meanings to involve the idea of a *group*.

There were cases in which a disputed matter of fact had to be established upon the evidence of men of the *gorvotref, i.e.* by men of the groups outside the tref in which the question in dispute arose. And this *gorvotref* was not merely the next adjoining tref or trefs, but it consisted of those *randirs* or divisions of neighbouring trefs of *uchelwrs*, or tribesmen, whose boundaries touched the tref in which the disputed facts arose. Neighbouring randirs of *taeog trefs, i.e.* the trefs of non-tribesmen, were excluded, presumably because the testimony of taeogs in matters relating to tribesmen was not relied on. But this compound of the word tref implies that its general sense was a group of homesteads. That, in general, trefs had defined boundaries, is clear from the fact that it was an offence to break them, and this applied also to the randirs or divisions of the tref.

Speaking, then, of the group generally known as a tref, we must regard it, not only as a taxable area, but also as the natural group known everywhere as a *trefgordd, i.e.* the natural group of the homesteads of relatives or neighbours acting together as a single community as regards their cattle and their ploughing.

The typical lawful *trefgordd* is thus described

> This is the complement of a lawful *trefgordd:* nine houses and one plough and one oven (*odyn*) and one churn (*gordd*) and one cat and one cock and one bull and one herdsman.

There is another passage [in the Denbigh Extent] which mentions the nine buildings in the tref.

> These persons do not forfeit life . . .
> The necessitous for the theft of food after he has traversed three trevs, and nine houses in each trev, without obtaining a gift though asked for.

So, in case of fire from negligence in a tref, the holder of the house in which it arose was to pay for the damage to the next houses on each side if they took fire. And again no indemnity was to be paid to the owners in a trefgordd for damages from the fire of a smithy if covered with shingles or tiles or sods, nor from the fire of a bath, provided always that the smithy and the bath were at least seven fathoms from the other houses in the trefgordd.

The description above quoted of the normal trefgordd suggests that the herd under the one herdsman did not belong to one person or homestead, but to many; and so far it seems to be consistent with the surveys which represent the villatae as occupied by the cattle of several family groups who had grazing rights therein.

And this, too, accords with what the Denbigh Extent tells us of the individual tribesmen, viz. that only some of them had homesteads. So-and-so *habet domum* or *non habet domum.* The young tribesman with his *da* thus may have joined in a common homestead with someone else—probably with his parents or near relatives.

Distinguishing, then, the tref as a taxable area from the trefgordd, and still confining attention to the trefgordd as a cluster of homesteads united for the practical purpose of occupation, let us recur to the things which bound the trefgordd into one group, viz. the one plough, the one oven, the one churn, the one bull, and the one herdsman.

Here are the two elements combined of pastoral and agricultural co-operation, and the trefgordd is the local and physical unit of this co-operation.

Taking first the pastoral element, the trefgordd was a working unit of co-operative dairy-farming. The cattle of several households or individuals were put together in a common herd with a common bull and under the care of a common herdsman (*bugeil*) and his dog. It may be regarded as a group of the homesteads of the persons in charge of such a herd, and the tribesmen of a gwely may have cattle in the herds of more than one trefgordd.

Three things were "ornamental" to a trefgordd, "a book, a teacher versed in song, and a smith (*gov*) in his smithy"; but a trefgordd herdsman was an "indispensable" of the *hendrev*,[4] and, when engaged with his herd in summer on the mountain, *his* "three indispensables" were "a bothy, his herdsman's dog, and a knife"; and the three indispensables of his bothy were a roof-tree, roof-supporting forks, and wattling, and he was at liberty to cut them in any wild wood he pleased.

So far, then, as the pastoral element was concerned, the trefgordd was occupied by a little group of tribesmen engaged in dairy-farming having charge of cattle in a common herd, with a common bull, and under the care of a common herdsman and his dog.

Custom, grown out of traditional experience of what a single herdsman and his dog could manage, had determined, it seems, the size of the normal herd. Thus in the Gwentian Code we are told that "a legal herd of cattle is 24 kine." And custom tenaciously adhered to tribal rules in such matters.

Thus in the Denbigh Extent it is mentioned that the whole villata of Arquedelok was *in manu domini* by reason of escheats and exchanges, and that a portion of it was let *ad firmam* to nine firmarii, each of whom held for a term of years 31 acres, with one bull and 24 cows, paying per annum 73s. 4d., and rendering to the lord at the end of his term the said bull and cows or their price, together with the land and a house built thereon. Here,

---

[4] The principal tref as contrasted with summer bothy on the mountains.

even in a case in which Henry de Lacy was introducing into Wales holdings and herds in severalty, and very possibly introducing English tenants, he adhered to the Welsh tribal rule of the one bull and 24 cows to the herd. So also in the survey of St. David's, under the head *Glaston* in Breconshire, the number 24 of *grossa animalia* is spoken of as the usual number *ab antiqua consuetudine,* and in the arrangement of common pasture one great animal is said to count as equal to twelve sheep.

The normal herd of the trefgordd was then 24 cows, or their equivalent in bullocks and sheep.

During the summer months the herdsman living out on the mountains was responsible with his dog for the cattle of the trefgordd. And his dog was worth as much as a cow or an ox, if it was one that "will go *before* the herd in the morning and *behind* them in the evening, and make three turns *round* them in the night."

Having no cattle of his own in the herd, the herdsman's testimony as to whose cattle were injured, and as to whose cattle had done the injury, was held, when such cases arose, to be sufficient to make the owner responsible, while as regards injuries done by the cattle of one trefgordd to those of another there was joint responsibility. There is common sense in such rules to begin with, and then, having grown into custom, they become perpetuated when custom is codified.

The trefgordd possessed further a common churn. This implies that the milk of the cows was thrown altogether into this one churn as in Swiss mountain communes now. One of the dues from a taeog tref, *i.e.* a group of *non*-tribesmen, was a cheese made from a day's milking of all the cows in the herd. So that we note in passing that the taeog tref, *i.e.* of non-tribesmen, also had its herd and was in fact a trefgordd.

In winter the cattle came down into the lowlands and grazed on the pastures near the tyddyns or homesteads of the tref, and as each of these had its corn and cattle-yard, we may conclude that each owner penned in his own cattle at night during the winter months or joined with some other tribesmen who had a homestead in doing so. The rules as to the divisions of the tyddyns probably referred to these winter homesteads so held in quasi-severalty.

We need not dwell upon the common *oven*. Every hamlet in Brittany possesses its common oven to this day, often in the middle of the village green. Nor need we more than mention the common plough, to the team of which the tribesmen contributed oxen for the *cyvar* or common ploughing of the portion of the waste agreed upon for each year's corn crop. The attempt to realise what this practical unit—the trefgordd —was, will not be thrown away if it should help us to understand how easily it lent itself to the arrangement of the chieftain's food-rents or tribute in after-times of taxation. Granted that some such system of trefgordds or clusters of trefgordds pretty generally prevailed, having grown up as a matter of convenience in a grazing community, it is obvious how easily it might become the unit of tribute or taxation. Just as in the Domesday Survey the number of ploughs affords such a unit, so in a tribal community a district might easily be fiscally estimated at so many herds, or so many churns, or so many ploughs. All these would mean so many trefgordds. And whatever the relations of the trefgordd to the villata of the surveys might be, and however much or often the actual residents, with their herds, might be shifted from one district to another, the district, as in the Denbigh Extent, would remain the permanent unit for payments.

In the early stages of tribal life, when the chieftain of the tribe moved from one district to another and received his food-rents in the actual form of "the night's entertainment," each customary place of encampment in his annual progress would become the centre at which the food-rents would be paid and services rendered for as many nights' entertainment as his accustomed stay in the place. In later stages, when the chieftain's dues were commuted into money, the "tunc pound" in lieu of food-rents easily became, as we find it in the surveys, a charge on the district rather than on the shifting tribesmen and their herds.

And when the power of the chieftain had grown with time, and instead of "nights' entertainments" obtained in the primitive way by the actual movement of himself and his retinue from place to place, the food-rents or the tunc pounds in lieu of them were delivered at his palace, he would become the recipient of a regular revenue. And out of this revenue it would become easy for him to reward a follower or endow a church by the transfer of so many food-rents or tunc pounds in lieu of them, or the revenue from such and such a district, or of so many of its trefgordds, without disturbing the internal working of the system or the daily life of the tribesmen and their herds. When Beowulf returns to his chieftain after his exploit and is rewarded by the gift of a palace and so many "thousands," we naturally ask of what, and how it could be done. We may not be able to say off-hand what the unit was, but we get from the Welsh example some rough idea of what tribal tribute and income were, and how these could be readily gathered and transferred.

The Method of Payment of Galanas between Kindreds

Postponing for a while the consideration of the position of the various classes of non-tribesmen, but still keeping in view the fact that in considerable numbers they were practically sharers with the tribesmen in the rights of grazing and occupation of land, we are now in the position to realise to some extent what happened when a murder had taken place.

If it was of some one within the kindred, there was, as we have said, no slaying of the murderer. Whether it were a parricide or a fratricide, or the murder of a near kinsman, under Cymric custom there was no galanas, nothing but execration and ignominious exile.

But if a tribesman of one kindred were killed by a tribesman of another kindred, then it was a serious matter of blood feud between the kindreds, or of the payment of the blood fine. The tribal conscience demanded vengeance or composition.

It sometimes happened that the murderer had fled to a church for safety, taking his cattle with him. For the clergy or monks at the place of refuge had a herd of cattle of their own, and with them the murderer's cattle were allowed to wander and graze so long as they returned nightly to the refuge.

There he remained presumably till the kindred of the murdered tribesman, through negotiation and arrangement of the chiefs of the kindreds, had agreed to accept the payment of the galanas, if it were the case of an *uchelwr* or full tribesman, of 126 cows. Six cows, as we shall see hereafter, were *saraad* for the insult, and

120 cows galanas for the murder. The saraad was paid first—six
cows or other cattle to the same value belonging to the murderer
were driven from the herd in payment.

The murderer's life was then safe, and presumably he might
return with his cattle to his place.

Within a fortnight, the tribesmen of the murderer's kindred
met to apportion the payment of the rest. They came from
trefgordds far and near, from the territories sometimes of various
higher territorial chieftains within whose districts they had grazing rights.

The collected tribesmen having apportioned the payment, fortnight after fortnight instalments must be paid till the whole
number in value of 120 cows was completed.

But by whom was the payment to be made?

Forty cows must first be found by the *murderer,* his *father,
mother, brothers,* and *sisters* with him. They doubtless helped one
another, but theoretically, in one or other of the common herds,
there must have been cattle belonging to the murderer, his father,
mother, brothers, and sisters, or how could they have paid their
shares? There was nothing unreal in this liability of each to pay
a share, for had the murderer been slain each one of them would
have received, instead of having to pay, a share in 40 cows.

The murderer himself had to pay a third of the 40 cows if he
had them. His father and mother between them paid the next
third, and the brothers and sisters the remaining third, the sisters
paying half what the brothers did.[5] The herds of many a trefgordd
must be thinned before this could be done.

The remainder of the galanas, viz. 80 cows, fell on the kindred,
to the seventh degree or fifth cousins. The paternal relations had
to find two thirds of it and the maternal one third, and these
kindreds embraced the descendants from the great-grandparents
of the great-grandparents on both sides.

In the first fortnight the kindred on the father's side had to find
half what was due from them. In the second fortnight they had to
find the other half, and in the third fortnight the maternal kindred

---

[5] Sisters paid for their possible children, and if these children were of
age they paid instead of their mothers. After the age at which they could
not have children, the sisters did not pay . . . the daughter after twelve
was independent of her father with *da* of her own.

had to find their share, till so at last the full tale of the 120 cows was paid. The oath of peace from the kindreds of the murdered man could then be given, and the murderer and his kinsmen be at peace.

But what happened if the murderer could not find the cattle for his third of the 40 cows which he and his immediate family had to find? He had yet a right, as a member of the greater kindred, to claim in aid a "spear penny" from all those male kinsmen descended from a common ancestor on his father's side two steps further back, *i.e.* still more distantly related to him than those included in the kindred to the seventh degree who had already paid their share. Even if the slayer were a woman, she had the same right of spear penny from the men of her kindred to help her to make her payment.

So this attempt to realise what was involved in the payment of an ordinary case of galanas brings us back to the recognition of the double aspect of the kindred in the structure of tribal society—its solidarity and joint responsibility, on the one hand, as against outsiders, the whole kindred being responsible in the last resort; on the other hand the individual responsibility of its members, graduated according to nearness of relationship, for the crimes of their relative.

In Cymric tribal society this was made possible by the broad fact that both males and females in the group of kindred, on both paternal and maternal sides, liable to pay, had cattle of their own in the common herd, each having received his or her *da* for maintenance by right of kin and descent from the common ancestor or chieftain of the kindred. The two things surely hang together. And therefore, if we find in the laws of other tribes somewhat similar rules regarding the payment of wergelds, it probably will be worthwhile to inquire further whether the corresponding structure of tribal society, or something more or less equivalent to it, may not be present also.

The Amount of the Cymric Galanas

In all the Welsh Codes the galanas, as already mentioned, is described in a peculiar form. It is a combination of two items, viz. the saraad, or payment for insult, and the galanas proper.

Thus the galanas of the innate *boneddig,* or young tribesman, accepted by the kindred as a tribesman of nine descents of Cymric blood, is described as "three kine and three score kine," that of the *uchelwr* or *breyr* as "six kine and six score kine."

The explanation of this is obtained from the following passage [in the Denbigh Extent]:

> What is the galanas of the breyr without office? Six kine and six score kine. The six score kine is the galanas and the six kine is for saraad of the corpse.

So also in the Gwentian Code:

> When a married man shall be murdered his saraad is first paid and then his galanas, for the wife has the third of the saraad, and she has no part of the galanas.

So also in the Venedotian Code:

> No one is killed without being first subjected to saraad. If a man be married, let a third of the man's saraad be given to his wife and let the two shares be placed with the galanas, and after that let the galanas be divided into three shares and let the third share go to the lord as exacting third.

The reason why the wife has a share in the saraad and not in the galanas has already been explained. She suffers from the personal affront or insult to her slain husband and shares in the saraad. But she has no blood relationship with her husband, and only the husband's kindred are therefore entitled to share in the galanas, as her husband's kindred alone would have been concerned in the feud.

The saraad and the galanas were therefore separate things and subject to separate rules, though both payable on the murder of a tribesman. The galanas proper is what must be regarded in any comparison with Continental wergelds.

The real galanas of the uchelwr or breyr, apart from the saraad, was 120 cows, and that of the young innate boneddig who had received his *da* but had no family was 60 cows. In one of the Codes his galanas when *married* is said to be 80 cows.

Now in what currency was the galanas paid? Formerly, according to the Codes, all payments were made in cattle, and the galanas proper was reckoned in scores of cows.

But of what cow? How was the normal cow for practical purposes to be defined? It is a question worth answering, because we may probably take the Cymric method, of valuing the cow as a unit of currency in cattle, as at any rate suggestive of the methods generally adopted by other tribes.

According to the Venedotian Code the cow was of full normal value when in full milk and until her fifth calf.

> And if there be any dispute concerning her milk, she is to be taken on the 9th day of May to a luxuriant place wherein no animal has been before her, and the owner is to milk her without leaving any for the calf, and put the milk in the measure vessel, and if it be full twice a day that is sufficient; and if it be not, the deficiency is to be compensated by oatmeal until the feast of St. Curic, thence until the feast of St. Michael by barley meal, and from thence until the calendar of winter by rye meal.

> Others say that the worth of the milk deficient in the measure is to be returned to the possessor of the cow; if half the milk be deficient, half the worth; if a third of the milk, a third of the worth; and that is the best mode.

Then the *milk measure* is described thus:

> The measure for her milk is, three thumbs at the bottom, six in the middle of the vessel, and nine at the top, and nine in its height diagonally (*enyhyd en amrescoeu*), and the thumb whereby the vessel is to be measured (in case of dispute) is the breadth of the judge's thumb.

In the Dimetian Code substantially the same rules are given, except that the measure of the cow's milking is smaller.

> The measure of a vessel for a cow's milk is nine thumbs at its edge, and three at the bottom, and seven diagonally from the off-side groove to the near-side edge in height.

The only difference is between the seven and the nine thumbs of diagonal measurement. Possibly there may be some error in the figures, and the measure may have been the same in both Codes.

Returning to the galanas; although it was reckoned in the Codes in scores of cows, a fixed equation had already been made between cows and silver.

The normal cow was equated in the Codes with "three scores of silver." And in the Latin version of the Dimetian Code the "score of silver" is translated by *uncia argenti*. The score of silver at the date of the Code was therefore an ounce of silver. So that the reckoning is the Frankish or Anglo-Saxon one of twenty pence to the ounce.

The score of pence of 32 wheat-grains would make the ounce of 640 wheat-grains: that is, the ounce of the pound of 240d., or 7680 wheat-grains—the pound in use in England after the time of Kings Offa and Alfred, and at the date of the Codes.

The galanas of the uchelwr or breyr being 120 cows, and the cow being reckoned at three scores or ounces of silver, the galanas would equal 360 scores or ounces, or thirty pounds of silver.

The ratio of gold to silver after the temporary disturbance under Charlemagne had, as we have seen, settled down again to the Imperial ratio of $1:12$.

Now thirty pounds of 7680 wheat-grains equal 230,400 wheat-grains, and this number of silver wheat-grains divided by twelve equalled exactly 19,200 wheat-grains of gold. So that this Celtic galanas of the Cymric uchelwr or breyr of 120 cows, like so many Continental wergelds, was apparently exactly equal to 200 *gold solidi* of 96 wheat-grains, *i.e.* the heavy gold mina of Imperial standard.

The Methods of Treatment of Strangers or Non-tribesmen

Another point upon which special inquiry is made in this volume regards tribal methods of treating strangers in blood and slaves.

There is no subject requiring more careful investigation than the combination of circumstances out of which arose what is roughly called serfdom, *i.e.* the attachment of tenants to the land rendering services to a lord. I shall not be suspected of suggesting that tribal customs and methods were the *sole* factors which produced serfdom and of ignoring the influences which came from Roman methods of managing landed estates, and from Roman law modified by ecclesiastical usage.

Indeed, I have insisted from the first that while, in the *Germania* of Tacitus, the germs may be found of an "embryo manor," both Roman and German elements probably combined in producing the later manorial system and serfdom which grew up in what were once the Roman provinces of Gaul and the two Germanies, and even also in Britain. But I think that in Cymric tribal custom we may find a fresh clue worth following in the attempt to gather from Continental evidence the methods likely to be used by conquering German or Anglo-Saxon tribes in the treatment of strangers in blood.

In Welsh tribal custom *alltuds* or strangers and their descendants (not necessarily otherwise unfree persons) having some special circumstances in their favour, being allowed to settle within the district of a greater or lesser chieftain upon land which, in a sense, may have been his demesne land, were free to remove and settle under another chieftain, unless and until they had remained on the same land or under the same lordship for four generations. But thereafter the great-grandchildren of the original settlers became *adscripti glebae*. And this fixture to the land, or rather to the lordship, was apparently not looked upon as in any way a degradation in rank, but on the contrary a step in advance towards the recognition of tribal rights. The great-grandson of the stranger did not indeed become a Cymric tribesman, but he gained the recognition of his status as the founder of a kindred of his own, the members of which in after-generations would, as kinsmen, be able to swear for and defend one another.

This being so in the case of free strangers coming into the country, the next question is what was the position of the semi-servile class, the *aillts* and *taeogs* of the Codes, who and whose ancestors for many generations had been born upon the land in a semi-servile condition?

The fixture to the land of the aillt or taeog was not the special mark so much of a semi-servile condition as of his *want of recognised kindred,* and under the local custom of South Wales it seems that he too, like the alltud, could sometimes arrive at the recognition of kindred, without indeed becoming a Cymric tribesman, at the end of four generations of residence under the chieftain of the land; and even to further recognition of it, involving a still better position as to rights, at the ninth generation. The ninth man in South Wales seems according to local custom in some districts to have, at last, climbed the highest rung of the ladder, and to have attained the right to claim the status of a Cymric tribesman.

This curious rise under Cymric custom, by steps of four generations, up the ladder towards the recognition of tribal rights, seems to have a suggestive correspondence with the reverse process under manorial usage of proving the serfdom of a *nativus* by showing that the great-grandfather was a *nativus* on the lord's land, the manorial rule being that settlement on servile land for four generations made the posterity of an original settler into *nativi*.

Once more let us try to realise what this meant, and what was the position of these Cymric non-tribesmen in regard to their settlement on land.

If under the guidance of the Codes we turn to the extents and surveys, we find them living, in some cases, not mixed up with the tribesmen, but in separate groups, or trefs, or trefgordds. There may be here and there exceptional alltuds or strangers of a higher class growing up, by the gradual process of intermarriage for four generations with tribeswomen, into the status of tribesmen. But the mass of the stranger class were aillts and taeogs living in separate *taeog trefs,* though, according to the surveys, sharing, often in common, certain rights of grazing over certain districts with gwelys of tribesmen. Now these groups of taeogs and aillts were, according to the Codes, as we have seen, of two classes, and we recognise the same two classes when we find in the surveys not only groups of taeogs in taeog trefs but also gwelys of non-tribesmen.

The normal group of the taeog tref differed from the free tref in the fact that in it no family rights were recognised. All the members of it shared in its rights and payments equally *per capita,* and not *per stirpes.* They were all liable as a body, few or many, for the whole amount of the dues to the chieftains. During their fathers' lifetime sons shared *pari passu* and equally with their parents, and other members of the group, in the pasture and common ploughing, except youngest sons, who remained with their fathers.

In the gwelys, on the other hand, as in the gwelys of tribesmen, there was recognition of family or blood relationships, and a patriarchal element.

There were thus under Cymric tribal custom various subordinate grades or classes. Beginning at the bottom of the ladder were:

(1) The slaves who could be bought and sold, and who were reckoned as worth one pound of silver.

(2) The taeogs and aillts or permanent *nativi,* born non-tribesmen, without recognised family rights.

(3) Non-tribesmen growing or having grown in four generations into gwelys of non-tribesmen with recognised family rights.

(4) Strangers of exceptional position who, having married into the tribe, had become tribesmen in the fourth generation by repeated intermarriage.

And once more the fact should never be lost sight of, that the gradual growth into tribal or quasi-tribal rights was not a growth into exactly what in a modern sense would be called individual freedom. It was accompanied by the growth of ties which bound the family to the chieftain, till at the moment that at the fourth generation the recognition of rights of kindred was attained, the family found itself, as we have seen, so closely tied to the chieftain and the land that the newly recognised gwely had become *adscriptus glebae.*

Finally, the tribal logic of the case was probably something like this:

The free tribesman is the man who belongs to a kindred who can protect him by oath and by sword. Until a stranger has kinsmen who can do this he is an odd or kinless man, protected only by his lord. If he be killed his galanas goes to his lord; he has no recognised kin to receive it. If, on the other hand, he is charged with slaying another, he has no kin to swear to his innocence, the oath of a non-tribesman not being held good as against a tribesman. If guilty, he has no kin bound to fight in the feud for him, or to help him to pay a galanas for his crime. So that even when at the fourth generation the descendant of the alltud becomes the founder of a gwely he has gained only half the status of a tribesman. It is not till the fourth generation of descendants in the gwely, *i.e.* the seventh generation from the original settler, that a complete kindred has grown up. It is not till then that the descendant of the original alltud is surrounded by a full group of relatives, born in his great-grandfather's gwely, whose oaths can be taken and who can protect him by oath and sword or in payment of galanas. All this time the alltud family have been more or less dependent on the protection of the chieftain, and rights and obligations are apt to be correlative.

The objcct of this essay is to inquire how far, in the case of other tribes, evidence may be found of the working of somewhat similar tribal instincts, resulting in customary rules more or less like those of the Cymry, so that at last, turning attention to the Anglo-Saxon laws, we may be able all the more fully to recognise and appreciate in them the traits of tribal custom, which among other factors went to the making of Anglo-Saxon England.

In the meantime, for future reference, the following list of the galanas of various classes will be found convenient:

The chief of kindred	180 cows	⎰ In Gwent and ⎱ Dimetia 540, and his family 180
The uchelwr	120 "	
Man with family without office	80 "	
The innate boneddig unmarried	60 "	
The alltud of the brenhin or chief	60 "	
The alltud of uchelwrs	30 "	
Bondman 1 lb. of silver or	6 "	
Bondman from beyond sea	4 "	

§§ 5

BEOWULF

Frederic Seebohm

The object of this short study of *Beowulf* is to learn what incidental information it may give of tribal usage regarding the *blood feud,* especially on points which, in the case of the substituted wergeld, present doubt and difficulty.[1]

Allusion has already been made to some of these points. Did the rule excluding galanas or blood-fine within the kindred extend beyond the gwely to the greater kindred? What happened to a tribesman in a feud between his paternal and maternal kindreds? Did he abstain from taking sides, or did a marriage so far unite two families or kindreds as to make them one for the purpose of blood-fine or feud, so as to prevent the feud or blood-fine from arising?

These are questions upon which we want light from the point of view of Welsh tribal custom, and upon which we approach *Beowulf* for light, with eyes open also to other matters of tribal usage as they may turn up.

Beowulf for the present purpose may be taken as an Anglian or Northumbrian recension of a story founded upon Scandinavian tradition, and designed for use or recital at some 8th century royal

From Frederic Seebohm, *Tribal Custom in Anglo-Saxon Law* (London: Longmans, Green, 1902), Ch. 3.

[1] In the quotation of passages from *Beowulf* I have mostly followed Professor Earle's translations.

court—possibly, if Professor Earle's suggestion be correct, that of King Offa.

The western horizon of the story extends to the Frisian shores, but the scene seems chiefly to lie in the Baltic.

The plot involves tribal relations between a chieftain of the Danes possibly of Zealand, and two Swedish chieftains. The two latter concern us most, and they seem to be the chiefs of two kindreds—Geats and Swedes—Beowulf himself being the link between them, his mother having married from one into the other kindred. This marriage at any rate was one *between* two kindreds.

There is no apparent effort on the part of the poet to enlighten the reader or those who heard him either upon the pedigrees of the persons mentioned in his story or upon the rules of Scandinavian tribal custom. But it happens that, by incidental hints dropped in the telling of the tale, the pedigree of each of the kindreds involved can be fairly made out, and has already been made out by translators and critics.

And as the story involves a homicide within Beowulf's maternal kindred, and fighting and bloodshed between the kindreds in spite of the marriage link, and as it deals also with outside feuds, it happens to present remarkable opportunities for studying the action of tribal custom in various cases.

The evidence it gives is made all the more valuable by its being an Anglian version of Scandinavian traditions, inasmuch as the poet, or his Anglian interpreter, assumes throughout that the laws of the game, under Scandinavian tribal custom, were too well known to need explanation to his Anglian audience. So that by inference it would seem that the customs of Baltic chieftains were familiar at the court of Offa, and not very far removed from those of Anglian tradition.

The poet introduces us first to a tribe of *Gar-Danes* and the clan or kindred of Scyldings. Scyld the son of Scef is the ancestor of the Scyldings. He is an Adeling who has torn their meadthrones from many tribes (*mægdum*) and in true tribal fashion compelled them to pay tribute. Surrounded in his old age by numerous descendants and other *gesiths* who have resorted to him, the chieftain has become a great hero in his tribe (*mægdh*).

A graphic description of the burial of Scyld in his ships by his gesiths is a fitting introduction to the poem. Let us mark in pass-

SCYLD
The great-grandfather

BEOWULF
(not of the story) The grandfather

HEALFDENE
The father

HEOROGAR — { HEOROWEARD

HROTHGAR
The Scylding
m. Wealtheow — { HRETHRIC
HROTHMUND
FREAWARE

HALGA
(youngest son) — { HRODULF

ELAN
daughter
presumably
married to
Ongentheow
the Scylfing — { ONELA
OHTHERE
"sister's sons"
to Hrothgar — { EANMUND
EADGIL

ing that the word *mægd* evidently may mean a much wider kindred than the near family of a great-grandfather's descendants (the Welsh gwely). One mægd conquers another and makes it pay tribute.

Again the word *gesith* evidently includes, with members of the near kin, such others, not necessarily blood relations, as may have joined the warrior band of the hero. They may or may not have been adopted into his kindred in becoming his men, but this extension of comradeship or kinship, as the case may be, to these gesiths adds to the greatness and power of his mægd.

The opening episode of the burial of Scyld is followed by a few lines which reveal something of the pedigree of his descendant Hrothgar the Scylding. The pedigree of Hrothgar, in true tribal fashion, makes Scyld his great-grandfather. He is Hrothgar the Scylding, may we not say, *because* Scyld was his great-grandfather, just as Hengist and Horsa were Oiscings according to Bede, who in stating their pedigree makes Oisc their great-grandfather, and just as in the Welsh surveys the gwelys still bear the great-grandfather's name though he be long dead, because the gwely hangs together till the fourth generation.

So far as it goes here is at least an indication that the nearer kindred (or gwely) might be much the same thing both in Celtic and Teutonic tribes.

But Hrothgar is not described only as chieftain of his nearer kindred. Success in arms had made him head of many *winemâgas* (blood friends) and he was surrounded by a mighty *mago-dright* (band of kin). He had built himself a famous *folk-stede,* or hall, called Heort, and all had gone well with him till the monster Grendel came upon the scene.

The deliverer from the monster was Beowulf, the hero of the story. He comes from another kindred, that of the Scylfings, whose pedigree, not fully given, seems to have been something like the following.

Scylf was the common ancestor of the Swedes or Scylfings. The tribe was divided into two families in the elder of which descended the chieftainship of the Scylfings.

At any rate the Scylfings seem to be divided into two families whose common ancestor was Scylf. But both Beowulf and Wiglaf

(1) Links not stated { ONGENTHEOW who presumably married Elan, sister of Hrothgar the Scylding } { ONELA, OHTHERE } { EANMUND, EADGILS }

Second family of WÆGMUNDINGS

(2) WÆGMUND { .... } { ECGTHEOW — BEOWULF who fled to Hrothgar, WIHSTAN — WIGLAF }

are spoken of as *Wægmundings*. The headship of the Scylfings had passed into the older of the two families, and this probably is the reason why Beowulf is never called Beowulf the Scylfing.

The reason why Beowulf appeared as the natural helper of Hrothgar from the monster Grendel was that his father Ecgtheow owed a debt of gratitude to Hrothgar. "Fighting out a mighty feud," Ecgtheow had killed Heatholaf the Wylfing, thereby raising another feud. Wherefore his own people fearing invasion, had caused him to flee over sea, thereby seemingly wiping their hands of him. He seems to have fled to Hrothgar just as the latter had become chieftain of the Scyldings on his brother Heorogar's death. Hrothgar compounded the feud with money, sending to the Wylfings over sea "ancient treasures." Whereupon Ecgtheow swore oath to Hrothgar and presumably became his "man." And Beowulf now, "at honour's call," had come to fight the monster, thereby confirming the friendship between Geats and Gar-Danes, requiting what Hrothgar had done for his father.

The details of the fight need not detain us. But the fact is important that Beowulf comes to the rescue not as a Scylfing or as representing his paternal kindred, but as the thane of his maternal uncle Hygelac, the chieftain of his mother's kindred.

He approaches Hrothgar with a band of fifteen chosen warriors. When asked from whence they came they said they were Geats, Hygelac's *hearthgeneats*. And the meaning of the word is illustrated further when the warriors accustomed to sleep in

Hrothgar's hall are spoken of as Hrothgar's *hearthgeneats*. When brought into the hall Beowulf himself calls his band Hygelac's *beod-geneats* (table geneats), and to Hrothgar he calls himself *"mæg and mago-thegn,"* literally "kin and son thane" of Hygelac. The daring deed accomplished, Beowulf's success is rewarded by many golden and other gifts from Hrothgar, and it is significant that on his return he lays all these at the feet of his maternal uncle Hygelac, his *heofodmagus*—chief of kin—whose man and kin he owns himself to be. His position in Hygelac's kindred thus demands careful study.

This seems to be the pedigree.

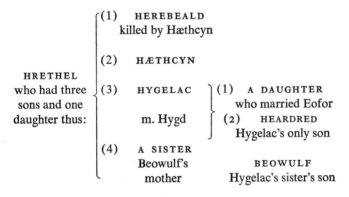

HRETHEL
who had three
sons and one
daughter thus:

(1)   HEREBEALD
      killed by Hæthcyn

(2)   HÆTHCYN

(3)   HYGELAC
      m. Hygd

(4)   A SISTER
      Beowulf's
      mother

(1)   A DAUGHTER
      who married Eofor

(2)   HEARDRED
      Hygelac's only son

BEOWULF
Hygelac's sister's son

Beowulf is made to say that, when seven winters old, Hrethel had received him from his father Ecgtheow and had kept him as his own child. "Remembering kinship" (*sippe gemunde*), the old chieftain held him in no less regard than his own three sons, Herebeald, Hæthcyn, and Hygelac. But Hrethel's old age was full of trouble. The worst tragedy that came upon him was the death of his eldest son Herebeald, killed by his second son apparently by accident.

> Hætheyn by arrow from hornbow brought him (Herebeald) down, his near kinsman. He missed the target and shot his brother.

Here, then, was an apparently accidental homicide within the family. How was it regarded?

One brother killed the other with bloody dart. That was a wrong past compensation. . . . Any way and every way it was inevitable that the Etheling must quit life unavenged.

The poet likens the father's grief to that of "an old *ceorle*" who should see his young son ride on the gallows-tree and can do nothing but wait while his son thus hangs, food for the ravens, as he cannot bring him help.

So did the crowned chief of the Stormfolk, in memory of Herebeald, carry about a tumult of heart-sorrow. He could not possibly requite the feud upon the man-slayer, neverthemore could he pursue the warrior with hostile deeds though not beloved by him. He then, with the sorrow wherewith that wound had stricken him, let go life's joys and chose the light of God.

Thus incidentally is revealed by the poet the depth of the tribal feeling that homicide can only be atoned for by avengement and feud, making it a hard struggle against nature for a father to withhold revenge upon a son for even accidental fratricide. As with the Cymry, it seems that there could be no feud or composition within the family. Nor in the case of accidental homicide was there apparently in the poet's mind the necessity of flight or outlawry, however great the craving for avengement. It is also significant that Hæthcyn, the slayer, is made to join with his brother Hygelac in the next warfare after Hrethel's death. The accidental slayer remains a tribesman.

This next warfare was a quarrel—"provocation and reprisal"— between Swedes and Geats, *i.e.* between the paternal and maternal kindreds of Beowulf. He himself, it is worth noting, did not engage in it. Onela and Ohthere, the sons of Ongentheow (Beowulf's paternal relation and chief of the Scylfings or Swedes), apparently began the quarrel. They recklessly broke the peace between the two families—Swedes and Geats. Hrethel was no longer living. Beowulf's maternal uncles, Hæthcyn and Hygelac, fought on one side, and Ongentheow and his two sons on the other. Hæthcyn fell on one side and Ongentheow on the other: the latter by the hand of Eofor—a comrade rather than kinsman of Hygelac, for he was rewarded by the bestowal of Hygelac's daughter. The quarrel seems to have been open fighting, possibly from the revival of the old enmities and in breach of tribal custom. Be this as it may, Beowulf himself took no part in the quarrel between his maternal and paternal kindreds. This disastrous and unnatural quarrel left Hygelac the only surviving son of Hrethel, and so the chieftain of Beowulf's maternal kindred.

All this irregular fighting, incidentally mentioned by the poet, was past before Beowulf's great enterprise against the monster Grendel. And, as we have seen, it was as the "man and kin" of Hygelac that Beowulf appeared at Hrothgar's court. And it was at the feet of Hygelac as his chief of kin, and at the feet of Hygd his queen, that Beowulf laid down his treasures on his return in safety. This exploit ended, Hrothgar thenceforth disappears from the poem, and the poet confines himself to Boewulf's nearer belongings.

The next event in order of date is a quarrel between Hygelac and the Frisians. This time Beowulf fights for his chieftain. But Hygelac is killed, and again the result reveals interesting traits of tribal custom.

Beowulf returns from Friesland to Hygd the widowed queen of Hygelac. She "offers him rings and throne, not daring to trust that her young son Heardred would be able to maintain the chieftainship against all stranger folk." Beowulf, however, declines to become *hlaford* over Heardred, but supports him in his chieftainship till he should be older.

Young Heardred, however, is not chieftain long. The old lawless quarrel between Beowulf's maternal and paternal relations rises up again.

The facts, when unravelled, seem to be these. Within Beowulf's paternal kindred trouble had arisen. For some cause not told, the grandsons of Ongentheow (sons of Ohthere) had been outlawed. They are described as *wräc-mäegas* and as having cast off allegiance to the chieftain of the Scylfings. These outlawed kinsmen of Beowulf's paternal family came to young Heardred's court, and whilst his guests (*on feorme*) the young chieftain fell by the sword of one of them.

It was Eanmund by whom this outrage was committed, and once more the crime remained apparently unavenged. The slayer was allowed to withdraw in safety, leaving Beowulf to succeed to the chieftainship of his maternal kindred. Again we ask why? Here was a crime committed by an outlawed paternal kinsman of Beowulf against the chieftain of his maternal kindred, of whom he was himself the guardian. and yet Beowulf did not avenge it! Was it because of the kinship, or because of the outlawry? Whilst nursing the remembrance of his chieftain's death, Beowulf is made to act with kindness to the other outlawed brother in his desolation, waiting for such avengement as might come at last in the course of things—as it did, according to the poet, when "with a band of warriors over sea Eadgils died in cold and painful marches."

Avengement is made to follow too in the same way upon Eanmund the murderer. It came from Beowulf's paternal uncle, Weohstan. But here again the poet is careful to record that it came not in a blood feud, but "in fair fight" with weapon's edge. And, as if to emphasise the fact that the outlawed kinsman had forfeited all tribal rights, the poet adds that "Weohstan from his kindred carried off the armour and sword of Eanmund, Onela [Eanmund's uncle] yielding them up to him *without a word about a feud,* although he [Weohstan] had slain his brother's son."

Evidently the poet means to make it clear that Onela's passive attitude was due to the fact that his nephew was a lawless exile, and so no longer entitled to protection from his kin.

> The old sword known among men as the relic of Eanmund [son of Ohthere], whom, when a lawless exile, Weohstan had slain in fair fight with weapon's edge; and from his kindred [*magum*] had carried off the brown mottled helmet, ringed byrnie, and old mysterious sword; which Onela yielded up to him, his nephew's war-harness, accoutrement complete. Not a word spake he [Onela] about the feud, although he [Weohstan] had killed his brother's son. He [Weohstan] retained the spoils for many a year, bill and byrnie, until when his own boy [Wiglaf] was able to claim Eorlscip rank, like his father before him, then gave he to him, before the Geats, armour untold of every sort, after which he gave up life, ripe for the parting journey.

Thus the restrained desire of avengement incidentally is made to find satisfaction at last as regard both the outlawed sons of Ohthere.

After these events the elder branch of the Scyldings passes out of the poet's interest. The only remaining heroes of the tale are the two Wægmundings—Beowulf and Wiglaf.

A long interval had elapsed between Beowulf's accession to the chieftainship of his maternal kindred and the final feat of daring which cost him his life. And it was Wiglaf, his nearest paternal kinsman, who in the last tragedy came to his aid bearing the sword of the outlawed Eanmund. Beowulf's dying words to Wiglaf were: "Thou art the last left of our kindred [*cynnes*] the Wægmundings. Fate has swept into eternity all my kinsmen [*mâgas*]—*eorls* among men! I must after them!" As he comes to the rescue, Wiglaf remembers the honour done to him by Beowulf, who had already passed on to him the hereditary right of the chieftainship of the Wægmundings.

Why had he done this? If we might tentatively use the clue given by ancient Greek tribal custom to elucidate a Scandinavian case, we should say that on failure of male succession the "sister's son" of Hygelac had been called back into his mother's kindred to become its chieftain, leaving Wiglaf, his next of kin on his father's side, to sustain the chieftainship of his paternal kindred. The right of the maternal uncle, known to have existed under early Greek law, to claim his "sister's son" if need arose, to perpetuate the mother's paternal kindred, suggests a similar explanation in Beowulf's case. Such a right, found as well in the Laws of Manu, may possibly have been inherent in Scandinavian tribal custom also. Such a suggestion would be at least consistent with the fact of Beowulf's having been brought up from seven years old in the household of his maternal grandfather, and treated by him as a son. It would be in harmony, too, with what Tacitus describes to have been the relation of the "sister's son" to the *avunculus* amongst the German tribes, and the peculiar value of the "sister's son" as a hostage.

Some indirect confirmation of the probable truth of such a suggestion may perhaps be also drawn from the fact that in *Beowulf,* when a man's father is no longer living, the poet sometimes seems to describe him as his maternal uncle's nephew instead of as his father's son.

Heardred, the young son of Hygelac and Hygd his queen, after his father's death is spoken of no longer as Hygelac's son, but as the *nephew of Hereric* (*nefan Hererices*). Now his paternal uncles were Herebeald and Hæthcyn, and it becomes an almost necessary inference that Hereric was a maternal uncle. Thus:

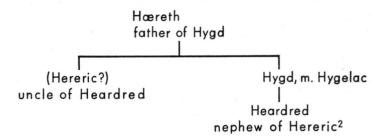

So also in the case of Hygelac himself. He was the son of Hrethel. The poet calls him son of Hrethel, and again *Hygelac Hrethling*. But after Hrethel's death he calls him "Hygelac of the Geats, *nephew of Swerting*" (*Hygelac Geáta nefa Swertinges*). Here again it seems likely that Swerting was the maternal uncle, though the poet, as in the other case, does not think it needful to explain that it was so. Otherwise, why the change of epithet?

We are here recording tribal customs as revealed in *Beowulf*, and not seeking for their origin in earlier stages of tribal life. We pass on, therefore, to consider what light the story throws on the customs of the Northern tribes as to marriage.

It is with the chieftains' grade of rank that we have mostly to do in *Beowulf*, and nothing is more strongly emphasised by the poet than the important place of marriage between two tribes or kindred as a link, recognised, however, to be a very brittle one, binding them together so as to end or prevent the recurrence of a feud.

When Beowulf, after his first exploit in aid of Hrothgar against Grendel, has returned to his maternal uncle and chief of kindred Hygelac, and is recounting his adventures, the poet at the first mention of Hrothgar's queen makes him call her the "peace bond to the people." And in the same breath, in telling how in Hrothgar's hall the daughter Freaware bore the ale-flagon, he stops to tell how "she, the young, the gold dight, was promised to the

---

[2] *Nefan* cannot mean son or grandson, for Hygelac was his father and his grandfather was Hrethel.

gay son of Froda; it having pleased the Friend of the Scylfings
that he, through that woman, should compose deadly enmities
and feuds." And the poet makes Beowulf moralise to the effect:
"Often and not seldom anywhere after deadly strife, it is but a
little while that the baneful spear reposes, good though the bride
may be!"

It would seem that Hrothgar had been formerly at feud with
the Heathobeards, that Froda had been killed in the feud, and
that the marriage of Freaware to Froda's son, Ingeld, was to close
the feud. But Beowulf repeats aside to Hygelac that he does not
think much of the chances of a long continuance of peace between Scyldings and Heathobeards.

> Well may it mislike the ruler of the Heathobeards and every
> thane of that people when the lady goeth into hall with a prince
> born of Danes, amidst the high company; upon him do glisten
> heirlooms of their ancestors, ringed harness, once Heathobeardic
> treasure, while they could keep the mastery of those weapons and
> until they in an unlucky moment led to that buckler play their
> dear comrades and their own lives. Then saith one over the
> beer, one who observes them both, an old lance fighter. . . . "Canst
> thou, my friend, recognise the blade, the precious steel, which thy
> father carried into battle, wearing his helmet for the last time,
> where the Danes slew him? . . . and the masters of the battle-
> field were the fiery Scyldings! Now here a boy of one of those
> banesmen walketh our hall . . . wearing the treasure which by
> right should have been thine!" So urged and egged on at every
> turn with galling words, at last the moment comes that for his
> father's deeds the lady's thane sleepeth bloodspattered after the
> falchion's bite, life-doomed! The other escapes alive! By-and-
> by the sworn oaths of the warriors on either side will be broken,
> when in Ingeld's mind rankle war purposes, and care has lessened
> his domestic sorrow! Therefore I deem not the loyalty of the
> Heathobeards nor the alliance with the Danes secure, or the
> friendship firm! (Slightly abridged.)

What a consistent light this passage throws incidentally on the
quarrels which, in spite of the Geats and Swedes being bound
together in friendship by the marriage of Beowulf's mother, broke
out again and again, according to the poem, between the two

kindreds—quarrels in which Beowulf himself is represented as taking no part, presumably because, according to tribal custom, his blood relationship to both kindreds was a bar to his taking up the feud or assuming the part of the avenger! And how the whole story of Beowulf's paternal kindred reveals the melancholy fact that, however great the force of tribal custom in controlling feuds, the wild human nature of hot-blooded tribesmen was wont to break through restraints and often ended in the outlawry of tribesmen and the breaking up of kindreds!

To sum up the results obtained from the study of tribal custom as incidentally revealed in *Beowulf*:

(1) There is no feud within the kindred when one kinsman slays another. However strong the natural instinct for avengement, it must be left to fate and natural causes. Accidental homicide does not seem to be followed even by exile. But murder within the kindred breaks the tribal tie and is followed by outlawry.

(2) Marriage between two kindreds is a common though precarious means of closing feuds between them. The son of such a marriage takes no part in a quarrel between his paternal and maternal relations.

(3) When a marriage takes place, the wife does not pass entirely out of her own kindred into her husband's. Her own kindred, her father and brothers, maintain a sort of guardianship over her, and the son in some sense belongs to both kindreds. He may have to join in his maternal kindred's feuds, and he may become the chieftain of his maternal kindred on failure of direct male succession, even though by so doing he may have to relinquish the right of chieftainship in his paternal kindred to another kinsman.

Finally, in passing from the blood feuds to the composition substituted for them, after what we have learned from *Beowulf* of tribal custom, there need be no surprise that maternal as well as paternal relations are found to be interested in them. We may fairly judge that tribal custom, in the stage in which we find it in *Beowulf* and later in the laws of various tribes, would not have been true to itself, had this been otherwise.

Part III

Law of Household
and Family

In this part we turn from the consideration of the larger social group, the community and the manor, to the family, which in most of its forms is numerically smaller. In brief compass, Vinogradoff brings together much that was known in his time of the Indo-European family. The terms "household" and "family" are far from perfectly identical. "Household" sometimes applied to cases in which non-kin or distant kin lived in a common residence and shared a common economy (the word "economy" is derived from the Greek *oiko-,* household, and *nom-,* from a root meaning to manage, regulate). "Family" refers only to close kin, whether gathered into a household or not.

"Patriarchal household" in Vinogradoff's usage was literally correct, patriarchy being rule by the father, the form of regulation of the ancient household with which Vinogradoff dealt. The term should not, however, be used to refer to a system of agnatic and patrilineal kinship, a usage in which Vinogradoff sometimes indulges.

Vinogradoff assumes as a matter of course that linguistic and cultural unity are coterminous, which is of course not the case. Although the linguistic unity of the Indo-European peoples is undoubtedly an accepted fact, their cultural unity is not. Par-

113

ticularly, the institution of the *zadruga* of some of the South Slavs, a community of agnatic kin, is not to be exactly paired with the Russian *mir* or *derevnya*. The existence of a Slavic linguistic unity, within the larger Indo-European language world, does not imply, despite Vinogradoff's contention, a common family and village organization.

However, Vinogradoff's chapter on the Indo-European joint family and the system of succession within family and household is a model of clarity of exposition and of learning.

Chapter 7, by Rudolf Huebner, deals with marriage and family organization among the ancient and medieval Germans. In these pages Huebner is most critical of the notion that a stage of mother-right or matriarchate precedes that of patriarchate. They should therefore be read in connection with Kovalevsky's views to that effect (Chapter 8). Huebner provides a straightforward account of the early German family and, in view of the renewed interest in early Indo-European kinship systems by Paul Friedrich and others, should add much to the current discussion of that subject. Of great importance is his examination of forms of marriage, which should serve to broaden our analysis of the relations between man and woman, and the status of woman in a society growing ever more complex in its organization.

Maxime Kovalevsky's work on the Russian family stands somewhat to the side of the group whose writings have so far been set forth in this volume. A Russian by birth, like Vinogradoff, he maintained his home in Russia, unlike Vinogradoff. However, he went to England at Maine's invitation to deliver lectures on the Slavic rural family and village. Our selection consists of one of these lectures.

Kovalevsky couples a keen analysis of Russian peasant customs with a somewhat mechanical application of a stage theory of social evolution. According to Kovalevsky and others, the kinship system current in nineteenth-century peasant Russia was an agnatic one, which must have been preceded by a system of mother-right or matriarchate. Human life, they held, did not move neatly from one stage of development to the next; rather, certain features of the last stage survived in the ensuing stage, which it was the task of the scholar to seek out, if possible, and identify. Moreover, one society might advance at a faster pace than another. Therefore, it was possible to examine such features in the more backward society in order to gain a greater understanding of the last stage of the more advanced society. Russia, even rural Russia, for example, was considered by Kovalevsky and Maine to be more advanced than rural Bulgaria. Therefore, the customs of rural Bulgaria might supplement the knowledge of early Russian rural life derived from other sources.

Leaving aside Kovalevsky's alleged mechanical application of this view, we may agree that nineteenth-century rural Russia was a stagnant or at least slowly changing society; that its past, even its distant past, was not unlike its then present; that features from the thirteenth century could be useful in studying the nineteenth, and vice versa if proper scholarly control were applied.

The parallels Kovalevsky draws between the Russian family system and the Serbian *zadruga* are not convincing. In Russia, the rights of individuals to participate in the fruits of the property, its crops, and natural riches, could be maintained only by those members who lived and worked on the family property. Those who left the family also abandoned their rights in its property. The *zadruga,* on the other hand, was a unit of family organization and tenure maintained by individual members, absent or not. For example, Serbian emigrants who left their natal *zadruga* were able to take up rights in it again even after being away for fifty years. Kovalevsky did not see the difference between a system in which both kinship and economic considerations were applied to rights and membership in the great family, as in Russia, and one in which kinship considerations were solely relevant, as in Serbia.

Kovalevsky is skilled in interpreting medieval legal documents, contemporary ethnographies, and literary sources, such as novels, to fulfill his aim—the composition of a meaningful picture of the family life of the Russian peasant in the nineteenth century. No methodological strictures can diminish this contribution.

L. K.

§§ 6

THE JOINT FAMILY

Paul Vinogradoff

We usually consider family ties and family property from the point of view of successive generations and of inheritance. This is, however, by no means a necessary or even a natural mode of approaching the subject. In ancient life the principal fact governing these relations was the continuity of a family organization, and there was no compelling reason for dissolving it in connection with the death of a particular member, even if the member in question happened to be the ruler or manager of the concern. We are quite familiar with the persistent maintenance of corporate units like the State, the Church, a town, a teaching institution, and there is no inherent reason for treating the combination of persons and things constituting a household unit in another way. As a matter of fact, every partition and dismemberment is bound to produce some loss and dislocation, and while such losses have to be incurred nowadays in order to satisfy the claims of individuals, the natural bent of ancient Aryan custom was in the direction of keeping up the unity of the household at the cost of curtailing individual tendencies. Strictly speaking, there should not have been any disruption of the family community by way of partition or inheritance, any more than there is a necessity for a

From Paul Vinogradoff, *Outlines of Historical Jurisprudence,* Vol. I (London: Clarendon Press, 1920), Ch. 6. By permission of the Clarendon Press, Oxford.

party meeting for a meal to alter or abandon that common meal every time one of the members has to leave the table. In connection with this prevailing idea, we find among all the branches of the Aryan race manifestations of the so-called united family or *joint family* arrangement. The most extensive and best described practices of this kind are to be found in India and among the Southern Slavs, but there are many traces of similar institutions in the history of the Germans, of the Eastern Slavs and of Romance nations. To begin with, let us consider the Indian data.

In the Rig Veda we read in a Hymn (x. 85, 46) of a bride who is invited to take charge of a household in which parents-in-law and other relations are mentioned as members. The Sutras often refer to the common management of families which have outgrown the stage of the primordial group of father, mother and children. The institution is considered in the Indian law books chiefly from the point of view of its possible dissolution by partition; but this does not mean in any way that partition was the normal consequence of the decease of a householder. On the contrary, the sons of a householder generally continued to manage their affairs in common as before, but it was advisable from a juridical point of view to anticipate the possibility of partition, and to lay down rules as to the relative rights of interested persons. The supposition that, in the ordinary course of affairs, common management remained the usual expedient is supported by the fact that right through recent history, and up to our times, Indian families keep together as far as possible and submit to division only with great reluctance. It has been argued sometimes that the possibility of claiming a partition places these united families in the category of voluntary associations. Such a reading of the evidence, however, perverts the true state of things; it represents exceptions as the rule and the rule as an artificial contrivance built up by help of the exceptions. In these cases, as in many others, we have to take into account not so much extreme possibilities as the customary or usual development of affairs. From this point of view it is highly characteristic that brothers, cousins and nephews in India strive to keep up, as far as possible, the household unit with which their claims are connected. During a recent visit to India I came

across many significant facts of this kind: *e.g.,* a large family
of some seventy relatives was keeping up its connection with the
central household of a judge of the High Court in Calcutta
(Justice Chaudhuri). I was told that great gatherings of the members took place twice a year, that most distant relatives looked
upon the household of the Judge as the principal stock on which
they could rely in case of need, that considerable property was
managed in common and that personal maintenance was provided
for spinsters, widows, minors and other members who could
not shift sufficiently for themselves. Similar arrangements could
be witnessed in the daily life of some professors of the Sanskrit
College, and of other Hindu householders with whom I came
into contact.

The modern practice of the institution as reflected both in its
customary peaceful development, and in occasional conflicts
before the Courts, is marked by specific juridical traits which
draw a definite line between this legal arrangement and forms of
association known to the modern West. I have chiefly in view
four consequences of the Joint Family system:

(1) The estimate of the shares held by the different members
in the common concern.

(2) The method of managing property.

(3) Rights of maintenance.

(4) The relations between common and self-acquired property.

1. The basis of the juridical conception in this case is the
corporate existence of the family: there is originally no privileged
right assigned to the father or to any senior member who acts
as his substitute. Taking the case of the father as the most
obvious, the fundamental fact is recognized that father and sons
stand on an equal footing as members of the Joint Family. In
this way the son cannot be said to be heir to his father, and does
not take after the father's death property which did not belong
to him before. The only change which occurs on the decease of
the father is the alteration which would follow from the fact that
a family, say, of five members, would shrink to a family of four
members and the surviving members would, therefore, each hold
a fourth instead of a fifth. The same effect would be produced
if one of the sons disappeared in his father's lifetime. This posi-

tion is quite clear in the older system represented by the Yâjñavalkya and Mitákshará, and it holds good at the present time in the greater part of India. In parts of the Bombay Province a more individualistic conception has taken root. According to the so-called *Dayabhaga* (partition) of this Western region, the father is recognized as the owner of the property during his lifetime. But even in this modernized arrangement the idea of the continuity of the family tradition is preserved, and there is no question of a purely individualistic treatment on the pattern of the Roman *dominium*.

Altogether the rights of members of a Joint Family appear as ideal shares: in order to understand the proportion in which these shares are allotted, we must keep clearly in view the fact that they follow the pedigree. Without going into the details of the question we have to notice that the right of representation holds good, so that the members of junior generations may have to wait for the realization of their individual claims till the decease of their parents, who, while alive, represent the whole branch. Such questions are, however, only particular applications of the general rule that shares are assigned to members in proportion to their relative seniority, and that the reckoning is carried out not *per capita*, but *per stirpes*.

2. As the father, or any substitute of his, acts as manager of the family and not as owner, his policy is subject to supervision and if necessary to correction by the body of members. There is a good deal of evidence in the Law Reports as to conflicts between managers and members. There are a good many disputed points as to the amount of discretion to be left to the managers in dealing with current affairs and with emergency cases, but on the whole it is an established rule that alienations of valuable property, or mortgages which produce heavy encumbrances, should not be carried out without the consent of the whole body of members. At the same time, the conditions in which such consent has to be given or can be withheld are not set out very clearly. The customary tendency is towards unanimity; in practice such unanimity cannot always be attained and dissent is sometimes overruled, but there are no definite rules as to decision by the majority.

3. The right of maintenance introduces a conception which is

quite alien to modern European views as to property. The nearest analogy might be found in English Law in the position of beneficiaries under a general trust, such as the inmates of a charitable institution. In Continental law a similar situation is met by the rules as to foundations for definite aims (the German *Stiftungen*). The point in these cases is that a certain amount of property or its income is set apart for the maintenance of certain persons and cannot be diverted from that destination; nevertheless none of the beneficiaries can exchange his right for anything else or realize it as an object of property. In the same way, in the case of the Indian Joint Family, the stock of material goods belonging to it is regarded primarily as the basis for the economic position of the members, but not as a complex of things to be treated as materials *in abstracto,* from the point of view of ownership and possession. It would hardly do to conceive of the institution on the lines of the abstract notion of "corporation" as understood in the West: the aim and essence of the arrangement is to provide the means of subsistence for its members.

Turning back to Indian Law, we may say that this peculiar colouring of the institution, although present right through, is especially noticeable in the case of those members who stand in need of help and protection. If we take the fully-qualified householders or their grown-up sons, the usual correspondence between requirements and services, between meals and means, is expressed more or less on the same lines as in ordinary corporate property, but the fact that the Joint Family aims directly at establishing a material basis for the personal existence of its members, is strongly brought out in the case of the weaker members of the institution. A widow is entirely dependent on the assistance of the imperishable household to which her late husband belonged. In the case of a spinster, it is the duty not only of parents but of the Joint Family, to arrange a suitable marriage. Perhaps the most striking cases arise in connection with the requirements of education. In this respect there can be no definite limitation of individual claims: they depend entirely on capacity and opportunity. A Joint Family would not think of refusing to spend money on an expensive course of education on the ground that the claimant was overdrawing his balance in the common fund. The other side of the matter appears when the community claims profits which are considered to be the result, not so much of individual exertions, but of the bringing-up by the help of the family.

4. This leads to the difficult question of drawing proper distinction between communal and self-acquired property within the sphere of action of a Joint Family. The development of modern economic ideas and relations is unquestionably breaking up the primitive conceptions of family solidarity, and it is unnecessary to consider in detail the various inroads which the interests of individuals make in the compact block of primitive conceptions as to property; but it ought to be noticed that the germ of the distinction is already definitely before us in the period of the Sutras. There is a famous saying in the Laws of Manu that a ploughed strip of reclaimed land belongs as much to the tiller as a deer brought down by an arrow belongs to the hunter. This saying has sometimes been cited in proof of the prevalence of private property in land in ancient India, but as a matter of fact it is nothing of the sort; it is neither land as such nor the animal as such that is claimed as property, but the result of the personal exertion of the tiller and of the hunter. We need not, I think, labour the point that a field which has not been appropriated by actual tillage would be out of the range of private ownership, in the same way as a deer which has succeeded in escaping from the arrow. As the stress is laid on concrete appropriation by some kind of exertion, the way is opened for a distinction between objects directly acquired by personal labour or prowess, and the store of goods which are potentially at the disposal of the family community.

Speaking in terms of modern economics, we may say that self-acquired property is directly derived from labour, while the capital from which labour starts remains in the hands of the community. But, of course, all such translations from one set of terms into another and more modern set are only intended to call attention to characteristic distinctions and could not be followed with safety in working out details.

A most interesting corroboration of the teaching as to the economic foundation and the natural history of the Indian Joint Family is provided by the fact that perfectly similar organizations arise on Indian soil in those cases where society is built up not on the patriarchal, but on the matriarchal principle. All the features which we have been examining in the life of the Mitákashará community recur in the practices of the Malabar *tarwads*. The only difference is that we should have to substitute connection through the females for the agnatic skeleton of the Mitákshará Joint Family. The *taiwazhi* runs from the mother instead of from the father, and the management of property is complicated by the addition of a male protector, the *karnavan;* but in other respects we are met by the same problems as to unity and partition, as to ideal shares and representation, as to limits on alienation, as to maintenance and self-acquired property, which we have noticed within the domain of the patriarchal system. This shows convincingly that the necessity of holding together in large clusters of relations is the natural consequence of the social situation in India, and that systems of relationship built up on opposite lines have to take these necessities into account in the same way.

No less instructive an instance is provided by the Southern Slavonic *zadruga*. It has been proved, in spite of some captious criticisms, that this institution goes back to the tribal settlements of the Slavs, right from the earliest times, and that it is endemic among all the branches of this race. But let us turn our attention first and chiefly to the development of the institution as presented by contemporary arrangements in Serbia, Montenegro, Bosnia, Herzegovina, Dalmatia and Croatia. Contemporary practices and absolutely trustworthy evidence as to the state of affairs in the earlier years of the nineteenth century make it possible to describe the working of the institution with great completeness and with clear indications as to the solution of problems which otherwise might have presented difficulties. In these regions, where the population had constantly to fight for existence against the Turks, the Albanians, sometimes the Hungarians, and where the economic struggle was also no easy matter in the absence of good roads, political security and commercial credit, the stress of social organization was laid emphatically on the communal principle as against individual action. According to a Croatian proverb, a single man does not get food nor work. Another saying likens a man devoid of communal support to a man without an arm.

As a result, all the provinces enumerated above were covered with Zadrugas, large families which had grown out of the narrow family, or *inokoshtina,* composed of father, mother and children. The *inokoshtina* itself presents the features of a family corporation in its structure, and the father is anything but the absolute owner and ruler of Roman Law. He is in truth the manager and senior member who leads the family, but is included in its corporate existence. In this way there is no break of continuity when, after the decease of the father, the brothers and eventually the cousins of different degrees develop the *inokoshtina* into a *zadruga.* The feature of the family hearth is still preserved in the central *ognisće,* round which the members congregate in the common hall. It stands usually in the centre of a settlement shaped like a horseshoe and is surrounded either by *Kleti,* the bedrooms of the single families which constitute the joint household, or by separate cottages. In the latter case relations with the central hearth are nevertheless kept up. These communities are very different in size according to topographical conditions and customs, but they may be said on the average to include some thirty or forty persons of both sexes, not counting the children. Sometimes these clusters number even from fifty to seventy. At the head stands the elder or headman, *Glavar Domaćin.* His election is not regulated in a very formal way, and it may be said that seniority is taken into account as far as possible, unless there are definite reasons for passing over persons who are either senile or of weak character. Sometimes a dying *glavar* may point out his successor, and his recommendation in such a case would be treated with due respect. Sometimes, again, an especially capable or strong personality would win the seat of *domaćin,* even against senior competitors, as a result of an expression of public opinion. This is, however, not connected with any regular election or vote by majority. By the side of the *domaćin* leader stands the *domaćica,* the lady manageress in charge of the keys of the storehouse, the dairy and other household arrangements. In the settlement of all important affairs a council of the heads of the constituent family meets. Its decisions are reached by unanimity. It may appear strange to us that this seemingly vague idea of unanimity should rule the proceedings, but what it really comes to is that votes are not counted but weighed, or rather that the moral influence of the elder and of the other leading family fathers is regarded with such respect that no action of the community is taken unless there is unanimity. The most prominent expression of this organic conception of management is to be found in the case of any alienation of property: it is impossible to imagine a *domaćin* acting in such cases by his single will without the assent of the other family fathers. On the basis of such an organization customary rules arise which are in principle identical with those obtaining in the Indian village communities. We might start from the position of the father in the narrow family (*inokoshtina*), as it contains the germs of further development. Professor Bogišić has summarized the customs in this respect in the following words:

(1) The father, while living in the same household as his grown-up sons, has not the right to dispose of the family property.

(2) He has not the right to dispose of it *mortis causa* without the consent of his sons.

(3) The father is the head of the administration, but on important occasions he acts in concert with his sons. If, for any reason, he is not equal to the task of administering the affairs of the community, one of his sons may be put in his place.

(4) Sons who are of full age, especially if they are married, may demand partition during the life of their father.

The relations between members of large *zadrugas* were usually ruled by the sense of common interest and solidarity. In the exceedingly valuable collection of answers from various districts inhabited by the Serbian race, which have been published by Professor Bogišić, stress is often laid on the obligation of the elders to keep the fortunes of the community intact, so that the growing generations should in any case not receive less than their forefathers had left to their parents. Altogether the *zadruga* communities present a striking instance of the spirit of comradeship and union in the management of social affairs.

The possibility of partition is always open. For a general division, the consent of most members of the *zadruga* would be required, but single members and small families are constantly observed leaving the large unions on account of overcrowding or quarrels. Nevertheless the fact remains that this institution was up to quite recent times regarded as the customary form of peasant life in the country of the Serbians and Croatians. We have here, therefore, a case in which custom holds its own tenaciously in spite of the legal possibility of dismemberment.

Similar communities are reported to have existed among the Alpine Slovenes of Carinthia and Istria, although in these parts of the country they gave way to more individualistic management under the influence of German colonization.

Important facts of the same kind have to be noticed in the early development of the Russian race, both in the Northern forests and in the Southern steppes. The population of the Northern provinces, colonized from Novgorod, consisted of peasants who made clearings in the vast forests and moors of the provinces of Archangel, Vologda, Viatka, etc. The settlements were achieved by clusters of kinsmen, and the form of these settlements were repeated over and over again with the regularity of bee-hives. The unit was the so-called *derevnia,* comprising a Joint Family which usually extended to second cousins and sometimes to their children. Each *derevnia* consisted of six or seven *dvors* (crofts or courts) forming the dwelling-house and adjacent orchards of the smaller households. Several *derevnias,* again, formed a higher union called *selo,* and common husbandry did not reach any further than this. The *selo* and the villages composing it (*derevnias*) held wide tracts of moor and forest and fisheries in common, allowing each of the component householders certain gangs or entries, i.e., rights of exportation for the purpose of fetching wood, fuel, hunting, fishing, etc. Such tillage as there was had to be carried on in fields "snatched" (*terebit*) from the wilderness. Each of the householders took a certain number of strips in the different fields, so that each holding was originally equalized as between the brothers or companions (*siabri,* cf. *sobrini*). In the succession of generations some of the holdings were parcelled up into smaller parts in consequence of the allowance of claims by *stirpes,* but the idea of keeping up the communal union was strongly held, and occasional redivisions might take place under the pressure of insistent claims by members of the younger generations. Later on, with the growth of population and subjection to the land-tax, the *mir* system grew out of these tribal settlements. . . . The South Russian arrangement is constructed on entirely similar lines, with the difference that the homestead is centred not in the *dvor* (court), but around the big oven (*pechische*). Again there recurs the fundamental feature of the enlarged household naturally growing out of the ordinary family on the death of the father. Similar arrangements are recorded in the history of the Poles and Czechs. I may refer readers for information on this subject to the excellent monograph of Professor Balzer of the University of Lwów. It is to be noticed, however, that with the Western Slavs *zadruga* arrangements gave way at an early period, and that from the fourteenth century the peasantry in those parts were organized on individualistic lines.

The same observation may be made to an even greater extent in the case of the Germanic peoples. The geographical features of the land and the troubled history of migrations and conquests led to individualization in the earlier Middle Ages, but yet we find widespread vestiges of a tendency towards common management of family affairs on the lines of enlarged households. In all territories inhabited by Germanic tribes we find the practice of joint management by co-heirs (*Ganerbschaft*) working in the same direction of solidarity in the difficult struggle for existence which is such a prominent feature in the life of *zadrugas*. The importance of voluntary co-operation and the more frequent partitions testify to a more mobile constitution of society than in the case of the Southern and Eastern Slavs. We read, for example, the following rule in the customary law of Skone: if a son is established with his wife in the household of his father, his property is added to that of his father. If he dies without having defined his property in severalty, his children share with grandfather and other co-heirs. It is clearly a case of a family which holds together under the authority of a grandfather after the marriage of some of its members. A similar rule may be cited from the legislation of Liutprand of Lombardy, and in the mediaeval Italian documents we often hear of *condomae* in the sense of joint households. Yet it is not always easy to say to what extent customary unions for the management of property, of which we get evidence in Romance countries, are to be traced to the gradual expansion of families, and in what measures they were the result of voluntary associations. Altogether the Joint Family presents an interesting example of the value of co-operative action, and of customary restrictions on the free play of individual self-determination.

§§ 7

GERMANIC LAW OF THE FAMILY AND MARRIAGE

Rudolf Huebner

Beginnings of the Germanic Law of the Family

The Patriarchal Family

In view of the present results of historical research it may be asserted with good reason that the primitive Indo-Germanic folk already lived under patriarchal conditions; and at any rate as regards the general Germanic and the German family law, there can scarcely remain any doubt that their historical point of departure was the patriarchal family organization. It prevailed among the primitive Germans (*Germanen*) in a pure and absolute form, so far as their conditions can be traced in the obscure origins of history.

During the dominance of the patriarchal system the family constituted a circle of persons all of whom were absolutely subjected to the power of the house-lord, the patriarch, and were united by this common bond of subjection into a social group. They participated in legal life solely through the mediacy of the "house-father"; he was their representative outside the group.

From Rudolf Huebner, *A History of German Private Law,* tr. F. S. Philbrick, with an Introduction by P. Vinogradoff (Boston: Little, Brown, 1918), pp. 584–603.

The Germanic languages and the Latin both took the name for this power of the house-lord from the most striking symbol of power, the hand, and named it therefore *Munt* (Old High G. *munt;* North Germanic and Old Norse *mund,* Latinized *mundium*). For the primary meaning of this word is "hand"; the Germanic *Munt* corresponds, etymologically and in meaning, to the *manus* of Roman family law. *Mundium* was originally a very broad conception, under which there seem to have been classed, in accord with the one-time actual extent of household authority, all possible relations of personal dependence; and which points backward to conditions when no public authority was recognized alongside of or superior to the authority of the family head. Even in medieval law, the meaning of the concept still extended far beyond the law of the family, embracing—in addition to the house-lord's authority over the family members dwelling in the house, and the servants—the relation of "a lord (*Schutzherr*) to his liegeman (*Mundmann*) and to his serf, of jurisdiction (*Vogtei*) over strangers, and over churches, and the representation of minors in law suits in so far as this was exceptionally permitted." However, this conception, originally unitary, assumed in time a varying character in the individual cases in which it was applied. For example, the mundium of husband, parents, and guardians, which rested upon relations of kinship, was differentiated as an independent legal institute. And within this mundium of the family law a further division took place: the power of the husband over his wife, of the father over his children, of the guardian over his ward, were each subjected to independent legal rules, differing unequally from their one-time common prototype. The original character of the institute was preserved in its purest form in the relation of a father to his children; the name was preserved, in the end, almost solely in the law of guardianship (*Vormund* = guardian; *Mündel* = ward; *mundtodt* = *entmündigt* = subject to guardianship). Its original character was that of an unlimited authority of the mundium-holder (*Muntherr*) over the persons subjected to his power. At an early day, and thereafter with ever increasing clearness, there were grafted upon this original concept of almost unlimited authority, first moral and then legal restrictions, which recognized a duty, in addition to the right, of the master. And thus "there

already appears in our earliest sources of information, the meaning of 'protection,' of 'peace.' " The house-lord became a lord-
protector, a *mundporo, foramundo, mundoaldus, Muntwalt,* of
the person subject to his authority; he was bound to exercise
such authority, not as formerly in his own interest alone, but
equally in their interest. With this step, wife and children ceased
to be mere things subject to his control. Nevertheless, the mundium of the house-lord, even in this mixed form of right and
duty that was characteristic of the Middle Ages, long continued
to signify "a power which we, according to our present views,
would call one of public law"; it continued to embrace a field into
which no public authority penetrated. For the state only the house-
lord existed, to him alone its commands were directed; he alone
long continued responsible under the criminal and the private
law for everything that happened within his house and through
the members thereof.

Membership of the Family

The Indo-Germanic family was probably a so-called "greater-"
(*Gross-*) family; a man's descendants remained together so long
as their common "truncal" (*Stamm-*) father, or common male
ancestor lived, or was capable of exercising physically and mentally
his household authority. This Indo-Germanic hearth-community
united "in one community not only parents and children, but
also the wives of sons, with their sons, and the wives and
descendants of the latter." In the greater-family of Old Russia
and in the Servian *Zadruga* this primitive family organization
has been preserved down to the present day. Among most of the
Indo-Germanic peoples, however, the greater-family developed
into the looser form of the sib; that is, into a group of persons
who, though conscious of union through common descent were
no longer bound together by the authority of their truncal father,
but constituted an association (*Genossenschaft*) of equal family
heads and the members of their households that far exceeded
in membership the "greater-" family. But the son, when he married, henceforth ordinarily lighted his own hearth fire. And thus
there existed within the sib, as the narrowest independent social
group, a separate (*Sonder-*) or "lesser-" family that was limited to

two generations: parents and children. Among the primitive and the later Germans we meet, in general, with this lesser-family only; though examples in which married children and grandchildren remained living in the parental household are not lacking, they are relatively rare. Nevertheless, in the peasant communities of collective hand common in the Middle Ages, which have persisted in some localities down to the present day, reminiscences were preserved of the original greater-family. In these communities, after the death of the house-father, the sons and their issue often remained united through many generations as an association. As contrasted with the associational sib and the community of collective hand, the lesser-family preserved the element of authority that was essential to the primitive greater-family. It was the circle within which the household mundium of the house-lord was exercised, over his wife and children as well as over the servants.

Marriage

The primitive patriarchal system did not necessarily involve the institution of marriage. But the family of the primitive Germans, like the supposititious family organization of the primitive Indo-Germans, rested upon marriage from the beginning. Marriage, however, was by no means synonymous with monogamy. On the contrary marriage acquired a special quality distinguishing it from other sexual unions merely from the fact that wife and children, notwithstanding their subjection to the unlimited mundium of husband and father, enjoyed in relation to him a position legally more secure than that of other women with whom he cohabited, and his offspring by such. Marriage was regarded as the legitimate sexual union. The "married" wife (*Ehefrau*) was distinguished from other wives (*Nebenfrauen*), concubines, and slaves by the fact that only she could bear him children of "full birth"; that is, above all, give her husband male issue who continued his line and family, performed the obligations of the blood-feud and, especially, were able to offer sacrifices for him when dead and thereby care for the peace of his soul. It was perfectly reconcilable with this religio-political purpose of marriage, however, that the husband might, in case his first wife remained childless, or for other reasons, acquire a second wife, or a third, or as many wives as his social, economic, and political associations made desirable and possible for him. Thus, among the primitive Germans, although according to the report of Tacitus (which was certainly in this respect accurate) they ordinarily contented themselves with one wife, a plurality of wives was by no means legally impossible. Among the northern Germanic races (*Nordgermanen*) the prevalence of polygamy long continued to be noteworthy; among their western branches it was still practiced even in Christian times, although only by the richest and greatest men, especially in royal houses—for example in those of Merovingians and Carolingians. Moreover, in addition to unions with several wives of equal rights there also existed among the primitive Germans a system of legal concubinage.

It was essential to the patriarchal marriage that the wife who lived with a man, either voluntarily or because compelled to do so, left her own household community forever, and abandoned all relation of kinship with its members; and also that the children she bore her husband thereby entered into relations of kinship with the father and the father's family only, and not with the house of the mother. Already in the Indo-Germanic period the family was therefore completely agnatic, as is particularly evidenced in the terminology of kinship. The same must be assumed to be true of the primitive Germans. The assumption that they lived originally in a condition of mother-law must be rejected. The expression "mother-right" (*Mutterrecht*) has been used since the epoch-making work of Bachofen to indicate conditions of very different character, as reported both in the accounts of ancient writers and in accounts of primitive peoples of the present time. Even if one understands by mother-law simply a form of family organization actually prevailing among a number of peoples—notably those of a low stage of culture—in which children are not counted with the father and the paternal kindred, but with the mother and the maternal kindred, and therefore possess rights of inheritance only in relation to the latter, such a condition would by no means constitute, as some were for a time inclined to believe, a necessary transitional stage in the social development of every people. Neither does it enjoy an exclusive authority, under all circumstances, where it exists. Still less does it involve, in itself, any peculiar legal position of the mother, or even a supremacy of mothers or of women (*Mutter-, Frauenherrschaft*); mother-right is therefore not the equivalent of matriarchy. At all events, in the present light of historical research we must start with the assumption that the Indo-Germanic peoples, from the beginning, never knew conditions of mother-right; nor the primitive Germans, either. It is true that several scholars (von Amira, Dargun, Ficker, Heusler, Opet, E. Mayer) have believed they had discovered traces of original mother-right in the primary monuments of Germanic law; and upon this basis it has been contended that primitive Germanic law was one of mother-right. Inasmuch as the arguments for this view (championed with most assurance by Ficker) that were derived from the law of inheritance, from the law of the marital community of goods, and from the legal status of illegitimate children have been convincingly disposed of, it now rests, at best, upon interpretations of the institute known as the "avunculate." Tacitus reports in a celebrated passage that the relation between nephews and uncles on the mother's side was quite as close as that between son and father, and that some persons, in giving hostages, treated the former relationship as the stronger security. Now, it is true that this powerful position of the maternal uncle is a characteristic feature of a society under mother-right. In order, therefore, to reconcile the unlikeness between the Germanic avunculate and the patriarchy which elsewhere prevailed among Indo-Germans, the hypothesis has been advanced that we have here a survival of pre-Indo-Germanic society—which lived under mother-right, as is provable from reports of the Lycians, Locrians, Etruscans, Cantabrians, the Balearians, and Picts. But it is not necessary to resort to this explanation. For the special honor of the maternal uncle may have been merely a consequence of the fact that the maternal kindred came, in time, to be considered along with the paternal, who were at first exclusively regarded; in other words, a consequence of the fact that the family's purely agnatic structure was replaced by a cognatic organization. In this appearance of the idea of cognatic relationship, which transformed in the same manner the family and the sib, the maternal uncle naturally played the most important rôle: he was the link between the families of the father and the mother, and he was primarily the person upon whom was incumbent, as the representative of the maternal sib, the protection of the wife as against her husband.

The Later Development

The beginnings of the Germanic and of the German family-law agree exactly with those we find among other Indo-Germanic peoples, and like the latter they can be derived and explained with a great degree of probability from the manners and law of an inferential primitive Indo-Germanic race. In its further development, also, from the earliest times down to the present day, German family-law has similarly followed the broad line marked by the general development of European civilization. True, it must not be forgotten that the family-law of a race is related with especial closeness to its particular mental genius; indeed it is precisely in this field that the law always finds its most important complement in manners and customs, and cannot be understood without attention to these. Despite this fact, however, the influence that has been exercised by the general development of economic and intellectual culture has been far stronger, in the long run, than the influence of national peculiarities. The former influence was greatly strengthened in the family-law by the fact that the most important part of this, the law of marriage, was withheld by the Church for many centuries from national legal development. The result was that an international ecclesiastical law took the place of a national secular law. In this medieval ecclesiastical law of marriage and also in the modern secular law that in turn displaced it, as well as in certain other portions of the family-law that remained more or less completely unaffected by the Church's influence—for example the law of the marital community of goods and the law of guardianship—certain general tendencies have prevailed among all nations of the Germanic-Romanistic circle of civilization, and have set identical ends to their legal development, however variant in detail the ways in which those ends were pursued and realized. At the same time, consciously or unconsciously, the development of all institutions of the family-law has undoubtedly been constantly directed toward a curtailment of the original patriarchal power of the husband, an equalization of husband and wife before the law, the legal security of children and other persons under mundium, and a reincorporation of the family-law in the secular law of the state.

The Contracting of Marriage

Although different varieties of sexual union were once not only actually practiced but also recognized by law, nevertheless marriage, as that form of sexual community which involved the most far-reaching legal consequences, was always distinguished by a special form observed in its creation, on the strength of which alone it was conceded its privileged rank of full legitimacy. The Germanic law, like the legal systems of other Indo-Germanic peoples, developed special forms for the creation of marriage; forms which were, of course, adjusted to the general principles regulating the conclusion of juristic acts. For even among the primitive Germans the contraction of marriage was regarded as a juristic act, although one that was consummated from the earliest times in an especially formal and solemn manner, because of its far-reaching consequences and its importance in religious and political life. This primitive and purely secular law of marriage contract, however, was later displaced by an ecclesiastical law of marriage, which as a part of the Canon law in the form finally given that by papal codification attained universal authority over the entire Christian population of Europe, until it was divided after the Reformation into special systems for different religious confessions or Territorial churches. It is only in the modern period that the State has again assumed control of the regulation of the marriage contract.

The Old Germanic Law of Marriage Contract

WIFE-ABDUCTION AND
WIFE-PURCHASE

There can be no doubt that, just as among the people of India, Greeks, Romans, Slavs, and many other non-Indo-Germanic races, so also among the primitive Germans the abduction of women (*Frauenraub*—"wife-rape") had at one time the effect of creating the marriage relation. Indubitable evidences exist of this fact. Like the Indian and Grecian epics, the sagas and poems of the primitive Germans ascribe to their most celebrated heroes the abduction of women by violence; and that this poetry rested upon a basis of reality—although indeed one which had for the most part already disappeared—is shown by historical examples, among which none is more celebrated than that of Arminius, who by abduction won in marriage Thusnelda, the intended wife of another. These reports are confirmed by the legal sources: in some of the Germanic folk-laws there still occur provisions according to which the *raptor* retained as wife a woman he had abducted against the will of her kindred from whom he captured her; or at least retained her when she herself acquiesced in the abduction or thereafter chose to remain with him. It can be proved that the abduction marriage was still known among the North Germans in the age of the Vikings, and in the peculiar statutory wife-abduction of northern legal sources it continued even much later. Reminders of this one-time institution of bride-abduction have been preserved also in many marriage customs among Germanic and Slavic races, widespread even today, which considerably increase the weight of other evidences. Thus, among rural populations the wooing of the bride frequently still has an apparently warlike character. Something like a simulated investment of the bride's house is undertaken by the friends of the bridegroom; often, the bride conceals herself after the marriage ceremony and must be captured, in which connection feigned battles take place among the boys and girls; throughout Germany, moreover, there is known as a marriage game a custom in accord with which the bride is abducted by the youth of the village. It is consistent with all this that the marriage ceremony (*Trauung, Hochzeit*) was known in the East and West Germanic laws as "bride-flight" (*Brautlauf, Brautlauft,* from *laufen, currere,* to run); these names reflect the fact that it was the bringing home of the bride that constituted the most essential element in the marriage contract.

There is a theory—wholly without basis, notwithstanding that it is championed by some Germanists (Dargun, Heusler)—that this rape-marriage was "the normal marriage of primitive law"; that the rape of women was originally the only valid form in which marriage could be consummated among the primitive Germans, and that only in time was there developed from it a peaceful, contractual mode in which marriage could be established. Schröder justly remarks that "marriage contracted between the children of neighbors with the knowledge and consent of their families must have been the starting point in the case of every race not wholly bestial." In the case of the primitive Germans the further fact is especially important that among them, as among many other primitive peoples, so-called endogamous marriages seem to have been the rule; that is, marriages between members of the same sib. The sib, however, was a frith-union, and excluded as between its members blood-feuds, hostilities, and acts of violence. In the case of such marriages, therefore, there must always have been a peaceful form of contract. Just as in the old law of India marriage by violent abduction of women was ordinarily permitted only to the members of the military nobility, so among the primitive Germans rape-marriage was doubtless never the rule but always an exception, and could have been especially common only when the question was one of winning in marriage the daughters of another sib, of an alien line (*Stamm,* family), or of a conquered race.

The original form of marriage contract among the primitive Germans was wife-purchase (*Frauenkauf*). We meet with it in the oldest legal sources as the prevailing, and the only legal, form in which marriage could be consummated. In this respect, also, the oldest Germanic law agrees exactly with conditions that are attested with equal clearness among most of the other Indo-Germanic races in their earliest antiquity, and which have been preserved among some of such races down to the present day; for example in India, where even today wife-purchase is widely prevalent in many regions as a form of marriage among the ordinary people and among the Russians, where marriage is still, in the mind of the rural folk and in reality, a matter of purchase, and is treated in the most matter-of-fact way as a question of goods and prices. Again among the early Germans the consummation of marriage was a juristic act, which was concluded between the bridegroom and his kindred on one side, and the father or guardian who held mandium over the bride and her kindred on the other side; and in which the bride herself participated solely as the object of the sale and not as a contracting party. Hence the Frankish folk-laws still spoke of *"uxorem emere," "feminam vendere," "pretium emptionis," "pretium nuptiale," "puella empta"*; and the Scandinavian law-books of *"kaupa," "byggja konu"* (to buy a wife, to bargain). In Germany the expression *"kaufen"* (to buy), for "to marry," long survived in many regions the custom itself, and has been preserved down to modern times, indeed even to the present day, as for example in Holland "where popular speech still designates the bride as 'purchased' (*verkocht, verkauft*)." It is true that older legal phraseology used the expressions *"Kauf," "kaufen"* in a far wider sense than that which is usual today, applying them to every bilateral contract; to every contract which in Amira's words can be called in any sense a "trade" (*Handelschaft*). Relying upon this circumstance, Maurer and Amira deny to the marriage of Germanic law the character of a purchase in the present sense of that word. But despite this pertinent definition of the term, it can scarcely be doubted that the primitive Germans, when they chose their wives by contract, saw in the transaction by which they so procured them nothing more than an actual purchase; that in their eyes there was no difference in the transaction, as such, whether they purchased a woman to be a wife or a servant. This conclusion is not inconsistent with the fact that the purchase of a wife was distinguished from all other purchases both by its object—a free woman—and by its purpose—the creation of a mundium that protected the entire freedom of the woman. Nor is it inconsistent with the fact that the will of the bride herself may also have come to be considered, at least in fact, at an early date. Although bride-purchase was therefore distinguished by the special agreements that accompanied it, and which were lacking in other contract forms for the purchases of women, there was nevertheless involved in it, as in every contract of sale, an exchange of goods and a purchase price. The purchase price was called dower (*Wittum, Widum;* Old High G. *widemo, widem;* A. Saxon *weotuma;* Burgundian *wittimon*) or hire-money (*Mietgeld;* Lombard *meta; Miete, Lohn*—hire, wage). In Latin it was known as *pretium nuptiale; pretium emptionis, dos.* To be sure, fixed statutory tariffs for the dower (*Wittum*) were declared in the folk-laws, at least in the Frankish period, but these probably had no absolute, but only a relative, significance; possibly that of a minimum limit. On the contrary free agreement was probably the original and ordinary form. Indeed we are frequently told, for example in the Scandinavian sagas, of a bargaining concerning the sum. The creation of the marital community for life by a transaction of sale—it nowhere appears in more repulsive form than in some of the Anglo Saxon laws—has to our feelings a cold-blooded and brutal character. But that can be no reason for doubting that the actual nature of this form of marriage was a sale; especially when one remarks how widespread this view has been and still is among races of the past and of the present day. Even now it cannot be regarded as extinct in many social strata of the German folk.

FORMAL REQUISITES OF A MARRIAGE CONSUMMATED BY CONTRACT

Since Sohm's investigations it has been certain that marriages consummated contractually were always controlled by the general rules of contract law. Indeed the study of the forms in which marriage was consummated has served to make clear the general principles and development of the Germanic-German law of contract. Marriage by contract, like every other legal transaction, and particularly every sale, was originally consummated as a non-credit transaction. This spot transaction was composed, indeed, of two different elements; but it combined these, exactly as did the oldest conveyances of land, into an act single in time and in law. When the offer of marriage, which ordinarily preceded the contract, had been accepted, and when an agreement had been reached concerning the conditions—particularly the price and the time—of the nuptials, then the legal ceremony, upon whose publicity great weight was laid, was consummated within the circle of blood "friends." For marriage was an affair of the sib; it was a marriage under the family-law. This legal act was so executed that the performances of the two parties followed alternatively: the bridegroom counted out into the hand of him who held mundium over the bride, for her sib, the price agreed upon, and he who held the mundium gave (*tradieren, trauen,* to deliver) the bride to the bridegroom. Thereupon followed the leading of the bride home to the house of the bride-groom—the bride-flight—where cohabitation (*Beilager*) was consummated in a public manner; and with this the marriage ceremony was concluded, and the existence of the marriage begun. The father, brother, or the next male relative of the sword-kin was empowered to betroth and to give the bride. If she were a widow it was the nearest male connection of her first husband in conjunction with her blood-friends; whose place was taken, in case of their refusal, by the kindred of the widow. The betrother (*Verlober*) received for his participation a marriage gift from the bridegroom.

This simple marriage act, which we must assume for the Germanic period, became divided in the Frankish period into two acts, the two elements theoretically involved in it being separated in time—exactly as was the case with the Sala and the investiture in conveyances of land.

The first act essential to the consummation of the marriage, which corresponded to the Sala, was the betrothal or *Verlobung* (*desponsatio;* A. Saxon *beweddung;* Old Norse *foestning*). This was the contract of alienation, which continued for a time to be concluded between the bridegroom and the bride's sib, represented by the holder of mundium over her. To be sure, under the influence of Christianity increasing respect was paid to the bride's will, but no importance was at first attributed to this legally. In accordance with the general rules of the law of contracts, this contract of alienation could originally be concluded only as a real-contract. That is, the bridegroom was bound to perform first the act incumbent upon him—the payment of the purchase price; he thereby obligated the other contracting party to the counter performance, which after the appearance of credit transactions was postponed to a later time. However, just as the payment of handsel, symbolic of the full purchase price and in place of complete pre-performance, came in time to be considered sufficient in a sale to obligate the other party to counter performance, so in the betrothal men were contented if the bridegroom delivered an earnest (*arrha*), a payment on the purchase price. Among the Franks this symbolic mundium-money (*Mundschatz*) amounted to a solidus (= 10 denarii) and one denarius; in the betrothal of a widow—in which connection it was known as a *Reipus* (ring-money)—three solidi and one denarius. The payment of this slight sum was preserved for centuries in regions of the French law as a marriage custom. At the marriage of Louis XVI and Marie Antoinette there still figured thirteen denarii—which, indeed, are reported to be still in use in some parts of France; and it is reported of the marriage of the Count of Paris, celebrated in 1864, that the Count, to conclude the same, handed to his young wife a few gold and silver coins.

Although the payment of the earnest might preserve to the betrothal the character of a real contract it nevertheless became possible to conclude it in the form of a wed-contract; that is, to consummate it as a formal, instead of a real, contract. In this case the bridegroom obligated himself to a later payment of the dower (*Wittum*) by handing to the mundium-holder of the bride a *wadia;* whereupon—since the staff did not have the effect of binding the other party—a *wadia* was likewise handed over by the guardian, in order to assure the bride's future delivery. Moreover, there might easily occur here, as in all cases, a confusion of earnest-money (*arrha*) and staff (*wadia*), of real and formal contract.

The nature of the betrothal was altered in still another respect. It became usual to regard the mundium over the bride, rather than her own person, as the object of the sale which the bridegroom must acquire with the purchase price. This explains the fact that among the Lombards the purchase price was also known as *mundius,* among the Frisians as *muntsket* (*Muntschatz*), and among the North Germans as *mundr*. At the same time, this change of view must have had rather theoretical than practical importance so long as the mundium continued to involve extensive powers of control.

On the other hand it was of the greatest practical importance that the purchase money came in time to inure to the bride herself instead of her sib. From the mundium-holder's custom of delivering to her the whole or a part of the *Wittum* there was developed a legal claim of the bride to that amount of property. By this change, however, the meaning and purpose of the performance incumbent upon the bridegroom was also altered: he no longer gave the sum agreed upon in order to purchase the bride from her sib, but in order to make her a gift (*Zuwendung*) which was intended to serve her as a maintenance-portion (*Leibgedinge*), as support for her when a widow. The *pretium* became a *dos;* the *puella empta* became a *puella dotata.* With this change the giving of the dower (*Wittum*), once essential under the Germanic law to the validity of the marriage, completely lost its importance from the 1100s onward.

To these changes was added the following. As already mentioned, the bride was originally simply the object of the betrothal contract, and it marked an advance when regard was also paid to her will (in the beginning at least actually, and later legally as well), and her consent required. But when the legal position of women began gradually to improve, this purely passive participation of the bride ceased, and the rôles of the parties were reversed. "Whereas the father (or guardian) of the bride had theretofore concluded the betrothal contract, though with the consent of the daughter, she now betrothed herself, a mere right of consent, that is a veto upon the contraction of the marriage, being conceded to her father (or guardian) as a remnant of his old right of betrothal." The father or guardian thenceforth appeared as the beholder only in the case of a bride under mundium. The betrothal thus became a contract concluded between bridegroom and bride; they were the contract parties who made the mutual promises of marriage. But in this form also, of course, the betrothal continued subject to the existing rules of contract law. Afterward as before, it was concluded either as a weakened real contract by the delivery of earnest-money by the bridegroom, or as a formal (a wed-) contract by the mutual delivery of staffs; in which connection, however, as already mentioned, staff and handsel might easily be confused with one another. Following Roman-Italian usage, a ring was the customary handsel in Germany (*subarrhatio cum anulo*). It was entirely consistent with the nature of the *arrha* that only *one* ring was originally given, and this by the bridegroom to the bride; for the ring, the betrothal ring, was the last remnant of the old purchase-money; with it the bridegroom betrothed the bride, and the bride, by putting it on her finger, obligated herself to marital fidelity. When the custom of exchanging rings later developed, the mutual gift and acceptance of the rings replaced the mutual delivery of staffs, and represented the formal act of a wed-contract. However, as in the case of other contracts so in that of betrothal the weaker forms of oath or hand-clasp also sufficed for its consummation.

The betrothal was followed, when the day agreed upon arrived, by the delivery of the bride from her mundium-holder to the bridegroom. This was the *Trauung* (*traditio puellae;* A. Saxon *gifta*), which, as already remarked, exactly corresponded in legal significance and outward form to the investiture in a conveyance of land. It was performed as a public and solemn act in the bride's home in the presence of the kindred of both parties. It was accompanied by the marriage feast. The legal formalities observed in this connection were long the same as those that once accompanied the original simple act by which marriage was consummated. They corresponded, in part, to the usages customary in adoption. Along with the bride there were delivered to the bridegroom certain symbols of espousal—preferably a spear, as the token of the mundium that passed therewith to him for the future; the hair of the bride, which she had until then worn loose, was done up, her head was veiled, a mantle was thrown about her, and so on; the bridegroom grasped her hand, and probably stepped upon her foot, or set her upon his knee as if she were an adopted child; frequently, also, he delivered to her a present. The final act, afterward as before, was the festive leading of the bride home to the bridegroom's house, where, at least in the North, a common cup once more rejoiced the entire marriage company. Thereafter came the occupancy of the nuptial-bed in the presence of witnesses, frequently by torch-light; a custom which remained usual throughout the Middle Ages, persisting longest in the case of princely marriages, but also among the laboring classes down into the 1600s. The Law Books of the zenith of the Middle Ages emphasized more frequently and with greater stress than did the Frankish sources the importance of marital cohabitation as the act most decisive for the consummation of the marriage's legal consequences. The beginning of the marital community of goods, in particular, was very often made dependent upon it. This moment was expressed by phrases of the most varied character ("when the woman gets into the man's bed"; "when the cover is drawn over them"; "when the woman disrobes before the man's bed," etc.).

The consequences of dividing the marriage ceremony into two

acts, the betrothal and the nuptials, was that neither of these alone sufficed to establish the marriage relation. Of course the betrothal, like all other contracts, produced certain legal effects. It obligated the guardian to perform the marriage ceremony at the time agreed upon, and it obligated the bridegroom to take home the bride and to pay the purchase money whose payment was temporarily respited. Whoever failed to perform these obligations was punished for breach of the betrothal contract; the guardian was ordinarily obliged to give back the *Wittum* in case this had already been paid, and to pay an equal amount in damages; the bridegroom lost the *Wittum*. In addition to this, the betrothal created a personal obligation of fidelity on the part of the woman; so long as she was a mere object of sale, this could have been created by giving her a present, and later it was created by the handsel that was given her. Under many legal systems an affianced woman who was guilty of sexual intercourse with another man might be punished as an adulteress. Her betrothed, as well as her mundium-holder, had an action against a third person who seduced her, with or without her consent. But the marriage relation was first created by the espousals, which, however, could be consummated only after betrothal.

That betrothal and nuptials were equally necessary preconditionals to the creation of a legally valid marriage, and continued to constitute one act legally, is shown by the generally prevalent custom of performing in connection with each the formalities that were usual in the other. So for example, under the Lombard law, in the case of betrothal, when the *meta* had been paid or wagered (given as a wed), the bride was delivered by her mundium-holder symbolically (*per baculum*), but then immediately handed back by the bridegroom. It was more common to repeat the formalities of betrothal in the nuptials: the bridegroom once more paid the simulated purchase price (the earnest-money) and the parties once more declared their will to marry, just as they had already done in the betrothal. In particular, a ring was delivered or rings again exchanged in the nuptials: with this step the engagement ring became a marriage ring (*mahelfingerlin*). This is also the explanation of the fact that expressions were employed to designate the married couple that were derived from the betrothal—*Ehegespons, promessi sposi, épouser,* to spouse, to

wed, *vermählen* (that is, to promise, to betroth; from *mahal* =
speech, address, modern *Gemahl*).

When, at the zenith of the Middle Ages, self-betrothal by the
bride took the place of betrothal by her guardian, the nuptial
"giving" in the sense of an investiture had outlived its usefulness.
The *traditio puellae* was transformed into a self-espousal (*Selbst-
trauung*) of the bride, into a mutual giving by the bridal couple.
To be sure, the influence of the older viewpoint of the law continued to be shown in a peculiar manner. For that form of self-
espousal which first became predominant was "a 'giving' through
a third person who was freely chosen by the bride, or as the case
might be by the bridal couple." This third person thus became a
Salmann or fiduciary (*Treuhänder*) to whom the bride gave herself "in trust" (*auf Treue*); that is, "merely to the end that he
should deliver her to her betrothed." Who the third person might
be was immaterial. He might be a near relative but that was not
necessary; any trustworthy man, preferably one of advanced age
but always a layman, was asked to assume this rôle. The essential
thing was that he was not, like the guardian, chosen to coöperate
because of any right of kinship, but merely by virtue of a com-
mission; he was no "born" (*geborener*) but a freely "chosen"
(*gekorener*) guardian. He consummated the nuptials by certain
words with which he pronounced the marriage benediction; they
were no longer completed by a marriage act but by a marriage
formula. The transition from the old to the new usage can be traced
in certain remarkable records of legal and cultural history. In a
Swabian nuptial-formula of the 1100s it is still the true, the
"born" guardian who as the nearest male relative gives
(*antwortet*) the bride to the bridegroom together with the
symbols of marriage—namely seven gloves (the *wadia* given by
the bridegroom), a sword, a golden ring, a penny, mantle, and
hat—pronouncing at the same time the words: "*wa ich iu bevilhe
mine muntadele* (*Mündel*) *ziweren triwun und ze iueren gnaden,
und bit iuch durch die triwe als ich si iu bevilhe, dar ir ir rehte
voget sit, und ir genadich voget sit, und daz ir nit palemunt*
(*treuloser Vormund*) *ne werdent.*" ("Because I give over to you
my ward to your faith and mercy and beg you by the faith by
which I entrust her to you that you will be her right and kindly
keeper and that you will not become faithless to your trust.")

On the other hand, in a nuptial-formula of Cologne of the 1300s there is talk merely of a certain "somebody" who consummates the marriage simply with the following words: *"Ich bevelen uch zô houff up Frentzer Erden myt Goulde ind Gesteynen, Silver ind Gould, beyde nâ Francken Wyse ind Sassen ee, dat urre geyn den anderen layssen en sall umb Leyff noch umb Leyt, noch um geyn Dynck dat Gott an eme geschaffen hait odir geschaffen mach layssen werden."* ("I enjoin you, on Frankish soil with gold and precious stones, with silver and gold, both according to Frankish manner and Saxon law, that neither of you shall leave the other for love or woe nor for any other thing that God has created in you or may create in you.")

THE MODERN RUSSIAN FAMILY

Maxime Kovalevsky

We believe that the theory of the matriarchate finds a solid basis in the past history of the Russian family. The present condition of the latter seems to prove that the next stage in its evolution was the household community, composed of persons united by descent from a common forefather and accompanied by that worship of ancestors which usually resulted from it. The complete subjection of the wife to the husband, and of the children to the father; community of goods and the common enjoyment of their produce by the relatives living under the same roof; the acknowledged superiority of old age and of direct descent from the common ancestor; the total absence of testamentary dispositions of property, and even of that mode of legal succession which supposes partition, and the exclusion of the more remote by the nearer kin; the elimination of women from participation in the family estate because marriage makes them aliens; all these features of the patriarchal family so ably illustrated in the works of Sir Henry Maine reappear in the modern constitution of the Russian family. I mean, of course, that of the country people, the middle and higher classes having already adopted European manners and customs, and being on that

From Maxime Kovalevsky, *Modern Customs and Ancient Laws of Russia* (London: David Nutt, 1891), Lecture II.

148

account subjected to a legislation which, on more than one point, is in direct opposition to customary law.

Let us study one by one the characteristic features of this family constitution by the peasant, a constitution more like that of the early Celts and Germans than that of any of the modern nations of Europe.

The great importance still attached by the Russian peasant to agnatism, that is to relationship on the father's side, is shown by the part which ancestor worship plays even now at the celebration of a country wedding. Before becoming a member of her husband's family, the bride must sever all the ties which have hitherto bound her to the house-spirits under whose protection she has passed her youth, and must solemnly adopt the worship of those of the family into which she is about to enter. This public manifestation of a change of worship is most clearly seen in the wedding ceremonies of the Southern Slavs. It is not so distinctly preserved in those of the Eastern Slavs. Both these races being identical as to their origin and nature, I will begin by first stating the religious customs, customs of an undoubtedly pagan origin—still in use at Bulgarian betrothals. "In Lika," says M. Bogišić, "the bride, before leaving her father's house, goes three times round the hearth, prostrating herself each time, as if to implore forgiveness." As you are aware of the intimate connection which has existed between the worship of the hearth and that of the family ancestors, I need not tell you that the act performed by the Bulgarian bride before leaving her parents' house has no other meaning than that of a last invocation of the house-spirits whose worship she is on the point of abandoning.

The spirits are supposed to be hurt by the decision she has taken to withdraw to her husband's homestead, and to be appeased by an act of humiliation on her part. When she is once in the bridegroom's house the maiden is obliged to perform another ceremony; she must seat herself close to the hearth, in order to keep up for a short time the fire burning thereon by pieces of wood thrown on to it with her own hands. The symbolical character of this ceremony may easily be perceived. The young wife is on the point of becoming a member of the house community of her husband, and as such, a participant in its family worship. Her acquiescence must be expressed by a symbol, and her keeping up the fire on the hearth is precisely such a symbol. The custom just described exists all over Bulgaria and has been more than once alluded to by modern ethnographers, M. Bogišić, Mr. Krauss, and others.

Let us now examine the corresponding customs of the Russian peasantry. In little Russia the bride, while her father is discussing the question of her marriage with the person sent by the bridegroom, is obliged by custom to remain near the hearth, towards which she stretches out her hand. By so doing she expresses her desire still to remain under the protection of the house-spirits of her family, the so-called *domovoi*. A century ago, according to the statement of Kalinovsky, the day on which the bride was taken to the house of her future husband, a great fire was lighted in the yard before it, and the young couple were obliged to cross it sitting in their carriage. This custom is still observed in certain parts of the Government of Kiev, but only in those cases in which the bride is known to have misbehaved before marriage. Heaps of straw are kindled on such occasions in the yard before the bridegroom's house, and the bride who has passed safely over these fires is considered to be purified. But this does not prevent her, as soon as she has entered the house of her husband, from seeking refuge at the hearth, where she stands for a while singing a carol, the meaning of which is that she laments her past bad conduct and promises to be a good wife.

I beg you to observe that the fires are lighted in the yard of the bridegroom's house and that they are to be considered as being in direct relation with the house-community to which he belongs. Not every fire has the power of purification, only that which represents the family hearth. It is to this hearth that the young wife appeals for protection, should she have any reason to fear any ill-treatment from her husband's family, on account of her former conduct; it is before this hearth that she confesses and repents and promises to be a good and faithful wife.

In a society, in which the interests of the family constantly prevail over those of the individual (and such is certainly the case in all patriarchal societies, and amongst them the Russian), there is no room for marriages contracted by the mutual consent of the young people. I do not mean to say that Russian parents, whose duty it is to find suitable matches for their sons and daughters, never take into account the feelings of those they intend to unite. I wish only to impress on you the idea that they are not obliged to do so by custom. On more than one occasion Russian customary courts have plainly expressed the opinion that a marriage contract concluded by the bride's father with that of the future husband is a legal act, for the infringement of which amends ought to be made by the restitution to the party wronged of the loss he or she may have sustained.

The clergy very early endeavoured to put an end to the arbitrary manner in which parents disposed of their children's future, but the force of custom and the feeling that supported it were so strong that the only measure which the ecclesiastical statute of Jaroslav (XIth century) introduced for the protection of the freedom of marriageable children was the one by which a fine which went to the bishop was inflicted on the parents of a daughter who, after a marriage contracted against her will, had committed suicide.

The country people still believe that a marriage without the parents' approval will call down the wrath of Heaven on the heads of the young couple. This moral sanction, the right of parents to decide the future of their children, has received from the customary law of Russia the support of a penalty in case of disobedience; the son and daughter who conclude a marriage without consulting their parents lose all rights to inheritance and dowry.

According to modern Russian law, marriage is a religious act; it cannot be performed without the help of the Church, and is regarded as a sacrament. But such is by no means the light in which the country people look on it, nor was it the view of the old Russian law. For many centuries the Russian clergy had to fight against the inveterate custom of our lower classes to contract unions without the sanction of the Church. The young couple saved the expense of a religious ceremony and thought their union legally established as soon as they were publicly joined to each other in the presence of the community, which was invited on the occasion to a sort of festival called the *vesselic*. No later than the end of the sixteenth century an assembly of Divines convened by Ivan the Cruel entered a strong protest against the custom which everywhere prevailed of omitting the religious consecration of the marriage tie, and strong measures were in consequence taken against those who did not comply with the requirements of the clergy. All, however, failed, and marriage remained in the eyes of the common people nothing more than a sort of civil contract, entered into in the presence of the community as a sign of its recognition and sanction.

That such generally was, and still is, the prevailing opinion of the Russian peasant may be seen from the following facts.

Among the Cossacks of the Don, not more than a century ago, people, as a general rule, were joined in marriage in the following way: The young couple, after previous agreement, went to the popular assembly of the village, or stanitza, this assembly being known by the name of *Majdan,* and declared that they had made up their minds to become husband and wife. "Be my wife," said the bridegroom to the bride. "Be my husband," she answered. "So be it," chanted the assembly. "We wish you good luck and happiness."

On the Don the absence of a religious ceremony may, to a certain extent, be explained by the scarcity of priests; but such is by no means the case in those provinces which were annexed to Muscovy in the middle of the seventeenth century, after ages of political dependence on Poland. I refer to the Governments of Kiev, Tchernigov, and Poltava, which constitute what in our days is known under the name of Little Russia. It is, therefore, very interesting to find that in those provinces the religious consecration of marriage is still considered by the peasants as a superfluous ceremony. Matrimonial life begins here after the nuptial festival, the *vesselic,* and weeks may pass before the couple find it necessary to be married at church. Facts of the same description have been noticed by Madame Efimenko in the extreme north of Russia, in the Government of Archangel, occupied by colonists from Great Russia.

The customary law of Russia, like the old German jurisprudence, established a difference between betrothal and marriage. Both are considered to be legal acts, and both ought therefore to have distinct legal effects. Betrothal is legally concluded as soon as the two families have come to an agreement, first, as to the amount of the marriage expenses each party is to bear, and secondly, as to the time fixed for the wedding. The expenses are of different kinds: they comprise, first, the *kladka* of the bridegroom, a sort of *pretium emptionis* paid to the bride's father, and the dowry which the bride receives from her family. Then come the presents to be made by each party to the parents of the bride and those of the bridegroom, and the amount of expense which the bridegroom has to incur on the occasion of the nuptial feast. All these are regularly discussed and settled by a sort of verbal agreement, known among the peasantry by the name of *riad*. In ancient Russia when agreements of this kind were entered into even by the higher classes, the *riad* was always put down in the form of a written contract, and this is still occasionally done in the northern Governments of Russia, especially in that of Archangel. Betrothal is considered to be legally concluded at the moment when the two parties, that of the bridegroom and that of the bride, have shaken hands. It is not without reason that I insist on the fact that it is this indefinite expression of the two parties which concludes the act of betrothal. I want to impress on your minds that the presence of the bridegroom's father is not considered necessary. An outsider, called *Svat,* may be authorised by the father to speak and act for him in a contract of this sort.

As soon as the ceremony of shaking hands is over neither of the contracting parties can break the engagement without incurring the obligation of pecuniary compensation for the wrong he does to the other party by his breach of contract. This compensation is of two different kinds: the one seems to have rather a moral, the other a purely monetary or material origin. If the bride's party breaks the contract, the bridegroom and his family consider themselves injured in their honour. If, however, the breach of promise has been made by the bridegroom, the case is more serious. Then it is not only the honour of the bride that suffers, but also the material interests of the family, since a bride rejected by the man whom she was on the point of marrying will generally experience great difficulty in finding another suitor. Such being the case, the customary court of the village usually accords to the party aggrieved the right to demand a pecuniary compensation "for the loss of honour the bride is supposed to have sustained" ("*za beshchestit,*" say our peasants). In case security has been received for a bridegroom's performance of his promise by a pledge or by the partial payment of the money which he owes to the bride's father, the question of compensation is easily settled, as the family of the bride retain for her own use the money already received; but if no payment has been made, the court must decide the amount to be paid. It very seldom happens that the sum demanded exceeds thirty roubles, at least, in the provinces of Great Russia. No extenuating circumstances are admitted on this occasion by the Court. A father having once declared that he was drunk when he gave his consent to the proposed marriage of his son, received no other answer but this: "You may be drunk, but you must be clever" (*bud' p'ian da umen*).

The breach of contract may have two different results: one, that which I have just mentioned, a compensation in money for the loss of honour; as to the other, I have already stated that the contract of betrothal contains certain engagements as to the amount of the *pretium emptionis,* of the dowry and of the different expenses to be incurred by each party on the occasion of the marriage. If certain of these engagements have been partly fulfilled before the breach of promise, the wronged party has the right to demand the restitution of the money which had been spent; the bridegroom receives back the presents which he has made to his bride, and the bride those given to the bridegroom. The Courts uniformly recognise the necessity for such mutual restitution, the only exception being when the money already paid serves to constitute the amount of compensation to either party for the wrong inflicted by the loss of honour.

The contract of marriage which follows that of betrothal cannot at the present time be dissolved; but we should be mistaken if we inferred from this fact that this indissolubility of marriage has always been recognised by the common law of Russia. Though the peasants are now known to use the following aphorisms: "Marriage is known but not unmarriage"; "A bad pope may marry you, but even a good one cannot unmarry you," the case was quite different in the past. Not longer ago than the end of the eighteenth century the Cossacks of the Don practiced divorce. A husband and wife who did not wish to live together any longer appeared before the popular assembly and made the following declaration: "This woman is no longer my wife"; "This man is no longer my husband." "Be it so," was the answer of the assembly, and the marriage tie ceased to exist. During the sixteenth century husbands in Great Russia were still accustomed to grant their wives full liberty to contract a new engagement, or, at least, to live apart from their legal lords. An archbishop of Novgorod, Theodosius, bitterly complained of this practice. Up to the middle of the eighteenth century the Russian clergy dissolved the marriage bond very often for no other reason than that of incompatibility of temper, this incompatibility appearing in the dissolute life of either husband or wife.

The memory of those days is still preserved among the country folk, and we can explain the part taken by the customary Courts, in direct contradiction to the law, only by the influence on them of tradition. They take part in the making of certain contracts in which husbands and wives who no longer wish to live under the same roof waive questions of interest, and agree to interfere no more with each other's existence.

The part which the community is called on to play in the contract and dissolution of marriage is strikingly manifested in certain peculiar ceremonies still in use at a Little Russian wedding. The tokens of the damsel's virginity are exhibited in much the same way as they were exhibited unto the elders of a Jewish city, as is described in the twenty-second chapter of Deuteronomy. The whole company then begin to shout loudly, congratulating the mother of the bride, and eulogising the maiden's virtue. In case the newly married wife is no longer a virgin, and her husband makes no statement as to his previous cohabitation with her, instead of praises and cheers, the most violent abuse is poured on the parents of the bride, and the most shameful songs are sung. They often go on to insulting acts, such as the following: spirits are offered in derision to the bride's mother in a glass with a hole in the bottom; the outside walls of the house are blackened with tar; a hole is made in the stove in order to show the stain which the hearth has suffered. Sometimes, also, one of the guests climbs up to the top of the house and begins to throw water down on all sides—a symbol of the liberality with which the new wife has distributed her favours to all those who asked for them. Very frequently, also, the parents of the bride are insulted by having yokes made of straw, previously besmeared with tar and dirt, placed by force on their necks.

The reciprocal rights and duties of husband and wife according to Russian customary law, and the position of children as regards their parents, are the next topics I intend to discuss in the present lecture.

The husband is acknowledged to be the master of the woman he has married. "The wife is in the power of her husband," so runs the common saying, and the fact of her complete subjection to his will is illustrated by certain symbolical acts performed at the time of the wedding. The bridegroom, while he is leading his bride to her future home, gives her from time to time light blows from a whip, saying at each stroke: "Forget the manners of thine own family, and learn those of mine." As soon as they have entered their bedroom, the husband says to his wife: "Take off my boots." The wife immediately obeys her husband's orders, and, taking them off, finds in one of them a whip, symbol of his authority over her person. This authority implies the right of the husband to control the behaviour of his wife, and to correct her every time he thinks fit, not only by words, but also by blows. The opinion which a Russian writer of the sixteenth century, the pope or priest Silvester (the author of *The Domostroy*), expressed as to the propriety of personal chastisement, and even as to its beneficial effects on the health, is still shared by the country people. In more than one popular song the wife is represented as bitterly complaining of the indifference of a husband who never on any occasion gives her a good beating. "I thrash those I love best," says a well-known Russian proverb. The customary Court seems to admit the use of such disciplinary proceedings by not interfering in the personal relations of husband and wife. "Never judge the quarrel of husband and wife," is a common saying, scrupulously observed by the village tribunals, which refuse to hear any complaint on the part of the aggrieved woman, at least so long as the punishment has not been of such a nature as to endanger life or limb. Where that is the case, the offender may be condemned to imprisonment, and the outraged victim allowed to retire for a time to the home of her parents. The customary law has, however, taken effectual measures for the protection of the wife's fortune. That husband and wife should each have entirely distinct property, with sole control over it, is still the leading principle at least in Great Russia. In the provinces which, like those of Little Russia, have been for centuries subject to the statute of Lithuania and the municipal law of Magdeburg, the system of a partial community of goods has prevailed. According to the customary law of Kiev, Poltava, and Chernigov, a widow has a right to the third part of the fortune left by her husband. In former times this third part was a sort of pledge for the security of the dowry of the wife.

A few words will suffice to give a general idea of the dependence in which the children are placed as regards their parents, and more especially their father. The patriarchal character of the Russian family plainly appears in the fact that no amount of bad treatment on the part of the parents justifies an appeal to the village tribunal, unless it involves danger to life or limb. In such cases, the nature of which makes it difficult to establish the facts before a Court of Law, the further maintenance of the child is generally committed to some near relative.

The complete dependence of the children upon their parents in respect to fortune is proved by the fact that neither son nor daughter can claim any portion of the family estate. The father can, as he pleases, give or refuse a dowry to his daughter. Should she marry against his wish no dowry is given, and she enters penniless into her husband's family. It equally depends upon the father's pleasure whether he shall transfer a portion of his property to a grown-up son, or maintain it intact in spite of his son's manifest wishes. An act of insubordination on the part of the son, as for instance, his marrying without permission, may become the occasion for his complete disinheritance by the father, at least so far as the father's fortune is concerned. I make this exception, inasmuch as, besides his share in the father's fortune, the son may be enabled to inherit from his mother's estate, or may possess property, the gift of some relative or friend. Such property must be scrupulously guarded by the father whose rights over it are only those of the natural guardian of his son's fortune.

Hitherto we have spoken of the Russian family as of a kind of natural society, created by marriage and continued by the birth of children; but side by side with this form of family organisation, differing only in detail from that of Western Europe, there exists in Russia a peculiar mode of family communism. In various parts of the country numerous persons, sometimes amounting to fifty and rarely to less than ten, are to be found united in a common household, living under the same roof and taking their meals at the same table. A family constituted after this fashion is known to English scholars under the name of "The Joint Family" or "House Community." Sir Henry Maine has made the notion of it generally familiar through his marvellous investigations in the early law of Ireland and the modern customs of Northern India. He has also correctly settled the question of its origin by appealing to natural increase and non-division as the real sources of its growth. He has even made an attempt to show that it was not limited to distinct peoples or races, but that, notwithstanding the immense distance which separates the Eastern or Hindoo branch of the Aryan race from the European branches, notwithstanding, also, the difference in the historical development which may be traced between its Celtic and Slavonic ramifications, joint households are as likely to be met with in the defiles of the Himalayas as in the plains of old Erin or of modern Servia. Taking advantage of the recent investigations made by Professor Bogišić in the customary law of the Southern Slavs, Sir Henry Maine has presented a lively picture of the interior organisation of the famous Servian *Zadruga,* which, as he shows, has more than one feature in common with the House Community of the Rajpoots. The barrier of language, of which he so often complains, prevented this master in the field of comparative jurisprudence from completing his studies of the patriarchal system of House Communities by investigating the Undivided Household of Great Russia. This Undivided Household has been recently the subject of numerous and serious inquiries on the part of Russian ethnographers; and the results of their investigations I desire now to lay before you.

First of all let me tell you that the undivided household of the Eastern Slavs is a very ancient institution. In the so-called Chronicle of Nestor, mention is made of the *gens* organisation of the Polians, a Slavonic tribe, dwelling on the banks of the Dnieper. The Polians are stated to live (I translate literally) "each ruling his own kindred or gens (*rod svoi*) and occupying

distinct localities." This rather obscure text authorises the supposition that the Polians were divided into independent house-
communities, each of which possessed its own piece of land.
Another reference is made to these Undivided Households in
one of the paragraphs of the Pravda of Jaroslav, a sort of Mirror
of Justice compiled in the middle of the eleventh century, by
order of the Grand Duke Jaroslav, son of that Vladimir who
introduced Christianity into Russia. The frequent occurrence of
South Slavonic terms in this the oldest Russian code, such, for
instance, as that of *bratouchada* (the son of the brother, the
nephew) confirms the hypothesis first put forth, so far as I know,
by the well-known professor of Russian history at Moscow, Mr.
Kluchevsky, that the work of codification had been entrusted to
some Southern Slav. This is the more likely as owing to the
recent introduction of Christianity and learning into Russia, there
was a lack of well-educated natives, so that the Byzantine Church
had frequently to have recourse to priests of South Slavonic
origin, in order to propagate the Gospel and the elements of
learning among their eastern and northern brethren. Old Russian
being much more like the language into which the Holy Scriptures
had been translated, and the Slavonic dialect of the translation
being that of the Southern Slavs, priests of Bulgarian or Servian
origin were the fittest persons in Russia to be employed in this
work. The translation of Greek texts, the transcription and
composition of Slavonic and Russian MSS., as also the first attempts at a written exposition of Russian customary law would
equally fall into their hands. The share of a Southern Slav in the
work of codification would explain the presence in the Pravda of
Jaroslav of a term which has led to much comment. The word in
question is *verv*. Various guesses had been made as to its meaning, when at last Professor Leontovitch had the good fortune to
find it used in an old South Slavonic customary, the statute of
Politza, and that in the sense of Undivided Household or House
Community. The sense agrees with the context of the two paragraphs in which the word is used in the Pravda. In one of them
mention is made of a case where the body of a man belonging
to the "following" of the duke has been found within the limits
of a *verv;* and the other says that in such a case the whole *verv*
must pay in common a fine similar to that which was inflicted in

England in such cases during the reigns of William the Conqueror and the early Plantagenets.

A *verv,* paying in common a sort of pecuniary composition for a crime supposed to have been committed by one of its members; a *verv* possessing its own proper limits, and therefore its own territorial possession, exactly corresponds to a house-community, in which several persons, living under the same roof and owning land in common, are jointly answerable for the crimes and misdemeanours committed within the limits of their possessions.

If from the eleventh and twelfth centuries, during which the different versions of the Pravda were drawn up, we pass to the end of the fourteenth and the beginning of the fifteenth centuries, we find the same village community mentioned, as well in the North Western principalities of Russia—that of Pscov, for example, as in those of the South West which were ruled by the Statute of Lithuania. The name under which the members of these communities are known to the Russian law is that of *siabri.* This term is employed both by the judicial charter of Pscov (1397–1467) and by the Statute of Lithuania (1529). This word *siabri* is also to be found among the Southern Slavs. The code of Servian laws, published by King Stefan Douschan in the year 1349, makes frequent use of it when speaking of the peasants.[1] The peasants of Servia, having always lived, and still living, in undivided households, the term meaning co-partners in the enjoyment of an undivided property, was very naturally applied to them and it is this meaning that the word still keeps in the judicial charter of Pscov, and also in the Statute of Lithuania. The latter was the chief source of the customary law of Little Russia, and the term *siabri* and the institution it calls to mind are often mentioned in the Little Russian documents of the last three centuries. A recent survey of these sources, made by Professor Louchitzky, has quite settled the question of the existence of House Communities even in those provinces of Little Russia where in our time division of property most prevails. Here as elsewhere individualism seems to have been preceded by a

---

[1] This word appears, for instance, in the following sentences: "No political assembly of the *siabri* ought to exist." "If any one convenes it, let him lose his ears."

sort of family communism like that of India, Ireland and the South Slavonian principalities.

The term *siabri* is not the only one used by Old Russian writers to designate the members of such a household. They are often spoken of in the financial surveys of the sixteenth and seventeenth centuries under the characteristic name of hearth, *pechische*. The so-called *piszoviia knigi,* a kind of survey very like the poll-tax rolls still preserved in the Record Office, speak of the hearth as the unit of taxation. The *pechische* of the fifteenth and sixteenth centuries corresponds to the *feu* of Burgundy and is even known by that name in some of the northern provinces of Russia. The private charters, which are still preserved by more than one family in the Government of Archangel, some of which were drawn up in the sixteenth and seventeenth centuries, when speaking of the house community always make use of the term *ognische,* a word which means the hearth-fire, thus showing that what constituted the tie between members of the same household was their cooking food at the same hearth.

Thus far we have shown the high antiquity of the institution which we are engaged in examining. Let us now proceed to the study of its characteristic features.

All over Russia, but particularly within the boundaries of the old Muscovite empire, communities of persons belonging to the same kindred and living under the same roof are still in existence. The number of persons belonging to their communities varies from ten, or even less, to fifty and upwards. In the Government of Koursk a community composed of about sixty persons has recently been noticed by Professor Samokvasov. But such cases are rare, and the number of persons living in common does not, as a rule, exceed twenty or thirty. Among them we find the grandfather and grandmother, the father and mother, sons and daughters, grandsons and granddaughters, brothers and sisters, nephews and nieces, with such other persons as may be united to them by ties of marriage, as daughters-in-law in right of their husbands, and sons-in-law in right of their wives. Persons incorporated into the family, working for the common good, and having shares in the family profits are often mentioned by writers on Russian folk-lore. Besides these others may perchance have become members, as for instance persons adopted into it, or the children of a widow contracting a new marriage with a member of the community, who, on account of her unwillingness to be separated from them, come to live with her under the roof of her new husband.

From this we see how various may have been the origin of those who were members of the Undivided Family. Blood-relationship, in the proper sense of the word, is not always required, it suffices that the members be *considered* as relatives; adoption takes the place of actual descent, and the fact of sharing the daily work very often gives a stranger the rights of a relative.

Undivided households are, as a rule, governed by the oldest members of the community, but in case of prolonged illness or want of mental power the oldest member may be superseded by another, sometimes elected by the whole community. The name given to the house-elder is *bolschack,* which means the greatest in power. His authority and functions perfectly correspond to those belonging, in a Servian *zadruga,* to the so-called *domachin.* Like the domachin, he is assisted in the difficult task of governing the female part of the house community by some aged woman, known by the name of *bolschoucha* (the greatest woman), who is not always his wife.

It would be a gross error to look upon the house-elder of a Russian Undivided Family as holding the same position as the Roman paterfamilias. The house-elder has neither the authority nor the amount of independence enjoyed by the paterfamilias in the administration of the family fortune. The Russian house-elder, like the Servian domachin, is but *primus inter pares.* All the grown-up members of the community constitute a sort of family council, whose advice must be regularly asked in matters of importance. The domachin has no right to dispose of the family possessions without the unanimous consent of all the persons for whom he acts. When I say *all,* I mean of course only the grown-up members, women as well as men. The women's opinion, though of less importance than the men's, is not to be disregarded, the more so on account of the influence which they exercise on their husbands.

The functions of the house-elder are of very various kinds. We must mention first of all his exclusive right to represent the community before the executive and judicial authorities of the village and district (*selo i volost*). It is he who regularly appears in the courts, either to answer the complaints against the community, or to insist on the recognition of rights which have been violated. It is to him also that the Government officials address their demand for the speedy payment of the taxes. It is his duty to attend to the execution of the law concerning military service, and to the carrying out of the different orders issued by the local and provincial authorities.

As to the duties which the domachin has to perform in connection with the interior administration of the household, they are of two different kinds: they concern either the persons who compose the house community, or the undivided property owned by them. All disputes arising between co-partners are settled by the house-elder, who is regularly assisted in such cases by the family council. His interference in the relations between husband and wife, between parents and children, sometimes exerts a highly beneficial influence, in so far as it prevents cases of gross abuse in the exercise of marital and paternal power; but it often happens on the other hand that disputes between married couples are embittered by the partiality of the house-elder for one or other party. On more than one occasion husbands have been known to inflict severe punishment on their wives because they were ordered to do so by the head of the community; instances, too, are very frequent in which the wife, encouraged by the support of the house-elder, disregards the rights of her husband, and lives in almost open adultery with the person whose chief duty ought to consist in the maintenance of a high moral standard amongst the persons over whom he exercises authority.

The house-elder has also, if not a casting vote, at least a consultative voice in such matters as the choice of a wife, or the giving of a daughter in marriage. As the amount of the dowry is always fixed by the family council, presided over by its chief, his decision very often settles the question as to the acceptance or refusal of the offer of marriage. It is also the duty of the house-elder to find occupation for the unemployed members of the household. If the community is too large to allow of all its members being employed in agricultural labour, the family finds it advantageous to permit a certain number of its members to seek their fortunes abroad, either in private service or as small traders or pedlars, travelling about the country with packs on their backs. Such petty hawkers, very numerous in our Eastern provinces, are known in Russia under the various names of *ofeni, chodebocschiki, korobhniki,* and *prosoli.* They render a real service to the country population, which, at least in places far distant from railways and markets, would without them have no means of procuring the most simple necessaries of life.

Young orphans find in the person of the house-elder their legal guardian; their moral and mental education depends solely on him; it is he who sends them to school, finds employment for them in the fields, or apprentices them to the different village artisans to learn a trade by which to earn a future livelihood.

As the administration of the family fortune, as I have already said, falls on the house-elder, he makes all arrangements that are needful to secure that every kind of agricultural labour shall be properly done, assigning to each his daily share in the ploughing, harrowing, and sowing of the fields, thrashing of the corn, and such like occupations. If the number of hands of which the family can dispose is not sufficient to answer all its requirements, he hires others to help them. When the time comes for the exchange of harvest produce for such articles as the peasants may need, it is again the business of the house-elder to sign contracts of sale or exchange. Those under his charge have in such cases the right to control actions and to demand a full account of all the moneys received or paid by him.

This control is particularly useful on those somewhat rare occasions when, in consequence of a series of bad harvests, the family is obliged to dispose of a part of its estate. On such occasions the whole family has a voice in the selection of the purchases. Their unanimous consent, plainly expressed in the act of sale, is necessary in order to render it legal.

The resources by which the family provides for all its requirements are of different kinds: some are derived from the lands it owns, others from the private earnings of its members. Widely separated though some of its members may be from the family, the travelling pedlar, the labourer who has hired himself out on some distant farm, the soldier and sailor fighting in some foreign country or sailing to some distant land, nevertheless they all look upon it as a duty to allow their family to share in their earnings.

On its part the House Community does not object to maintaining the wife and children of an absent member, or to paying the amount of his yearly taxes. The communistic character of the great Russian family is shown by the ease with which the household gets its members who are temporarily separated from it to pay over to it the gains which they make. These, as a rule, make no claim to keep their earnings for themselves. The *peculium castrense* and *quasi castrense,* formerly known to the ancient Romans, appear still to exist among the members of the Russian house communities of the present day. If a movement in favour of the establishment of private property can be detected it is only in the private earnings made by the women and girls in their leisure hours. These earnings accumulated hour by hour and day by day form, as a rule, the principal part of the future dowry, the father and mother making but a small addition to the sum got together by the industry and thrift of a maiden who for many years has been preparing for her marriage. The Undivided Household of Great Russia may in this respect be compared to the house community of India, for it also secures to an unmarried woman the right of providing a *peculium* apart, a sort of independent fortune, the so-called *stridhana,* by the accumulation of the small savings she regularly makes by needlework.

Now that I have traced, though only in its general outlines, that peculiar institution known in Russia under the rather vague term of "The Great Family," let me call your attention to the advantages and disadvantages which this institution presents. Its great merit certainly consists in the fact that it develops to a far larger extent than the small families of our day the feeling of mutual dependence and joint relationship without which no system of social reform can have any chance of success. Possessing as they do no other but common property and having an equal share in all the material enjoyments of fortune, the members of these communistic bodies escape from the disheartening influence of economic competition.

The conditions of this existence necessarily develop in them all the consciousness of mutual responsibility, and the conviction that without reliance on one another they cannot overcome the dangers and difficulties of life. It would be a study of high psychological interest to analyse the character of a people which

had grown up under such conditions, and to show how far the
inborn selfish instincts of man have been moderated by the soften-
ing influence of a state of society which, to a certain extent, does
away with the necessity for an uninterrupted struggle for life.
The Russian novelists, conscious of what might properly be
expected of them, have more than once tried to give a picture
of the Russian *moujik* who is so unlike the French *paysan,* that
petty owner of a small piece of land jealously watched and
guarded from the encroachments of his neighbour and from those
of the State.

The life-like characters drawn by our great author, Tourgenieff, in his vivid *Sketches of a Sportsman* are, I believe, the
best illustrations that have ever been given of the thoughts and
feelings of our people—a people who, though rough and rude,
yet enjoy the great blessing of being unconscious of the need of
securing their individual happiness by a constant struggle and
by the pursuit of egotistic ends. The reliance shown by the Russian peasant on the community, his conviction that the *mir* is
always just and reasonable, and that truth is nowhere to be
found but in the unanimous opinion of the people, have certainly
developed estimable qualities and have helped to make the
Russian *moujik* a communist. That this is really the case, and
that his character has been modified by the system of the Great
Family, is proved by the fact that wherever a division of the
common property has taken place, wherever the peasant has been
reduced by his own will to depend entirely on his personal industry for his success in life, he has become the pushing, un-
scrupulous man whom the American novelist has rendered so
familiar to us. Two great Russian writers, Mr. Ouspensky and
Mr. Slatovraczky, both equally unknown to the English public
although their popularity amongst my countrymen almost equals
that of Tourgenieff or Tolstoi, have recently published two widely
different accounts of the social and psychological condition of
our peasants. Mr. Ouspensky has spoken of the peasant as a
creature whose ethics almost entirely depend upon the regular
performance of agricultural labour. As long as he remains a
proprietor his morals are sound, but let him once lose the piece
of land which he has made fruitful by the sweat of his brow and
he is sure to fall into debauchery and vice. Mr. Slatovraczky has

depicted him as a kind of unselfish philosopher, who thinks that the products of the earth are the common inheritance of all men, and that the chief duty of a Christian is to help his neighbour, sometimes even at his own expense.

Now, what may seem hardly credible is that both authors have been applauded by the same public—applauded, moreover, because both were equally correct in their statements. The key to the mystery is to be found in the fact that it is a different life which is pictured by each—the first having chosen his hero from among the members of a broken-up house community; the second among those still living in common. Our thoughts and feelings being directly influenced by our social conditions, Mr. Ouspensky's hero presents to us all the features of a hard worker, pursuing no other object than his own interests and welfare, whilst Mr. Slatovraczky's hero appears to be "a person living not after the word of man but after the word of God," caring for his fellow-creatures almost as much as for himself.[2]

There is exaggeration in the way in which both authors represent the modern Russian *moujik;* for the sense of proportion which was so highly valued by the ancients is not always possessed by my countrymen; but even taking into account this partiality for certain social forms and institutions, I believe they have rendered us a real service by pointing out the intimate correspondence that exists between the moral character of our peasantry and their ancient mode of life.

I must, nevertheless, confess that morality, that at least which is concerned with the relations between the sexes, has not much to gain from the close packing under the same roof of persons differing in sex and age. I leave to Mr. Anatole Leroy Beaulieu the task of instructing you on this subject: *"Chez un peuple pauvre et chez des hommes grossiers,"* says this acute French observer, *"tout n'est point profit et vertu sous le régime patriarcal. On sait combien de maux de toutes sortes dérivent dans les grandes villes d'occident, de l'étroitesse des logements et de l'entassement des individus. Les inconvenients ne sont pas moindres en Russie. Quand une étroite izba (chaumière) réunit*

---

[2] The two novels to which I allude are *The Power of Land*, by Ouspensky, and *The Solid Base (Oustoi)*, by Slatovraczky.

plusieurs générations et plusieurs ménages, que durant les longues nuits d'un long hiver les pères et les enfants, les frères et leurs femmes couchent pêle-mêle autour du large poêle, il en résulte une sorte de promiscuité aussi malsaine pour l'âme que pour le corps. Chez le moujik, alors même que les enfants mariés habitaient plusieurs izbas disposées autour de la même cour, l'autocratie domestique était un danger pour l'intégrité et la chasteté de la famille. De même que le propriétaire noble sur les serves do ses domaines, le chef de maison s'arrogeait parfois une sorte de droit du seigneur sur les femmes soumises à son autorité. Le chef, désigné du surnom le Vieux, qui, grâce à la précocité des marriages, avait souvent à peine quarante ans, prélevait sur ses belles filles un tribut que la jeunesse ou la dépendance de ses fils leur défendait de lui contester. Il n'était point rare de voir ainsi le foyer domestique souillé par l'autorité qui en devait maintenir la pureté.

It may also certainly be questioned how far the loss of a spirit of personal enterprise, and the removal of a strong feeling of self-reliance ought to be considered beneficial. I have no doubt that if modern Russia produces on the minds of foreign observers an impression as of a land of paupers, the reason of it, or at least one of the reasons, is to be found in the prevalence of these old communistic institutions. We must not forget that it is the principle of self-help that has created the material growth of England and of the United States of America. But in entering on these discussions I trench on very uncertain ground. The relative advantages and disadvantages of individualism and of communism have furnished matter for warm controversy from the time of Plato down to the time of Ruskin and of Spencer, and we need not discuss them here. I think it better to state that the Russian peasant, at least in our time, is not insensible to the advantages of individualism, as is well shown by the fact that between two and three million divisions of House Communities have been effected since the day when the liberated serf obtained the right to make them. If divisions of family property were rare before 1861, the year of the abolition of serfdom, the reason lies in the fact that the manorial lords and the State were alike interested in the preservation of the system of Undivided Households. The natural responsibility of the members for the payment of taxes and for the execution of those various kinds of agricultural labour which serfs were bound to perform on the lands of the manor, were advantages far too precious to be easily abandoned. It was, and it still is, for the interests of the national treasury that these divisions should not take place. It is for this reason that the Government, concealing its real designs under a show of good-will towards an old and venerable institution, has recently taken measures to prevent further divisions. It is no longer with the majority that the decision is to rest in questions of this kind, but with the chief of the household, a person who is, of course, as a rule, interested in the maintenance of non-division.

The reasons which are brought forward by the peasants to justify their breaking up of Undivided Households are generally the following: Non-division, they say, causes the able and laborious to work for the idle and incapable. It is unjust to force an unmarried person to divide his savings with a relative enjoying the pleasures of married life and a numerous progeny, who, on account of their youth, are not yet able to earn anything by the work of their hands. They also affirm that, as the dwelling-place is too small to accommodate a large family, they are forced to divide in order to live with decency.

It is also often said that disputes among the women are the direct cause of separation, while, again, some peasants frankly avow that they insist on leaving their communistic mode of life in order to have their own homes and to be their own masters. If the objections just mentioned are not those of individualism, I do not know what individualism is.

It is in the most fertile regions of Russia—in Little Russia and New Russia—that divisions have been most numerous. In these parts small families are already the general rule, as the black soil of those districts is rich enough to pay the taxes that are levied, and the peasant is not alarmed by the prospect of being deprived of the aid of his relatives. The spirit of independence of the Cossacks, which all those who are acquainted with them readily acknowledge, explains to a great extent the reason why the undivided household is dying out in the southern and south-western parts of Russia.

The northern provinces will certainly sooner or later follow the same path, and the patriarchal house community will disappear in Russia, just as it has disappeared in France, Italy, and Spain, and as it is disappearing in our day in Servia and Croatia. For we must not think that this system was altogether unknown to the people of Western Europe. Not only in Ireland, where its previous existence had been recognised by Sir Henry Maine, but also among the German and Latin races, the Undivided Household was, a few centuries ago, a still living institution. Guy Coquille, a legal writer of the sixteenth century, speaks of them in the province of Nivernais, and they have recently been discovered in the old charters of Berry. The *consorteria* of mediaeval Tuscany, the *genealogiae* of the old Alemannic law, and the still existing *Companias* of Spanish Galicia, are but different names to designate the Undivided Household. If these have disappeared, or are likely to disappear, in the near future, it is because they have been forced to yield to the requirements of individualism. I see no reason why the same thing should not happen in Russia.

Part **IV**

Succession, Inheritance, and Descent

Frederick Pollock and Frederic W. Maitland—or, more properly, Maitland with Pollock's assistance—composed a monumental *History of English Law.* Our selection comprises most of a chapter on the part of that history which treats of family law, inheritance, and descent. It is mainly a factual work; theorizing is confined to a few representative cases. Those cited are placed in their contemporary context and then linked historically. But that is as far as Maitland permits himself to go. Inheritance is discussed with a terminological exactitude to which little need be added even after two generations of subsequent research and debate.

The matter that Maitland deals with is that most basic concern to an agricultural society, land: who owns it, how it is bequeathed, and how it is alienated by sale, legal initiative, etc. His fundamental finding is that in the early Middle Ages the English system of land tenure was laid down for the succeeding eight to ten centuries. In accordance with this system, land is passed from father to eldest son—a not surprising conclusion, for the kinship system was agnatic and patrilineal in that day—and kinship and inheritance are closely related. This finding is important because it shows that land was not held by the family as such in England, in the early period which Maitland discusses, as it was elsewhere. The practice of the *zadruga,* for instance, was one by which land was held by an entire family and could not be further divided or assigned.

Property in land, real property, descended in many ways other than from father to eldest son in England, although the law of primogeniture had its effect on the ownership of land, on the international relations of England in its wars and peace making, and in the evolution of English society.

The presentation in Chapter 9 offers certain nice problems in kinship analysis: in the formation of kinship relations, in the application of these relations to matters of genealogy and—always—ownership of property or rights. Blood ties have a practical, not an antiquarian, meaning in these pages.

L. K.

§§ 9

INHERITANCE AND DESCENT

Frederick Pollock

Frederic W. Maitland

Antiquities

If before we speak of our law of inheritance as it was in the twelfth and thirteenth centuries we devote some small space to the antiquities of family law, it will be filled rather by warnings than by theories. Our English documents contain little that can be brought to bear immediately or decisively on those interesting controversies about primitive tribes and savage families in which our archaeologists and anthropologists are engaged, while the present state of those controversies is showing us more clearly every day that we are yet a long way off the establishment of any dogmas which can claim an universal validity, or be safely extended from one age or one country to another. And yet so long as it is doubtful whether the prehistoric time should be filled, for example, with agnatic *gentes* or with hordes which reckon by "mother-right," the interpretation of many a historic text must be uncertain.

It has become a common-place among English writers that the family rather than the individual was the "unit" of ancient law.

From Frederick Pollock and Frederic W. Maitland, *The History of English Law* (2nd ed.; 2 vols.; Cambridge, England, 1899), Vol. II, pp. 237–81, 293–306.

That there is truth in this saying we are very far from denying—
the bond of blood was once a strong and sacred bond—but we
ought not to be content with terms so vague as "family" and
"unit." It may be that in the history of every nation there was a
time when the men and women of that nation were grouped
together into mutually exclusive clans, when all the members of
each clan were in fact or in fiction bound to each other by the
tie of blood, and were accounted strangers in blood to the members of every other clan. But let us see what this grouping implies. It seems to imply almost of necessity that kinship is
transmitted either only by males or only by females. So soon as
it is admitted that the bond of blood, the bond which groups men
together for the purpose of blood-feud and of *wergeld,* ties the
child both to his father's brother and to his mother's brother, a
system of mutually exclusive clans is impossible, unless indeed
each clan is strictly endogamous. There is a foray; grandfather,
father and son are slain; the *wer* must be paid. The *wer* of the
grandfather must be paid to one set of persons; the *wer* of the
father to a different set; the *wer* of the son to yet a third set. If
kinship be traced only through males or only through females,
then we may have permanent and mutually exclusive units; we
may picture the nation as a tree, the clans as branches; if a twig
grows out of one branch, it cannot grow out of another. In the
other case each individual is himself the trunk of an *arbor
consanguinitatis.*

Now it is not contended that the Germans, even when they first
come within the ken of history, recognize no bond of blood between father and son. They are for the more part monogamous,
and their marriages are of a permanent kind. The most that can
be said by ardent champions of "mother-right" is that of "mother-
right" there are distinct though evanescent traces in the German
laws of a later day. On the other hand, we seem absolutely debarred from the supposition that they disregarded the relationship
between the child and its mother's brother. So soon as we begin
to get rules about inheritance and blood-feud, the dead man's
kinsfolk, those who must bear the feud and who may share the
wergild, consist in part of persons related to him through his
father, and in part of persons related to him through his mother.

It was so in the England of Alfred's day; the maternal kinsfolk paid a third of the *wer*. The *Leges Henrici,* which about such a matter will not be inventing new rules, tell us that the paternal kinsfolk pay and receive two-thirds, the maternal kinsfolk one-third of the *wer;* and this is borne out by other evidence. It is further clear that marriage did not sever the bond between a woman and her blood-kinsmen; they were responsible for her misdeeds; they received her *wer,* and we are expressly told that if she committed homicide vengeance was not to be taken on "the innocent family" of her husband. It would even seem that her husband could not remove her from the part of the country in which her kinsmen lived without giving them security that he would treat her well and that they should have an opportunity of condoning her misdeeds by money payments. Now when we see that the wives of the members of one clan are themselves members of other clans, we ought not to talk of clans at all. If the law were to treat the clan as a unit for any purpose whatever, this would surely be the purpose of *wer* and blood-feud; but just for that purpose our English law does not contemplate the existence of a number of mutually exclusive units which can be enumerated and named; there were as many "blood-feud groups" as there were living persons; at all events each set of brothers and sisters was the centre of a different group.

From this it follows that the "blood-feud group" cannot be a permanently organized unit. If there is a feud to be borne or *wer* to be paid or received, it may organize itself *ad hoc;* but the organization will be of a fleeting kind. The very next deed of violence that is done will call some other blood-feud group into existence. Along with his brothers and paternal uncles a man goes out to avenge his father's death and is slain. His maternal uncles and cousins, who stood outside the old feud, will claim a share in his *wer.*

This is what we see so soon as we see our ancestors. About what lies in the prehistoric time we can only make guesses. Some will surmise that the recognition of the kinship that is traced through women is a new thing, and that in the past there have been permanently coherent agnatic *gentes* which are already being dissolved by the action of a novel principle. Others will argue that the movement has been not from but towards agnation, and has now gone so far that the spear-cousins are deemed nearer and dearer than the spindle-cousins. Others, again, may think that the great "folk-wandering" has made the family organization of the German race unusually indefinite and plastic, so that here it will take one, and there another form. What seems plain is that the exclusive domination of either "father-right" or "mother-right"—if such an exclusive domination we must needs postulate —should be placed for our race beyond the extreme limit of history. To this, however, we may add that the English evidence as to the wife's position is a grave difficulty to any theory that would start with the patriarchal family as a primitive datum. That position we certainly cannot ascribe to the influence of Christianity. The church's dogma is that the husband is the head of the wife, that the wife must forget her own people and her father's house, and yet, despite all preaching and teaching, the English wife remains for what has once been the most important of all purposes a stranger to her husband's kin, and even to her husband.

It is quite possible that in England men as a matter of fact dwelt together in large groups tilling the land by co-operation, that the members of each group were, or deemed themselves to be, kinsmen in blood, and that as a force for keeping them in these local groups spear-sibship was stronger than spindle-sibship:—their relative strength could be expressed by the formula 2:1. We get a hint of such permanent cohesive groups when we find King Æthelstan legislating against the mægð that is so strong and so mickle that it denies the king's rights and harbours thieves. The whole power of the country is to be called out to ride against these offenders. The law will, if possible, treat such a mægð as a "unit" by crushing it into atoms. But in no other way, so far as we can see, will its unity be legally recognized. The rules of blood-feud that the law sanctions are a practical denial of its existence. Unless it be endogamous, it can have no claim to the whole wer of any one of its members; every one of its members may have to pay wer along with persons who stand outside it.

Again, if we would paint a picture of Anglo-Saxon society as of one in which the land-owning unit is not an individual but a mægð, a clan, or gens, we shall have to meet the difficulty that at an early period land is being inherited through women. The rules of inheritance are very dark to us, but, so far as we can see, the tendency in the historic period is not towards an admission of the "spindle-kin," but towards a postponement of their claims to those of the "spear-kin." Already in the eighth century the Anglo-Saxon settler wishes to create something like the estate in tail male of later times. And the law takes his side; it decrees that the form of the gift shall be respected. Now if for a moment we suppose that a clan owns land, we shall see a share in this land passing through daughters to their children, and these children will be on their father's side members of another clan. Our land-owning clan, if it still continues to hold its old lands, will very soon cease to be a clan in any tolerable sense of the term; it will be a mere group of co-proprietors, some of whom are bound by family ties, the sacred tie of blood-feud, more closely to those who stand outside than to those who stand inside the proprietary group.

We must resist the temptation to speak of "the *mægð*" as if it were a kind of corporation, otherwise we have as many corporations as there are men and women. The collective word *mægð* is used by the law as interchangeable with the plural of the word *mæg*, which signifies a kinsman. When a man has been slain, those who are bound and entitled to avenge his death will, it is probable enough, meet together and take counsel over a plan of campaign; but so far as we can see, the law, when first it knows a *wergeld*, knows the main outlines of a system which divides the *wergeld* among individual men. There is in the first place a sum called the *healsfang*, which is due only to those who are very closely related to the dead man; then there is the rule that gives two thirds to the spear and one to the spindle. Again, when the "kindred" of a lordless man is ordered to find him a lord, we need not think of this as of a command addressed to corporations, or even to permanently organized groups of men; it may well be addressed to each and all of those persons who would be entitled to share the *wergeld* of this lordless man; every one of them will be liable to perform this duty if called upon to do so. A fatherless child "follows its mother"; apparently this means that, as a general rule, this child will be brought up among its maternal, not its paternal, kinsmen; the guardianship, however, of its paternal goods is given by ancient dooms to its paternal kinsmen. But such texts do not authorize us to call up the vision of a *mægð* acting as guardian by means of some council of elders; the persons who would inherit if the child died may well be the custodians of the ancestral property. But even if in any given case a person's kinsmen act together and, for example, find a lord or appoint a guardian for him, it is only by reason of their relationship to him that they constitute a unit. There may be a great deal to show that in England and elsewhere strong family groups did form themselves and that the law had to reckon with them; but they had to struggle against a principle which, explain it how we will, seems to be incompatible with the existence of mutually exclusive *gentes* as legal entities.[1]

We turn to the popular theory that land was owned by families or households before it was owned by individuals. In what sense are we to understand it? We can not think that at the present day any one who has made a serious study of legal history and who weighs his words will assert that land was owned by corporations, that is by ideal persons, before it was owned by natural persons. The first man was of the earth earthy; the first person was of nature natural. But if there was ownership, and this ownership was not attributed to ideal persons, then it was attributed to men, and men are "individuals." Now co-ownership, and co-ownership which has kinship for its cause, is certainly not a phenomenon that is peculiar to the ruder stages of law. If at the present day an Englishman dies intestate leaving three daughters as his only descendants, the whole undivided mass of his property passes to them and they become co-owners of it. We do not—unless we are speaking very loosely—say that the lands and goods which once were his are now owned by his family; we say that they are owned by three women. Land would be owned "by individuals" even if every plot of it was always held *pro indiviso* by two or more persons.

---

[1] Heusler argues that the German sib does not show us even the germ of a juristic person. The contrary, and at one time more popular, opinion is stated with special reference to the Anglo-Saxon evidence by Gierke. When Bracton says that an infant sokeman is *sub custodia consanguineorum suorum propinquorum,* we do not see a family council; why should we see one when a similar phrase occurs in an Anglo-Saxon doom?

But co-ownership may take various forms. In the later middle ages it took here in England at least four. There was the tenancy in common. In this case when one co-tenant died, his own undivided share descended to his heir.[2] There was the joint tenancy. In this case when one co-tenant died, his share did not descend to his heir, but "accrued" to the surviving co-tenant or co-tenants. There was the co-parcenary occasioned by the descent of lands to co-heiresses. In this case there had been doubt whether on the death of one co-tenant without issue there would be inheritance or "accruer by survivorship." The intimate union between husband and wife gave rise to a fourth form, known as tenancy by entireties. We can not *a priori* exhaust the number of forms which co-ownership may take. Nor is it only on the death of one of the co-owners that the differences between these forms will manifest themselves. In a modern system of law, and in many a system that is by no means modern, every one of the co-owners may in general insist on a partition either of the land itself or, it may be, of the money that can be obtained by a sale of it; or again, without any partition being made, he can without the consent of his fellows transfer his aliquot share to one who has hitherto stood outside the co-owning group. Demonstrably in some cases, perhaps in many, these powers are of recent origin.[3] Let us for a moment put them out of account. Let us suppose that on a father's death his land descends to his three sons, that no son can force his brothers to a physical partition of the inheritance, that no son can sell or give away his share. Let us make a yet further supposition, for which there may be warrant in some ancient laws. Let us suppose that if one of the three sons dies leaving two sons, these two will not of necessity inherit just their father's share, no more, no less; on the contrary, there will be a redistribution of the shares into which the land has hitherto

---

[2] We are speaking briefly, and are therefore supposing that the co-tenants hold in fee simple.

[3] It is not until the reign of Henry VIII (Stat. 31 Hen. VIII c. 1) that one of several joint tenants can compel his fellows to make partition. But the co-parcener has had this power from a remote age. This is very remarkable: the co-ownership created by inheritance can, the co-ownership created by the act of a feoffor can not, be destroyed against the wish of one of the co-owners.

been ideally divided, so (for example) that these four persons, namely the two uncles and their two nephews, will have equal shares. The land is still owned by individuals, by four men.[4] Let the number of co-tenants increase until there are forty of them; the state of the case is not altered. Individuals do not cease to be individuals when there are many of them. But if there are many of them, we shall often spare ourselves the trouble of enumerating them by the use of some collective name. If John Smith's land has descended to his seven daughters who are holding it as co-parceners, we shall in common discourse speak of it as the land of the Smiths or of the Smith family, or, if we prefer medieval Latin to modern English, we shall say that the land belongs to the *genealogia Johannis Fabri*. If these ladies quarrel with their neighbours about a boundary, there may be litigation between two families (*inter duas genealogias*), the Smiths, to wit, and the Browns; but it will be a quarrel between "individuals"; this will be plain enough so soon as there is any pleading in the action.

No one is likely to maintain, even as a paradox, that the ownership of aliquot shares of things is older than the ownership of integral things. If nothing else will restrain him, he may at least be checked by the reflection that the more ancient institution will inevitably become the more modern within a very few years. He distributes the land to families. So soon as by the changes and chances of this mortal life any one of those families has but a single member, "individual ownership" will exist, unless to save his dogma he has recourse to an arbitrary act of confiscation.

To deny that "family ownership" is an ownership by individuals of aliquot shares is another expedient. But this in truth is a denial of the existence of any law about partition. If there is any law which decides how, if a partition be made, the physically distinct

---

[4] Some such plan of a repeated redistribution *per capita* among brothers, first-cousins and second-cousins seems to have prevailed in Wales; but the redistributions of which we read in Welsh law seem to be redistributions of physically divided shares. Apparently in ancient Germany the rule was that within the joint family the sons, however numerous, of a dead co-proprietor would upon partition get no larger share than their father would have taken had he lived. In other words, while the family is still "joint" there is inheritance of ideal quotas. Maine speaks of a distribution *per capita* occurring in the most archaic forms of the joint family.

shares ought to be distributed, then there is already law which assigns to the members of the group ideal shares in the unpartitioned land.[5] But to seek to get behind a law for the partition of family estates without passing into a region in which there is no ownership and no law does not in Western Europe look like an endeavour that is destined to succeed. Such evidence as we have does not tend to prove that in ancient times the "joint family" was a large one. Seldom did it comprise kinsmen who were not the descendants of a common grandfather; in other words, the undivided family rarely lived through three generations.[6] But supposing that there is no law about partition, we still have before us something that, if we agree to call it ownership, is ownership by individuals. We have land owned by four, or by forty individuals, and at any moment a war, a plague or a famine may reduce their number to one.

To our thinking then, the matter that has to be investigated is not well described as the non-existence of "individual ownership." It would be more correctly described as the existence and the origin of "birth-rights." Seemingly what we mean when we speak of "family ownership" is that a child acquires rights in the ancestral land, at birth or, it may be, at adolescence; at any rate he acquires rights in the ancestral land, and this not by gift, bequest, inheritance or any title known to our modern law. The Roman term *sui heredes* is a compendious expression of this.

Now that such rights once existed in England and many other parts of Western Europe is not to be denied. When the dark age is over, they rarely went beyond this, that the landholder could not utterly disinherit his expectant heirs either by will or by conveyance; the father, for example, could not sell or give away the ancestral land without the consent of his sons, or could only dis-

---

[5] We read of two rival schools of Hindu lawyers, the one maintaining the theory of "aggregate ownership," the other that of "fractional ownership." The same two theories have divided the German antiquaries. But it seems reasonable to say with Heusler that if there is law which upon a partition will assign to each co-proprietor some definite aliquot share of the land, then there is law which gives him an ideal fraction of the land while it still remains undivided, though it assigns him no certain share in the profits of the undivided land.

[6] Heusler says that in the oldest German documents even first-cousins are seldom "joint."

pose of some "reasonable" part of it. If he attempted to do more than this, then when he was dead his sons could revoke the land. However, it was not unknown in some parts of Germany that even while the father lived the sons could enforce their rights and compel him to a partition.[7]

It is natural for us to assume without hesitation that those forms of birth-right which are least in accord with our own ideas are also the most archaic, that the weaker forms are degenerate relics of the stronger, that originally the child was born a land-owner, that a law which only allows him to recall the alienated land after his father's death is transitional, and that his right has undergone a further and final degradation when it appears as a mere *droit de retrait,* a right to redeem the land which his father has sold at the price that has been given for it. According to this doctrine the law of intestate succession has its origin in "family ownership." It is an old and a popular doctrine. Before however we allow to it the dignity of a proved and universal truth, we shall do well to reflect that it attributes to barbarous peoples a highly commendable care for the proprietary rights of the *filius familias,* and if for his proprietary rights then also for his life and liberty, for the state of things in which a father may lawfully reduce the number of his co-proprietors by killing them or selling them into slavery is not one that we can easily imagine as a normal or stable stage in the history of mankind.

The suggestion therefore may be admissible that at least in some cases "family ownership," or the semblance of it, may really be, not the origin, but the outcome of intestate succession. We have but to ask for a time when testamentary dispositions are unknown and land is rarely sold or given away. In such a time a law of intestate succession will take deep root in men's thoughts and habits. The son will know that if he lives long enough he will succeed his father; the father will know that in the ordinary course of events his land will pass from him to his sons. What else should happen to it? He does not want to sell it, for there is no one to buy it; and whither could he go and what could he do if he sold his land? Perhaps the very idea of a sale of

---

[7] In Germany within historic times the stronger forms of birth-right seem to have been peculiar to the South German (Alaman and Bavarian) nations.

land has not yet been conceived. In course of time, as wealth is amassed, there are purchasers for land; also there are bishops and priests desirous of acquiring land by gift and willing to offer spiritual benefits in return. Then the struggle begins, and law must decide whether the claims of expectant heirs can be defeated. In the past those claims have been protected not so much by law as by economic conditions. There is no need of a law to prohibit men from doing what they do not want to do; and they have not wanted to sell or to give away their land. But now there must be law. The form that the law will take will be determined by the relative strength of various conflicting forces. It will be a compromise, a series of compromises, and we have no warrant for the belief that there will be steady movement in one direction, or that the claims of the heirs must be always growing feebler. That this is so we shall see hereafter. The judges of Henry II's court condemned in the interest of the heir those testamentary or quasi-testamentary dispositions of land which Englishmen and Normans had been making for some time past, though the same judges or their immediate successors decided that the consent of expectant heirs should no longer be necessary when there was to be an alienation *inter vivos*. Thus they drew up the great compromise which ruled England for the rest of the middle ages. Other and different arrangements were made elsewhere, some more, some less favourable to the heirs, and we must not assume without proof that those which are most favourable to the heirs are in the normal order of events the most primitive. They imply, as already said, that a son can hale his father before a court of law and demand a partition; when this can be done there is no "patriarchalism," there is little paternal power.

In calling to our aid a law of intestate succession we are not invoking a modern force. As regards the German race we can not go behind that law; the time when no such law existed is in strictest sense a prehistoric time. Tacitus told his Roman readers that the Germans knew nothing of the testament, but added that they had rules of intestate succession. They were individualistic rules, that is to say, they did not treat a man's death as simply reducing the number of those persons who formed a co-owning group. Again, they did not give the wealth that had been set free to a body consisting of persons who stood in different degrees of relationship to the dead man. The kinsmen were called to the inheritance class by class, first the children, then the brothers, then the uncles. The *Lex Salica* has a law of intestate succession; it calls the children, then the mother, then the brothers and sisters, then the mother's sister. These rules, it may be said, apply only to movable goods and do not apply to land; but an admission that there is an individualistic law of succession for movable goods when as yet anything that can be called an ownership of land, if it exists at all, is new, will be quite sufficient to give us pause before we speak of "family ownership" as a phenomenon that must necessarily appear in the history of every race. Our family when it obtains a permanent possession of land will be familiar with rules of intestate succession which imply that within the group that dwells together there is mine and thine. But the *Lex Salica* already knows the inheritance of land; the dead man's land descends to his sons, and an express statement that women can not inherit it is not deemed superfluous.

Now as regards the Anglo-Saxons we can find no proof of the theory that among them there prevailed anything that ought to be called "family ownership." No law, no charter, no record of litigation has been discovered which speaks of land as being owned by a *mægð*, a family, a household, or any similar group of kinsmen. This is the more noticeable because we often read of *familiae* which have rights in land; these *familiae,* however, are not groups of kinsmen but convents of monks or clerks.

But, further, the dooms and the land-books are markedly free from those traits which are commonly regarded as the relics of family ownership.[8] If we take up a charter of feoffment sealed in the Norman period we shall probably find it saying that the donor's expectant heirs consent to the gift. If we take up an Anglo-Saxon land-book we shall not find this; nothing will be said of the heir's consent.[9] The denunciatory clause will perhaps

---

[8] What can be said on the other side has been said by Mr. Lodge, *Essays on Anglo-Saxon Law,* pp. 74–77.

[9] Cod. Dipl. 1017 (v. 55), Birch, i. 394, on which Mr. Lodge relies, is a forgery. It is to be remembered that we have but very few land-books which do not come from kings or bishops, but we seem to have just enough to enable us to say with some certainty that a clause expressive of the heir's consent was not part of the "common form," and that the best forgers of a later time knew this.

mention the heirs, and will curse them if they dispute the gift; but it will usually curse all and singular who attack the donee's title, and in any system of law a donee will have more to fear from the donor's heirs than from other persons, since they will be able to reclaim the land if for any cause the conveyance is defective.[10] Occasionally several co-proprietors join to make a gift; but when we consider that in all probability all the sons of a dead man were equally entitled to the land that their father left behind him, we shall say that such cases are marvellously rare. Co-ownership, co-parcenary, there will always be. We see it in the thirteenth century, we see it in the nineteenth; the wonder is that we do not see more of it in the ninth and tenth than our Anglo-Saxon land-books display.

In the days before the Conquest a dead man's heirs sometimes attempted to recover land which he had given away, or which some not impartial person said that he had given away. They did so very frequently in the thirteenth century; they sometimes do so at the present day. At the present day a man's expectant heirs do not attempt to interfere with his gifts so long as he is alive; they did not do this in the thirteenth century; we have no proof that they did it before the Conquest.[11]

Expectant heirs do not like to see property given away by will; they sometimes contest the validity of the will which contains such gifts; not unfrequently, as every practitioner in a court of probate

---

[10] In the middle of the eighth century Abbot Ceolfrith with the king's consent gives to the church at Worcester land which has descended to him as heir of his father. The charter ends with this clause "*Si quis autem, quod absit, ex parentela mea vel externorum, malivola mente et maligno spiritu instigatus, huius donationis nostrae munificentiam infringere nititur et contraire, sciat se in die tremendo . . . rationem redditurum.*" Here is a man who has inherited land from his father, who gives it away though he has a *parentela,* and who is no more careful to protect the church against claims urged by his kinsmen than he is to protect it against the claims of *externi.*

[11] Mr. Lodge relies on Cod. Dipl. 195 (i. 238). King Egbert gave land to Aldhun, who gave it to the church of Canterbury. King Offa took it away, "*quasi non liceret Ecgberhto agros hereditario iure scribere.*" Another and an earlier charter, Cod. Dipl. 1020 (v. 61), distinctly alleges that Offa's resumption was based, not on an infraction of family law, but on a royal or seignorial claim. Egbert had given the land to his *minister* Aldhun; Offa revoked it, "*dicens iniustum esse quod minister eius praesumpserit terram sibi a domino distributam absque eius testimonio in alterius potestatem dare.*"

will know, the legatees are compelled to compromise their claims.
All this happened in the days before the Conquest; but when we
consider that the testamentary or quasi-testamentary gift was in
that age a very new thing, we certainly can not say that such
disputes about wills were common.[12]

A doom of King Alfred speaks thus: "If a man has book-land
which his kinsmen left him, we decree that he is not to alienate it
outside his kindred, if there is writing or witness that this was
forbidden by those who first acquired it and by those who gave it
to him; and let this be declared with the witness of the king and
the bishop in the presence of his kinsfolk." We may argue, if we
will, that this is an attempt to impose upon the alienable book-
land some of those fetters which have all along compressed the
less alienable folk-land or "family-land"; the *forma donationis* is
to be observed and restrictive forms are not unknown. Nevertheless, here, about the year 900, we see the current of legislation
moving, at least for the moment, in favour of the expectant heirs.
Either a new law is made for their benefit or a new sanctity and
precision are given to an old law.

We may well suppose that often enough a man's co-heirs left
his land unpartitioned for some time, and that for more than one
generation his male descendants and such of his female descendants as were not married continued to live together under one
roof or within one enclosure as a joint, undivided household. We

---

[12] The best cases are collected at the end of the Essays on Anglo-Saxon
Law, Nos. 4, 8, 14, 16, 30. Mr. Lodge's argument (p. 76) about Æthelric's
will Cod. Dipl. 186; Birch, i. 438, 440) is not one that we can adopt.
"The necessity of family consent is shown by the provision in Æthelric's
will, that the land could be alienated *cum recto consilio propinquorum*."
There is no such provision. Æthelric gives land to his mother for life,
and on her death it is to go to the church of Worcester. But he has reason to fear that a claim will be put in by the church of Berkeley. So he
desires that the church of Worcester shall protect the mother, and adds
"*et si aliquis homo in aliqua contentione iuramentum ei decreverit contra
Berclingas, liberrima erit ad reddendum cum recto consilio propinquorum meorum, qui mihi donabant hereditatem et meo quo ei dabo.*"
Whatever this may mean, it is not the land but an oath in defence of title
that is to be given (*reddendum*). Apparently the *propinqui* who have
given Æthelric his *hereditas* are already dead: the testator himself, by
whose "counsel" the oath is to be given, will be dead before it is given.
The devisee is to be free to swear that she acquired the land by the gift
of Æthelric, and that he came to it by the gift of ancestors who had it
to give.

may guess that when, to take one out of many examples, ten thegns hold three hides in parage, they are cousins; but the partition of an inheritance among co-heirs, or rather as it happens co-heiresses, appears at an early time, and we have nothing to show that when an inherited estate remained undivided and one of the parceners died, his share did not pass to his own descendants according to the same rules of inheritance that would have governed it had it been physically partitioned and set out by metes and bounds. No one word is there to show that a son at birth was deemed to acquire a share of the land that his father held. Need we say that there is no one word to show that the law treated the father as a trustee for his children, or as the attorney or procurator of his family?

"Only God can make a *heres* not man"—said Glanvill. But far back in remote centuries Englishmen had seen no difficulty in giving the name *heres* to a person chosen by a land-holder to succeed him in his holding at his death. And so with the English word for which *heres* has been used as an equivalent. It was not inconceivable that a man should name an *yrfeweard* to succeed him. We are far from believing that this could be done of common right, or that this nominated *yrfeweard* was a *heres* in the Roman sense of that term: but while in Glanvill's day it would have been a contradiction in terms to speak of an heir who was not of the blood of the dead man, this had not been so in the past.[13]

We must admit that most of our evidence relates to book-land, and we have often argued that in all likelihood book-land is an exotic and a superficial institution, floating, as it were, on the surface of English law. Of what went on below the surface among those men who had no books we can learn very little. But what we see happening among the great folk is not unimportant, and it is this: the Anglo-Saxon thegn who holds book-land does not profess to have his heir's consent when he gives part of that land to a church; his successor, the Norman baron, will rarely execute a charter of feoffment which does not express the consent of one

---

[13] It is possible to contend that the clause in the land-books which enables the donee to bestow the land upon such *heres* as he pleases, gives him what modern lawyers would describe as a limited power of testamentary appointment among his kinsmen. But the history of the clause does not favour this interpretation. We start with forms that say nothing of heirs.

heir or many heirs. Our record is miserably imperfect, but as it stands it tends to prove that among the rich and noble there was a period when the rights of the expectant heir were not waning but waxing. In the end, as we shall see hereafter, the heir succeeds in expelling the testamentary or *quasi*-testamentary gift of lands from the common law.

We have not been arguing for any conclusion save this, that in the present state of our knowledge we should be rash were we to accept "family ownership," or in other words a strong form of "birth-right," as an institution which once prevailed among the English in England. That we shall ever be compelled to do this by the stress of English documents is improbable; nor at this moment does it seem very likely that comparative jurisprudence will prove that dogma the universal validity of which we have ventured to doubt. To suppose that the family law of every nation must needs traverse the same route, this is an unwarrantable hypothesis. To construct some fated scheme of successive stages which shall comprise every arrangement that may yet be discovered among backward peoples, this is a hopeless task. A not unnatural inference from their backwardness would be that somehow or another they have wandered away from the road along which the more successful races have made their journey.

About the rules of intestate succession which prevailed here in the days before the Conquest we know very little; they may have been different in the different folks, and at a later time they may have varied from shire to shire. We know much more of the rules that obtained among our near cousins upon the mainland, and by their aid we may arrive at a few cautious conclusions. But we are here met by a preliminary question as to the nature of inheritance. For a time we must disregard that canon of later English law which bids us use the words "inheritance" and "heir" only when we are describing the fate which awaits the lands, or to speak more nicely, the "real estate" of the dead. This canon we can not take back with us into the distant age that is now before us; but applying these terms to movables as well as to immovables, and assuming for a while that we know who the dead man's heirs must be, we have still to ask, What is the nature of inheritance?

It is the more necessary to ask this question because we might otherwise be misled by modern law and Roman law into giving it a tacit answer that would not be true. To us it must seem very natural that when a man dies he should leave behind him some representative who will bear, or some few representatives who will jointly bear, his *persona.* Or again we may be inclined to personify the complex of rights and duties which are, as it were, left alive, though the man in whom they once inhered is dead; to personify the *hereditas.* We Englishmen do something of this kind when we speak of an executor owing money to or having claims against "the estate" of his testator. To do something of this kind is so natural to us, that we can hardly imagine a time when it was not done.

But our own modern law will remind us that even in the nineteenth century there is no absolute necessity compelling the whole *persona,* or whole estate, of the dead man to devolve upon one representative, or one set of representatives who will act in unison. In the case of intestacy the "realty" will go one way and the "personalty" another. This is not all; it is conceivable that the realty itself should fall into fragments, each of which will descend in a different course. Not only does our law respect ancient local customs, but it also still retains in an obscured form the old rule which gives *paterna paternis, materna maternis.* As an exercise for the imagination we might construct a case in which the intestate's realty would be broken into twelve portions, each of which would follow a different path.[14] Thus even in our own day we have not yet found it needful to decree that some one man or some set of conjoint persons shall succeed *in universum ius defuncti.*

But why do we demand that the dead shall be represented? The law of inheritance seems to answer two purposes, which can be distinguished, though in practice they are intimately blended. The dead man has left behind him a mass of things, and we must decide what is to be done with them. But further, he has gone out of the world a creditor and a debtor, and we find it exceedingly

---

14 The *propositus* inherited land from his (1) paternal grandfather, (2) paternal grandmother, (3) maternal grandfather, (4) maternal grandmother, and in every case the land inherited contained acres subject to (*a*) the common law, (*b*) the gavelkind rule, (*c*) the Borough English custom.

desirable that his departure should make as little difference as
may be to his debtors and creditors. Upon this foundation we
build up our elaborate system of credit. Death is to make as little
difference as may be to those who have had dealings with him who
has died, to those who have wronged him, to those whom he has
wronged.

Now the first of these needs must be met at a very early stage
in legal history. If there is to be peace and quiet, a scramble for
the dead man's goods can not be suffered; law must have some
rule about them. On the other hand we can not say with any
certainty that the second purpose will become visible until there
is a good deal of borrowing and lending. But it is only this second
purpose that requires any representation of the dead. It may be
allowed indeed that so soon as land is inherited the heir will in
some sort fill the place of his ancestor. The land, when it becomes
his, must still bear the same burdens that it has hitherto borne.
But here there seems to be no representation of the ancestor;
rather we have a personification of the plot of land; it has sustained burdens and enjoyed easements in the past, and must
sustain and enjoy them still.

We have therefore grave doubts as to whether any widely general dogma about these matters will deserve a ready assent. So
much will depend upon religion. In this province of law the
sacral element has in various ages and various lands been strong.
We have to think not only of what is natural but also of what is
supernatural. Among one rude people the representation of the
ancestor by the heir may appear at a very early time because the
son must perform sacrificial duties which have been incumbent on
his father. Among another and a less rude people there may be
no representation until commerce and credit demand it. Of Germanic heathenry we know little, but the Christianity which the
Germans have adopted when first they are writing down their
laws is not a religion which finds its centre at the family hearth.
Much might be done by a pious heir for the good of his ancestor's
soul, and the duty of doing this was sedulously preached; but the
heir could not offer the expiatory sacrifice, nor would it be offered
in his house; no priesthood had descended upon him. There is
therefore no religious nucleus that will keep together the *universum ius defuncti;* the churches would prefer that the dead

man's lands and goods should never reach the hands of the heir but be dissipated by pious gifts.

In the early age which is now before us the person or persons who succeeded to the lands and goods of the dead man had few, if any, debts to pay or to receive. Most of the pecuniary claims that could be made good in a court of law would perish at the death of the creditor and at the death of the debtor. We may perhaps gather from the so-called "wills" of this period that there were some claims of which this was not true, for a testator sometimes says that his debtors are to be forgiven or that his creditors are to be paid. In the former case however we can not be certain that there has not been an express promise that the creditor "or his heir" shall have the money. In later days this phrase becomes part of the common form of a written bond for the payment of money; and there is much both in English and in continental documents to suggest that the mention of the heirs has not been idle verbiage. A promise to pay money to Alfred is no promise to pay money to Alfred's heir, just as a gift of land to Alfred will hardly give him heritable rights unless something be said of his heirs. As to the hereditary transmission of a liability, this we take it was not easily conceived, and when an Anglo-Saxon testator directs that his debts be paid, this, so far from proving that debts can normally be demanded from those who succeed to the debtor's fortune, may hint that law is lagging behind morality. If the heir paid the ancestor's debts, he did a pious and a laudable act, perhaps an act as beneficial for the departed soul as would be the endowment of a chantry: this is a feeling that will grow stronger as time goes on. At any rate our law, when at the end of the thirteenth century it takes a definite form, seems to tell us that in the past many debts have died with the debtors. We have every reason to believe that claims *ex delicto* would seldom, if ever, survive the death of the wrong-doer or of the wronged. For one moment the blood-feud and the wergild may induce us to think otherwise; but in truth there is here no representation. The wergild was not due to the slain man and it is not paid to one who represents him. At least in the common case it is not even paid only to those persons who are his heirs, for many persons are entitled to a share in the wergild who take no part of the inheritance. The slain man's brothers, uncles and cousins as well as his children have been wronged and atonement must be made with them. And when an attack is made upon the slayer's kinsmen or the wergild is demanded of them, they are not pursued as his representatives—he himself may be alive—they are treated rather as his belongings, and all that belongs to him is hateful to those who hate him. Gradually as the feud loses its original character, that of a war, the heirs of the slayer may perhaps free themselves from all liability by rejecting the inheritance, but this is an infringement of the old principle, and in the region of blood-feud there is not much room for the development of representation. Lastly, as regards the wrongs which do not excite a lawful feud, such as insults, blows, wounds, damage to land or goods, we must think of them as dying with the active and dying with the passive party. Only by very slow degrees has our law come to any other rule, and even now-a-days those causes of action which were the commonest in ancient times still die with the person.

If there is to be no representation of the dead man for the purpose of keeping obligations alive, then there is no great reason why the things that he leaves behind him should all go one way, and early Germanic law shows a tendency to allow them to go different ways. It sees no great reason why some one person or some set of conjoint persons should succeed *in universum ius defuncti.* Thus the chattels may be separated from the land and one class of chattels from another. Among some tribes the dead man's armour, his *heriot,* follows a course of its own and descends to his nearest kinsman on the sword side. Then it is said that in the *Lex Salica* we may see the last relics of a time when movable goods were inherited mainly or only by women, and all along through the middle ages there are German laws which know of certain classes of chattels, the clothes and ornaments of a woman's person, which descend from woman to woman to the neglect of males. At all events, already in the *Lex Salica* there is one set of canons for chattels, another for land; a woman can not inherit land.

But the little more that can be said of these obscure matters will be better said hereafter. It is time that we should turn to an age which is less dark and speak of the shape that our law of inheritance takes when first it becomes plain in the pages of Glanvill and Bracton and the rolls of the king's court. And the first thing that we have to do is to leave off using the words "inheritance" and "heir" in that wide sense in which we have hitherto used them: they point only to the fate of land and of those incorporeal things that are assimilated to land; they point to a succession which is never governed by testament.

The Law of Descent

At the end of Henry III's reign our common law of inheritance was rapidly assuming its final form. Its main outlines were those which are still familiar to us, and the more elementary of them may be thus stated: The first class of persons called to the inheritance comprises the dead person's descendants; in other words, if he leaves an "heir of his body," no other person will inherit. Among his descendants precedence is settled by six rules. (1) A living descendant excludes his own descendants. (2) A dead descendant is represented by his own descendants. (3) Males exclude females of equal degree. (4) Among males of equal degree only the eldest inherits. (5) Females of equal degree inherit together as co-heiresses. (6) The rule that a dead descendant is represented by his descendants overrides the preference for the male sex, so that a grand-daughter by a dead eldest son will exclude a younger son. Here for a while we must pause, in order to comment briefly upon these rules.

The preference of descendants before all other kinsfolk we may call natural, that is to say, we shall find it in every system that is comparable with our own. A phrase that is common in the thirteenth century makes it prominent. A man who dies without leaving a descendant, though he may have other kinsfolk who will be his heirs, is often said to die "without an heir of (or from) himself" (*obiit sine herede de se*). It is only when a man has no heir *de se,* that his brother or any other kinsman can inherit from him.

A preference for males over females in the inheritance of land is strongly marked in several of the German folk-laws. The oldest form of the *Lex Salica* excludes women altogether. Some of the later codes postpone daughters to sons and admit them after sons, but a postponement of daughters even to remoter male kinsmen is not unknown. As to England, we may say with some certainty

that, in the age which immediately preceded Harold's defeat,
women, though they could inherit land, were postponed at least
to their brothers. Domesday Book seems to prove this sufficiently.
In every zone of the system of landholdership as it stood in the
Confessor's day we may find a few, but only a few, women as
tenants.[15] On the other hand, already at the beginning of the ninth
century we see a clear case of a king's daughter inheriting his
land,[16] and other cases of female heirs are found at an early
date.[17]

In later days the customs which diverge from the common
law, for instance the gavelkind custom of Kent, agree with it

---

[15] There are some three or four cases in which a sister seems to be
holding in common with brothers, but these may be due to gifts or
bequests.

[16] King Kenulf of Mercia died leaving as his heiress his daughter
Cwenthryth and was succeeded in the kingship by Ceolwulf, who seems
to have been his brother. A legend gives Kenulf a son (St. Kenelm)
whom Cwenthryth, aiming at the kingdom, treacherously slays. This is a
late fable, but the fact that she inherited some of her father's land seems
beyond doubt.

[17] Opet argues that the Anglo-Saxon law did not postpone women to
men of equal degree. He has hardly proved his case. As to such ancient
texts as Hloth. and Ead. c. 6 and Ine, c. 38, we can only say that they
are neutral. So again are Cnut II., c. 70 and 72. In neither chapter is
Cnut laying down a law of inheritance. In the former he says that the
lord is to take no more than his right heriot, but is to divide the dead
man's property according to right among his wife, children and near
kinsmen, to each according to his relationship. The king is in no way
concerned to define the rules of inheritance, and does not say or suggest
that all children shall have equal shares, or that sons shall not exclude
daughters. Nor is cap. 72 a law of inheritance. "Where the housefather
has sat undisturbed by any suit, there let his life and children sit undisturbed." This is a rule of limitation, perhaps an occasional measure for
the pacification of the land and the quieting of titles. A claim which
would have been good against the dead man will be invalid against his
heirs; it will have been "tolled" by the "descent cast." Only in the
roughest manner does the law indicate that "wife and children" will
probably be the successors of the dead man. Of what is said in the *Leges
Willelmi* and *Leges Henrici* we speak below: it is of little value. Opet
also relies on a story told in the *Historia Eliensis,* which he interprets
to mean that two sisters had shared with a brother the inheritance of
another brother. The *Historia Eliensis* however is but a poor witness to
the old law, and the phrase that it uses may well mean that the dead
brother had bequeathed the land to his sisters: "*terram . . . moriens
eis dimisit.*"

about this matter: males exclude females of equal degree.[18] This precedence is far older than feudalism, but the feudal influence made for its retention or resuscitation.[19] At the same time, the feudalism with which we are concerned, that of northern France, seems to have somewhat easily, when once the *beneficium* had become hereditary, admitted the daughter to inherit if there was no son. In England, so soon after the Norman invasion as any law becomes apparent, daughters, in default of sons, are capable of inheriting even military fees. In 1135 it is questionable— and this is the extreme case—whether a king's daughter can not inherit the kingdom of England.[20]

A rule which gives the whole of a dead man's land to the eldest of several sons is not a natural part of the law of inheritance. In saying this we are not referring to any fanciful "law of nature," but mean that, at all events among the men of our own race, the law of inheritance does not come by this rule if and so long as it has merely to consider what, as between the various kinsmen of the dead man, justice bids us do with his land. When it decides that the whole land shall go to one son—he may be the eldest, he may be the youngest—and that his brothers shall have nothing, it is not thinking merely of the dead man and his sons, and doing what would be fair among them, were there no other person with claims upon the land; it has in view one who

---

[18] Customs which put the daughters on a level with the sons seem to be exceedingly uncommon. The instances alleged in modern books, namely the customs of Wareham, Taunton and Exeter, are borough customs.

[19] The law of the Lombard *Libri Feudorum* excludes women as a general rule; but the original feoffment may make the *feudum* a *feudum femineum*. In Germany also women were excluded from the inheritance of fiefs for some time after fiefs had become heritable among males.

[20] That in 1100 women could inherit knight's fees is sufficiently proved by a clause in the coronation charter: "*Et si mortuo barone vel alio homine meo filia heres remanserit, illam dabo consilio baronum meorum cum terra sua.*" The Pipe Roll of 31 Hen. I shows the sale of female wards. We must leave to genealogists the discussion of the few cases in which Domesday Book shows that already since the Conquest a great lady has acquired lands. A daughter of Ralph Tailbois and a daughter of Roger de Rames appear among the tenants in chief; but the father of the latter seems to be living. The English fief of William of Arques, a Domesday tenant, seems to have passed to his daughter and then to her daughters.

is a stranger to the inheritance, some king or some lord, whose interests demand that the land shall not be partitioned. It is in the highest and the lowest of the social strata that "impartible succession" first appears. The great fief which is both property and office must, if it be inherited at all, descend as an integral whole; the more or less precarious rights which the unfree peasant has in a tenement must, if they be transmissible at all, pass to one single person. But these tendencies have to struggle against a mighty force, the dictate of what seems to be natural justice, the obvious rule that would divide the inheritance among all the sons. Perhaps we see this best in the case of the kingship. So soon as the kingship became strictly hereditary it became partible. Over and over again the Frankish realm was partitioned; kings and the younger sons of kings were slow to learn that, at least in their case, natural justice must yield to political expediency.[21] Brothers are equals, they are in parage; one of them can not be called upon to do homage to his peer.[22]

Happily for the England of the days before the Conquest the kingship had never become so strictly hereditary as to become partible. On the other hand, we have every reason to believe that the landowner's land was divided among all his sons. We are here speaking of those persons who in the Norman classification became *libere tenentes*. It is not improbable that among those who were to be the *villani* and the *servi* of Domesday Book a system of impartible succession which gave the land to the eldest or to the youngest son was prevalent; but for a while we speak of their superiors. In the highest strata, among the thegns, though we do not see primogeniture, we do see causes at work which were favouring its growth. Causes were at work which were tying military service to the tenure of land, and it would be natural

---

[21] It is possible, as argued by Maine, that "the examples of succession by primogeniture which were found among the benefices may have been imitated from a system of family-government known to the invading races, though not in general use." But the link has yet to be found, and had such a system of family-government been known to the Frankish nation, those ruinous partitions of the kingdom would hardly have taken place.

[22] Richard Coeur de Lion refused to do homage to his brother Henry, "the young king," saying, "It is not meet that the son of the same father and the same mother should admit that he is in any way subject to his elder brother."

that the king, who had theretofore looked to one man for a unit of fighting power, should refuse to recognize an arrangement which would split that duty into fractional parts: he must have some one man whom he can hold responsible for the production of a duly armed warrior. It is to this that point the numerous entries in Domesday Book which tell us of two, three, four, nine, ten thegns holding land "in parage." They are, we take it, co-heirs holding an undivided inheritance, but one of them is answerable to the king for the military service due from the land. This is the meaning of "tenure in parage" in later Norman law. The younger heirs hold of the oldest "in parage"; they do him no homage; they swear to him no fealty; they are his peers, equally entitled with him to enjoy the inheritance; but he and he alone does homage to the lord and is responsible to the lord for the whole service of the fee. As will be said below, this phenomenon appears in the England of the twelfth and thirteenth centuries when an inheritance falls to co-heiresses. There are several texts in Domesday Book which seem to show that the Norman scribes, with this meaning of the term in their minds, were right in saying that some of the Anglo-Saxon thegns had been holding in parage. It is not unnatural that, if one of several brothers must be singled out to represent the land, this one should usually be the eldest. In Buckinghamshire eight thegns were holding a manor, but one of them was the *senior* of the others and was the man of King Edward. Probably he was their *senior* in every sense of the word, both their elder and their superior; he and only he was the king's man for that manor. The state then is beginning to look upon one of several brothers and co-heirs, usually the eldest, as being for one very important purpose the only representative of the land, the sole bearer of those duties to the state which were incumbent on his father as a landholder. The younger sons are beginning to stand behind and below their elder brother. By a very powerful king this somewhat intricate arrangement may be simplified. He and his court may hold that the land is adequately represented by the first-born son, not merely for one, but for all purposes. This will make the collection of reliefs and aids and taxes the easier, and gradually the claims of the younger sons upon their eldest brother may become merely moral claims which the king's court does not enforce.

It is by no means certain that in 1066 primogeniture had gone much further in Normandy than in England. True that in all probability a certain traditional precariousness hung about the inheritance of the military fiefs, a precariousness which might become a lively force if ever a conquering duke had a vast land to divide among his barons. But we can not argue directly from such precariousness to primogeniture. We may say, if we will, that primogeniture is a not unnatural outcome of feudalism, of the slow process which turns an uninheritable *beneficium* into a heritable *feodum*. It is as a general rule convenient for the lord that he should have but one heir to deal with; but as already said, the lord's convenience has here to encounter a powerful force, a very ancient and deep-seated sense of what is right and just, and even in the most feudal age of the most feudal country, the most feudal inheritances, the great fiefs that were almost sovereignties, were partitioned among sons, while as yet the king of the French would hardly have been brought to acknowledge that these *beneficia* were being inherited at all. It is the splendid peculiarity of the Norman duchy that it was never divided. And, as this example will show, it was not always for the lord's advantage, that he should have but one heir to deal with: the king at Paris would not have been sorry to see that great inheritance split up among many co-heirs. And so we can not believe that our Henry III was sorry when his court, after prolonged debate, decided that the palatinate of Chester was divisible among co-heiresses. A less honest man than Edward I would have lent a ready ear to Bruce and Hastings when they pleaded for a partition of Scotland. That absolute and uncompromising form of primogeniture which prevails in England belongs, not to feudalism in general, but to a highly centralized feudalism, in which the king has not much to fear from the power of his mightiest vassals, and is strong enough to impose a law that in his eyes has many merits, above all the great merit of simplicity.

In Normandy the primogenitary rule never went beyond securing the impartibility of every military tenement, and even this impartibility was regarded as the outcome of some positive ordinance. If the inheritance consisted of one hauberk-fief, or of a barony, or of a serjeanty, the eldest son took the whole; he was bound to provide for his brothers to the best of his ability;

but this duty was only a moral duty, for an ordinance had forbidden the partition of a fief. If there were two fiefs in the inheritance and more than one son, the two eldest sons would get a fief apiece. Other lands were equally divided; but the eldest son would have no share in them unless, as we should say, he would "bring into account" the military fief that he was taking. It is put as a very possible case that the value of a share in the other lands will exceed the value of the fief; if so, the eldest son need not take the latter; he has first choice, and it is possible that the knightly land will be left to the youngest and least favoured son. In short, Norman law at the end of the twelfth century prescribes as equal a partition of the inheritance among sons as is compatible with the integrity of each barony, serjeanty or military fief, and leaves the sons to choose their portions in order of birth. Indeed, subject to the rule about the impartibility of military ficfs, a rule imposed by the will of the duke, Norman law shows a strong desire for equality among sons. Any gift of land made by a father to one of his sons is revoked by the father's death; no one is to make one of his expectant heirs better off than the rest. Not upon the Normans as Normans can we throw the burden of our amazing law of inheritance, nor can we accuse the Angevin as an Angevin.

We may believe that the conquest of England gave William an opportunity of insisting that the honour, the knight's fee, the serjeanty, of the dead man was not to be divided; but what William and his sons insisted on was rather "impartible succession" than a strict application of the primogenitary rule. The conquest had thrown into their hands a power of reviving that element of precariousness which was involved in the inheritance of a *beneficium* or *feodum*. There is hardly a strict right to inherit when there is no settled rule about reliefs and the heir must make the best bargain that he can with the king.[23] What we see as a matter of fact in the case of the very great men is that one son gets the

---

[23] In Germany the old rule seems to have been that all the sons had equal claims upon the dead man's fief; the lord however was only bound to admit one of them, and, if they could not agree who that one should be, then the choice was in the lord's hand. At a later time the primogenitary rule was gradually adopted; but the eldest son if he took the fief had to "collate" its value if he wished to share in the general inheritance.

Norman, another the English, fief. On the death of William Fitz Osbern, for example, the king "distributed his honour among his sons and gave Breteuil and whole of the father's possessions in Normandy to William and the county of Hereford in England to Roger." "Roger of Montgomery died; his son Hugh of Montgomery was made earl in England and Robert of Bellême acquired his whole honour in Normandy, while Roger of Poitou, Arnulf, Philip and Everard had no part of the paternal inheritance." We may believe also that in the outer zones of the feudal system the mesne lords insisted on the impartibility of the knight's fee and of the serjeanty, and that these as a general rule passed to the eldest son; but we can not say with any certainty that if the dead man held two different fees of different lords, his eldest son was entitled to both of them. Norman law, as already said, is in favour of as much equality as is compatible with the integrity of each military fee.

Two of the authors who have left us *Leges* for the Anglo-Norman period approached the topic of inheritance; neither of them knew what to make of it. The "bilingual" *Leges Willelmi* say, "If a man dies without a devise, let his children divide the inheritance equally," but this occurs among sentences of Roman origin, and if its maker had any warrant for it, he may perhaps have been speaking only of movables.[24] The author of the *Leges Henrici* goes all the way to the ancient *Lex Ribuaria* for a canon of inheritance, and fetches thence a rule which we should be rash in applying to the England of the twelfth century, for it would exclude a daughter in favour of the remotest male kinsman, to say nothing of admitting father and mother.[25] He says this however, and it is to the point: In the first place the eldest son takes

---

[24] *Leg. Will.* I. c. 34s "*Si home mort senz devise, si depertent les enfans lerité entre sei per uwel.*" The Latin translation gives *pueri* for *enfans;* but *pueri* may stand for children of either sex (Calend. Genealog. i. 204: "omnes alii pueri eius erant filiae"), and perhaps *enfans* may stand for *sons.* But we can allow hardly any weight to this part of the "bilingual code."

[25] *Leg. Henr.* 70 § 20. The writer tampered with the end of the passage that he borrowed, and it is possible that what looks at first sight like an exclusion of women is merely the rule *paterna paternis.* "*Et dum virilis sexus extiterit, et hereditas ab inde sit, femina non hereditetur*": an inheritance which comes down the paternal line will not fall to the maternal line if there be any sword-cousin living.

the father's *feodum*. What exactly he would have given to the eldest son, or what he would have done if the inheritance comprised two *feoda*, we do not know.[26] The conquest and the clash of national laws have thrown all into confusion, and the king will profit thereby.

It may well be that Henry II spoke his mind in favour of primogeniture both in England and in Normandy; his son Geoffrey in 1187, just when Glanvill was writing, decreed that in Britanny the knight's fee should pass intact to the eldest son. But already in Glanvill's day English law had left Norman law behind it. "According to the law of the realm of England," he says—and probably he is here contrasting the kingdom with the duchy—the eldest son of the knight or of one who holds by knight's service succeeds to all that was his father's. With such a military tenant he contrasts the "free sokeman." The free sokeman's land is divided among all his sons, but only if it be "socage and partible from of old." If it has not been partible from of old, then by some customs the eldest, by others the youngest son will inherit it.

In the many commentaries on this text it has hardly been sufficiently noticed that the sphere of primogeniture is already defined by very wide, and the sphere of equal division by very narrow words. Glanvill does not say that a knight's fee is impartible among sons; he says that land held by military service is impartible. Of the serjeanties he here says nothing; of them it were needless to speak, for a serjeanty is the most impartible of all tenements, impartible (so men are saying) even among daughters. But if we leave serjeanty and frankalmoin out of account, by far the greater number of the free tenures that exist in England at the end of the twelfth century fall within the sphere of primogeniture; they are in name and in law military tenures. True that the tenant may be a mere peasant who will never go

---

[26] *Leg. Henr.* 70 § 21: "*Primo patris feodum primogenitus filius habeat.*" At present there seems to be no warrant for the reading *Primum* which some of our older writers have adopted. The rubric to c. 70, *Consuetudo Westsexae*, probably refers only to the first sentence of the chapter, and neither the rubrics nor the division into chapters can be treated as of high authority. Here the writer is thinking primarily, not of the order of inheritance, but of the law concerning alienation; the *feodum* is contrasted with the acquests and may mean the family land, the *hereditas aviatica*. On the other hand, it may mean a military fee.

to the wars; but if he pays one penny by way of scutage his tenure is military, and usually when lords make feoffments they take care that the burden of scutage shall fall upon their tenants. By far the greater number of the countless new feoffments that are being made day by day are creating military tenures. It is not usual for the feoffor to assume as between himself and his tenant the ultimate incidence of the uncertain war-tax. The greater number of those very numerous tenures in "free and common socage" which exist in the last of the middle ages, have, we believe, their origin in the disappearance of scutage and the utter oblivion into which the old liability for scutage fell. But then again, Glanvill does not say that socage land is partible among sons. For one thing, it is partible only if it has been treated as partible in time past. Every new tenure therefore that is created after Henry II's day, albeit a tenure in socage, adds to the number of estates which obey the primogenitary rule. But more; the estates which according to Glanvill are partible, are only the estates of the "free sokemen." Now while in his day the term "socage" was just beginning to have that wide meaning which would ultimately make it cover whatever tenure was non-military, non-eleemosinary, non-serviential, there was no similar extension of the term "sokeman." The free sokeman whom he has in view are a small class, and one that is not increasing. They are to be found chiefly on the ancient demesne of the crown; a few may be found on other manors, for the more part in the eastern counties; but these are disappearing. On the one hand many are lapsing into villeinage; on the other hand some are obtaining charters, which perhaps make them in name and in law military tenants, but at any rate give them a new estate and one that has never been partitioned. Therefore after Glanvill's day there was no further change in the law; Bracton uses almost the self-same words that his predecessor used.[27]

---

[27] With Glanvill, as with Bracton, the only partible land is the socage land of a sokeman which has been divided from of old. Thus the common opinion that there was a change in the law after Glanvill's day does not seem to us to be warranted. The judges in the early Year Books do not lean strongly against partibility. If the plaintiff asserts partibility he must prove partition; but if he proves partition he may perhaps succeed in making even a knight's fee partible. Y. B. 30–31 Edw. I 57; 33–35 Edw. I 515. Glanvill's rule needs no extension; it is so very wide.

Consequently there is very little litigation about this matter, and what there is comes from very few countries. We can refer to seventeen cases from the reign of John and the early years of Henry III which make mention of partible land; of these seven come from Kent, five from Norfolk, three from Suffolk, one from Northamptonshire, one from Rutland. Leaving Kent out of account, it is the land which the Domesday surveyors found well stocked with "free men" and sokemen that supplies us with our instances. In later days it may be possible to find a few isolated examples of partible land in many shires of England; but, outside Kent, the true home of partibility is the home of that tenure which the lawyers of Edward I's day distinguished from "socage" by the term "sokemanry."[28]

The problem which is set before us by the gavelkind of Kent is not a problem in the history of the law of inheritance, but a very difficult problem in the general history of English law, and one which is of an economic rather than of a purely legal character. It belongs to the twelfth century. It is this: How does it come about that at the end of that period there is in Kent, and not elsewhere, a strong class of rent-paying tenants who stand well apart from the knights on the one side and the villeins on the other, a class strong enough to maintain a *lex Kantiae* which differs at many points from the general law of the land? . . . On the one hand it seems to us that the matter of the Kentish custom is in part very old. The law of inheritance shows a curious preference for the youngest son. When his father's house has to be divided, the hearth (*astre*) is reserved for him. We may say with some certainty that a rule which had its origin in the twelfth century, if it gave a preferential share to any son, would give it to the eldest. Again, some parts of the custom enshrined ancient English proverbs, which the scribes of the fourteenth century could not understand and which make reference to institutions that must have been obsolescent in the twelfth, obsolete in the thirteenth century.[29] On the other hand, we can not think that the

---

[28] A great deal of Norfolk seems to have been partible, and partibility reigned in several of the great "sokes" of the Danelaw, *e.g.* the soke of Rothley in Leicestershire and the soke of Oswaldsbeck in Nottinghamshire.

[29] We find a proverb about the wife who loses her free-bench by unchastity, another about the descent of the felon's land, a third about the

Kent of 1065 was a county in which the tillers of the soil were peculiarly well off. Unless the terminology of the Domesday surveyors was far more perverse and deceptive than we can believe it to have been, Kent differed little from Sussex, widely from Norfolk, and in 1086, not Kent, but the shires of the Danelaw must have seemed the predestined home of a strong free yeomanry tenacious of ancient customs. Nor again can we think that Kent suffered less than other districts at the hands of the Norman invaders. The best theory that we can suggest is that in the twelfth century the unrivalled position of Kent as the highway of commerce induced a wide-spread prosperity which favoured the tillers of the soil. An old system of "provender rents" may have passed into the modern system of money rents without passing through the stage in which the lord places his main reliance on the "week work" of his tenants. A nucleus of old customs expanded and developed; even the lowest classes of tenants were gradually brought within its range, until at length it was said that every child born in Kent was born free.[30]

---

process called gavellet. The last of these is obscure. The lord after a long forbearance has had the tenement adjudged to him, because of the tenant's failure to pay his rent. The tenant has however a *locus poenitentiae* allowed him. The proverb seems to say that, if he will get back his land, he must pay the arrears of rent nine times (or perhaps eighteen times) over, and, in addition to this, must pay a *wergild* of five pounds. In the Anglo-Norman reckoning five pounds will do well enough as a ceorl's *wer* (*Leg. Will.* I c. 8) and the nine-fold payment is like the eleven-fold payment which we find in the account of the Bishop of Worcester's customs in Domesday Book, i. 174. According to old Kentish law a nine-fold geld was payable to the king in some cases. Seemingly the proverb means in truth that the tenant will lose the land for good and all. It is one of those humorous rules of folk-law which, instead of telling a man that he can not have what he wants, tell him that he may have it if he will perform an impossible condition. As to the more famous proverb "the father to the bough, the son to the plough," the oldest form of this sends the father to the bowe, the son to the lowe, that is apparently, to the fireside, the *astre,* which is, if we may so say, the centre of the inheritance.

[30] The printed custumal professes to be a record of the customs approved in the eyre of 1293; but no official or authoritative text of it has been found. See Robinson, *Gavelkind* (ed. 1822), p. 355. Almost all the customs mentioned in it are however evidenced by earlier records. Somner, *Gavelkind,* Appendix, gives several ancient charters conveying land to be held in gavelkind. In the earliest of our plea rolls we find brothers sharing land in Kent and the name *gavelingude* appears: Rolls of King's

It is only to modern eyes that the inheritance partible among sons is the central point of gavelkind. In the thirteenth century a custom which allowed the sons of the hanged felon to inherit from their father must have seemed a far more striking anomaly. Still the partible inheritance was beginning to attract attention. Archbishop Hubert Walter, who presided in the king's court during years critical in our legal history, obtained from King John a charter empowering him and his successors to convert into military fees the tenements that were holden of their church in gavelkind. The archbishop's main object may have been to get money in the form of rents and scutages, instead of provender and boon works, "gavel-corn" and "gavel-swine," "gavel-erth" and "gavel-rip"; and we have here an illustration of those early commutations of which we have been speaking, and an important illustration, for a great part of Kent was under the archbishop and his example would find followers.[31] It is possible however that Glanvill's nephew and successor also intended to destroy, so far as he could, the partible inheritance. Such at any rate was the avowed object of Edward I when in 1276 he "disgavelled" the lands of John of Cobham. In the charter by which he did this we have perhaps the oldest argument in favour of primogeniture that has come down to us, for when Bracton tells us that the first-born son is "first in the nature of things" this is hardly argument. "It often happens," says Edward, "that tenements held in gavelkind, which so long as they remained whole

---

Court (Pipe Roll Society) pp. 39, 43. Thenceforward we often find the name. Thus in John's reign, Select Civil Pleas (Selden Society) pl. 157; Placit. Abbrev. p. 56. The peculiarities of the widow's free-bench soon appear: Select Civil Pleas, pl. 128; Note Book, pl. 9, 1338. So the peculiarities of the widower's free-bench: Robinson, *Gavelkind*, p. 179. Bracton speaks of gavelkind on f. 276 b, 311, 313, 374. On the whole, most of the known peculiarities can be traced as far back as Bracton's time. The statement that there is no villeinage in Kent is made in 1302: Y. B. 30–31 Edw. I p. 169, as well as in the custumal of 1293: Statutes vol. i. p. 224.

[31] Robinson, *Gavelkind* (ed. 1822), p. 66: Hubert Walter grants that a certain tenant, who hitherto has held a yoke and ten acres in gavelkind, shall henceforth hold in frank fee by the service of a twentieth part of a knight's fee and an annual rent of 28 shillings. In after days the power of the king and of the archbishop to change the mode of descent was denied.

were sufficient for the maintenance of the realm and provided a
livelihood for many, are divided among co-heirs into so many
parts and fragments that each one's part will hardly support
him"; therefore as a special favour Cobham's gavelkind lands
are to descend for ever as though they were held by knight's
service.[32]

We are far from saying that there were no sound reasons of
state to be urged for the introduction and extension of the
primogenitary rule. Englishmen in course of time began to glory
in it, and under its sway the England of Edward I's day had
become a strong, a free, and a wealthy state. But we miss one
point in the history of our law unless we take account of its
beautiful simplicity. Granted that each military fee should
descend as an impartible whole, a hundred difficulties will be
evaded if we give all the dead man's lands to his eldest son—
difficulties about "hotchpot," difficulties about the contribution
of co-heirs to common burdens, difficulties about wardships and
marriages to which a "parage" tenure must, as we shall see
hereafter, give rise. We cut these knots. That when one man
leaves the world one other should fill the vacant place—this is
an ideally simple arrangement. The last years of Henry II were
the years that decided the matter for good and all, and they were
years in which a newly fashioned court, unhampered by precedents, was with rude, youthful vigour laying down its first
principles. Here as elsewhere its work is characterized by a bold,
an almost reckless, simplicity. Nor must we fail to notice that
here as elsewhere it generalized the law of the great folk and
made it common law for all free and lawful men, except some
ancient and dwindling classes which had hardly come within its
ken. When we balance the account of our primogenitary law
we must remember that it obliterated class distinctions.[33]

---

[32] Already in 1231 we hear that one messuage is often divided into
three or four messuages "*sicut gavelikinde*": Note Book, pl. 666. Edward
allowed the Welsh to retain the partible inheritance, insisting only that
bastards must not be admitted, and that women must be admitted in
default of males; but then "Edward's power lay in the strength of
Kentishmen and the weakness of Welshmen."

[33] It is fairly clear that in Henry II's day the primogenitary rule was
not popular among those classes with which the royal court had to deal.
Glanvill has to regret that men are too fond of their younger sons. A

The manner in which our law deals with an inheritance which falls to the dead man's daughters may give us some valuable hints as to the history of primogeniture. If we look merely at the daughters and isolate them from the rest of the world, their claims are equal and the law will show no preference for the first-born. This principle was well maintained, even though some of the things comprised in the inheritance were not such as could be easily divided, or were likely to become of less value in the process of division. For example, if there was but one house, the eldest daughter had no right to insist that this should fall to her share, even though she was willing to bring its value into account. No, unless the parceners could agree upon some other plan, the house itself was physically divided. And so again if there was but one advowson in the inheritance, the eldest sister could not claim the first presentation as her own; all the parceners must join in a presentation, otherwise it would lapse to the ordinary. There were however certain indivisible things; a castle could not be partitioned, nor the messuage which was the head of a barony. This passed as a whole to the eldest of the sisters, but she accounted for its value in the division of the rest of the inheritance. To explain this however, a maxim of public law is introduced: were partitions made of these things, earldoms and baronies would be brought to naught, and the realm itself is constituted of earldoms and baronies. So again it is Bracton's opinion that a tenement held by serjeanty ought not to be divided, and this opinion seems to have been warranted at all events by the practice of an earlier age.[34] But the king's claim to prevent the partition of a great fee has in the past gone far. In 1218 a litigant pleads that ever since the conquest of England it has been the king's prerogative right that if any of his barons dies

French chronicler tells a curious story of a parliament held by Henry III and Simon de Montfort in which there was debate as to the abolition of primogeniture and the adoption of the French rule. England, so it was said, was being depleted and agriculture was suffering since the younger sons of the English gentry were driven to seek their fortunes in France. This chronicler shows himself very ignorant of English history, and the story, as he tells it, must be false. What we learn from him is that a Frenchman of the fourteenth century thought the English rule unjust and impolitic.

[34] But in 1221 Henry III permits co-heiresses to hold a serjeanty.

leaving daughters as his heirs, and the elder-born daughters have been married in their father's lifetime, the king may give the youngest daughter to one of his knights with the whole of her father's land to the utter exclusion therefrom of the elder daughters.[35] There is a good deal in the history of the twelfth century to show that the king had held himself free to act upon some such rule. The law of later times about the abeyance of titles of honour is but a poor remnant of the right which he has thus assumed. When of old he "determined an abeyance in favour of one of the parceners," he disposed not merely of a "title of honour" and a "seat in the House of Lords," but of a great tract of land.[36]

But though the division among the co-heiresses was in general a strictly equal division, we see the oldest daughter or her husband standing out as the representative of the whole inheritance for certain feudal purposes. The law about this matter underwent an instructive change. We will suppose that Henry, who holds of Roger, dies leaving three daughters, whom in order of birth we call Alice, Barbara and Clara, and that a partition of the land is made among them. Now two different feudal schemes may be applied to this case. On the one hand, we may decide that each of the three women holds her land of Roger; on the other, that Alice holds the whole inheritance of Roger, while her sisters hold their shares of her. Roger has apparently something to gain and something to lose by the adoption of either scheme. On the one hand, he may wish to treat Alice as his only tenant, for he will thus have one person to whom he can look for the whole service due from the whole land; but then, if this theory is adopted, can he fairly claim any wardships or marriages in the lines of which Barbara and Clara are the starting points? This however seems to have been the old theory; Alice will hold of Roger; her husband, and no one else, will do homage to Roger for the whole land; her sisters will hold of her; they will "achieve" (*accapitare*) to her, that is, will

---

[35] But this contention seems to be over-ruled, and as a matter of fact a partition seems to have been made.

[36] Geoffrey Fitz Peter, the chief justiciar, having married one of the co-heiresses of the last of the Mandeville earls of Essex, obtained the whole Mandeville fief.

recognize her as their head. For three generations (of which they are the first) they and their descendants will do no homage, swear no fealty, and pay no reliefs; but the third heir of Barbara or Clara must pay relief to, and become the man of, Alice or her heir.[37] We have here the Norman tenure in parage.[38]

The reason why no homage is done until a third heir has inherited we can not here discuss; but it soon becomes apparent that the king is dissatisfied with this arrangement and that the law is beginning to fluctuate. In 1236 the English in Ireland sent to Westminster for an exposition of the law. Of whom do the younger sisters hold? The answering writ, which has sometimes been dignified by the title *Statutum Hiberniae de Coheredibus,* said that if the dead man held in chief of the king, then all the co-heirs hold in chief of the king and must do him homage.[39] If the lands were held of a mesne lord, then that lord has the marriages and wardships of all the parceners, but only the eldest is to do homage, and her younger sisters are to do their services through her hands. The eldest daughter, the writ says, is not to have the marriage and wardship of her sisters, for this would be to commit the lambs to the wolf. This last provision looks like new law, if it means that the wardships and marriages of Barbara's descendants are to belong to Roger, and not to Alice or her descendants. In 1223 we may find the daughter of an elder sister claiming the marriage of the son and heir of a younger sister. A judge of Edward I's day tells us of a *cause célèbre* in which the wardships and marriages of the heirs in the younger line had in generation after generation gone to the representatives

---

[37] Glanvill, vii. 3.

[38] In Normandy the parage endures until the "sixth degree of lineage" has been past. It seems possible that this means much the same as what Glanvill means, and that the discrepancy is caused by divers modes of reckoning. According to Glanvill the great-great-grandson of the dead man is the first person who does homage to a cousin. Six degrees of Roman computation divide the great-grandson in the one line from the great-grandson in the other line; thus in the normal case there would be seven (Roman) degrees at least between the person who first does and the person who first receives homage. According to Bracton, the younger sisters do swear fealty to the elder; according to Glanvill they do not.

[39] For some time past the king had habitually taken the homage of all the parceners.

of the older line; but all this was held null and void at the suit of the lord.[40] Bracton gives the law as it was laid down by the writ of 1236, and in his day we still see the younger daughters holding of their sister, holding without homage until the third heir has inherited. Britton knows that the lord can not be compelled to take the homage of any but the eldest daughter, and that, when this has been done, he can and must look to that sister for the whole of his services; but Britton advises the lord to accept the homage of all, for should he not do so, he may find some difficulty in getting wardships and marriages in the younger lines. The lords from this time forward had their choice between two courses. As a matter of fact they took Britton's advice, followed the king's example and exacted homage from all the sisters. Very soon, if we are not much mistaken, the old law of parage began to fall into utter oblivion.[41]

The lesson that we learn from this episode is that the lord's interest has been powerful to shape our law of inheritance. At one time it looks as if even among women there would be what we may call an external primogeniture, so that the eldest of the daughters would be the only representative of the fee in the eyes of the lord and of the feudal courts. Had this principle been consistently applied, the rights of the younger daughters might have become merely moral rights. But in the thirteenth century wardships and marriages were of greater importance than knight's service and scutage, and first the king and then the other lords perceived that they had most to gain by taking the homage of all the sisters.

It is by no means impossible that the spread of primogeniture to tenements that were hardly military save in name, and then to tenements that were not military even in name, was made the easier by the prevalence of "impartible succession" among the holders of villein tenements. We have already said that in the

---

[40] Y. B. 32–33 Edw. I p. 301: Bereford, J. says: "I have seen a case where the father, grandfather and great-grandfather have been seised of the homage, wardship and marriage of their parceners, and yet all this was set aside by reason of the parcenry, and the chief lord recovered his services. This I saw in the case of Sir Edmund the king's brother, for parceners ought not to 'murder' another's right of seignory among themselves. . . ."

[41] So in France Philip Augustus tried to suppress parage tenure.

thirteenth century such tenements do very often pass from ancestor to heir. There is a custom of inheritance which is known to the manorial court and is maintained by it as against all but the lord. That custom seems generally to point to one person and one only as entitled to succeed to the dead man's tenement. In a manorial extent it is a rare thing to find the names of two brothers or even of two sisters entered as those of the tenants of a tenement.[42] On the other hand, it is a very common thing to find that the tenant is a woman. Often she is a widow and it is clear that she is holding the virgate of a dead husband. But putting the widow out of the case, then, if there were several sons, either the eldest or the youngest seems usually to have succeeded to his father to the exclusion of his brothers. In later days very many copyholds follow the primogenitary rules of the common law, and we can not think that those rules have been thrust upon them in recent days by the king's courts, though no doubt those courts have required strict proof of abnormal customs. We imagine therefore that from a remote time many villein tenements have descended in a primogenitary course. On the other hand, it is certain that a scheme which gave the land to the youngest son was common.

A mere accident—for we think that it was no better—has given the name "borough English" to this custom of ultimogeniture. In the Norman days a new French borough grew up beside the old English borough of Nottingham. A famous case of 1327 drew the attention of lawyers to the fact that while the burgages of the "burgh Francoys" descended to the eldest son, those of the "burgh Engloys" descended to the youngest. It was natural for the lawyers to find a name for the custom in the circumstances of this case, to call it the custom of the borough English, or the custom of borough English, for this custom came before them but very rarely. Without saying that it never ruled the descent of tenements held by the free socage of the common law, we seem fully entitled to say that, if we put on one side what in the thirteenth century were distinguished from socage as being burgage tenures, and if we also put on one side the "sokemanry"

---

[42] Among such manorial plea rolls as have been printed we have observed no instance even of two women claiming to be co-heirs of a villein tenement.

of the ancient demesne, then a freehold tenement descending to
the youngest son was an exceedingly rare phenomenon; and in
1327 the Westminster courts had as yet had very little to do
with the inheritance of burgages and sokemanries. The true
home of ultimogeniture is the villein tenement; among villein
tenements it has widely prevailed; in Bracton's day its appearance raised a presumption that the tenements which it governed
were not free.[43]

It is hardly to be explained without reference to the lord's
interest and the lord's will. But what has thus to be explained is
not really the preference of the youngest son, but the impartible
inheritance. If once we grant that the tenement is not to be
divided, because the lord will have but one tenant, then in truth
the preference of the youngest is quite as natural as the preference of the eldest son. Perhaps if the lord had merely to pursue
his own interest he would as a general rule choose the first-born,
for the first-born is the most likely of all the sons to be of full
age at the time of his father's death. Were there military service
to be done, there would be good reason for selecting him. But
if we look at the matter from the tenant's point of view there is
something to be said in favour of the youngest son. Of all the sons
he is the one who is most likely to be still dependent on his
father at the hour of his father's death. Add to this—and it will
count for something—that he is the son most likely to be found

---

[43] As a fair selection of copyhold customs, which have been reduced to
writing in comparatively modern times, we may take those collected in
Watkins, *Copyholds* (3rd ed.), ii. p. 228 fol. Dymock, Gloucestershire:
no inheritance beyond heirs of the body. Yetminster, Dorset: widow
has rights but there is no true inheritance. Weardale, Durham: eldest son,
and failing sons, daughters jointly. Mayfield, Sussex: yard-lands to
youngest son, and failing sons, youngest daughter; assart lands to eldest
son, or failing sons, eldest daughter. Framfield, Sussex: the like; primogeniture or, as the case may be, ultimogeniture prevails even when the
descent is to remote relations. Stepney, Middlesex: partible between sons
and, failing sons, between daughters; partible between remoter kinsfolk
of equal degree whether male or female. Cheltenham, Gloucestershire:
youngest son and, failing sons, youngest daughter. Taunton, Somerset:
widow inherits in fee from her husband to the exclusion of children.
Robinson, *Gavelkind* (last chapter), gives a list of places, mostly in the
south-east of England, where "borough English" has prevailed in modern
times. That an eldest or youngest daughter should, in default of sons,
take the whole land was not uncommon.

in the house at his father's death; he will be at the hearth; he is the fire-side child. The ancient customs of free tenements will sometimes respect this idea: the land is to be equally divided among the sons, but the house, or, if not the house, at least the hearth, is given to the youngest. Perhaps we may see in this a trace of an ancient religion of which the hearth was the centre. If then we suppose a lord insisting on the rule "One tenement, one tenant" and yet willing to listen to old analogies or to the voice of what seems to be "natural equity," it is not at all improbable that, with the general approval of his tenantry, he will allow the inheritance to fall to the youngest son.

A good illustration of the conflicting principles which will shape a scheme of descent among peasant holders is afforded by a verdict given in 1224 about the custom which ruled the descent among daughters in the "ancient demesne" manors of Bray and Cookham: The jurors have always seen this custom, "that if any tenant has three or four daughters and all of them are married outside their father's tenement, save one, who remains at the hearth, she who remains at the hearth shall have the whole land of her father, and her sisters shall recover no part thereof; but if there be two or three or more daughters and all of them are married outside their father's tenement with his chattels, whether this be so before or after his death, the eldest daughter shall have the whole tenement and her sisters no part; and if the daughters are married after their father's death with his chattels, and this without protest, and one of them remains at the hearth, she at the hearth shall retain the whole tenement as aforesaid."[44] Subject to the rule that the tenement must not be partitioned, we seem to see here an attempt to do what is equitable. If really there is no difference between the daughters—no such difference as can

---

44 "Within the manor of B. [Bray] in the county of Berks, there is such a custom, that if a man have divers daughters, and no son, and dieth, the eldest daughter shall only inherit; and if he have no daughters, but sisters, the eldest sister by the custom shall inherit and sometimes the youngest." In two Sussex manors we find the yard-lands (the old original villein tenements) governed by ultimogeniture even among daughters, while the assart lands (lands brought into cultivation at a later time) are governed by an equally strict primogeniture; but (and this is very instructive) if a tenant has lands of both kinds, they must all go together either to the eldest or to the youngest; the tenement that he acquired first will carry with it the other tenement.

be expressed in general terms by a rude rule of law—then we fall back upon primogeniture; but if the other daughters have been married off, the one who is left at the hearth is the natural heir.[45] But already in the thirteenth century ultimogeniture was becoming unpopular: Simon de Montfort granting a charter of liberties to his burgesses at Leicester abolished it. The reason that he gave is curious: the borough was being brought to naught by the default and debility of heirs.[46] By the common assent and will of all the burgesses he established primogeniture among them. We may believe that what moved the burgesses was not so much any ill effects occasioned by the old mode of inheritance as the bad repute into which it had fallen. It was the rule for villeins, explicable only by the will of the lord. The burgesses of Leicester mean to be free burgesses and to enjoy what is by this time regarded as the natural law for free men.

We would not suggest that in no case can a custom of ultimogeniture have arisen save under the pressure of seignorial power. In a newly conquered land where land is very plentiful, the elder sons may be able to obtain lands of their own and, they being provided for, the father's lands may pass to the fire-side child; and again there may conceivably have been a time when the pressure which made for impartial succession was rather communal than seignorial. But as a matter of fact, whether we look to England or to other European countries, we shall hardly find ultimogeniture save where some lord has been able to dictate a

---

[45] The verdict is a good typical verdict about a customary mode of descent. It leaves many cases unprovided for. In the imperfection of all ancient statements of the rules of inheritance to copyholds our common law has found an opportunity for spreading abroad its own rules. Thus jurors state in the custumal that a youngest son excludes his fellows, but says nothing of a descent to brothers, uncles, cousins. Hence perhaps the not uncommon result that in modern times there is ultimogeniture among sons, primogeniture among brothers. But the reason for giving the land to a youngest son hardly extends to the case of a youngest brother. He is not so likely to be found at the dead man's fire-side.

[46] Jeaffreson, Index to the Leicester MSS. p. 66: "*propter defectum heredum et debilitatem eorum iam multo tempore [villa] fere ad occasum declinavit et ruinam.*" This of course can not refer to a "default" of heirs in the ordinary sense of that term. What is suggested is that the heirs are weaklings.

rule of inheritance to dependent peasants.[47] It seems to have been so in medieval Germany. The common land law divides the land among all the sons, giving perhaps to the eldest, perhaps to the youngest a slight preference[48]; the noble fief will often pass undivided to the first-born; the tenement of the peasant will go as a whole either to his eldest or to his youngest son, and as a matter of geographical distribution the primogenitary will be intermingled with the ultimogenitary customs: "The peasant," says a proverb, "has only one child."[49] For all this, however, we are not entitled to draw from ultimogeniture any sweeping conclusions as to the large number of slaves or serfs that there must have been in a remote past. The force which gives the peasant's tenement to his youngest or his eldest son is essentially the same force which, in one country with greater in another with less success, contends for the impartibility of the military fee. Somehow or another it has come about that there is a lord with power to say, "This land must not be divided." The persons to whom he says this may be slaves, or the progeny of slaves, who are but just acquiring an inheritable hold upon the land; they may be mighty barons who have constrained him much against his will to grant them "loans" of land; they may be free landowners over whom he has acquired jurisdictional powers, which he is slowly converting into proprietary rights. . . .

The canons which regulate the course of inheritance among the collateral kinsfolk of the dead man are worthy of observation. Our English law has been brought to bear upon a brisk controversy that has been carried on in Germany. What was the main principle of the old Germanic scheme of inheritance? Was it a "gradual" or a "parentelic" scheme? Proximity of kinship may be reckoned in divers ways. The calculus which will seem the

---

[47] We here speak of a rule which gives the whole land to the youngest son. Rules which divide the land equally among the sons but reserve "the hearth" or house for the eldest or youngest are quite a different matter and may perhaps have their origin in a religious cult of the hearth.

[48] A rule which gives the father's house to the youngest son seems to have been very common in Germany. Stobbe cites a Frisian rule which, like the Kentish rule, gives the youngest son the hearth, *den Herd*.

[49] Ultimogeniture has been found in every quarter of Germany, from Switzerland to Holstein, and from Bohemia to the Rhine.

most natural to us in modern times is a "gradual" calculus. Each act of generation makes a degree and we count the number of degrees that lie between the *propositus* and the various claimants. It is probable that any system of inheritance with which we have to deal will prefer the descendants of the dead man to all other claimants; we will therefore leave them out of account. This done, we find in the first degree the dead man's parents; in the second his grand-parents, brothers and sisters; in the third his great-grandparents, uncles, aunts, nephews, nieces; in the fourth his great-great-grandparents, great-uncles, great-aunts, first cousins, great-nephews, great-nieces; and so forth. Our English law of inheritance has a very different scheme. In order to explain it we had better make use of a term to which modern disputants have given a technical meaning, the term *parentela*. By a person's *parentela* is meant the sum of those persons who trace descent from him. My issue are my *parentela,* my father's issue are his *parentela*. Now in our English scheme the various *parentelae* are successively called to the inheritance in the order of their proximity to the dead man. My father's *parentela* is nearer to me than my grandfather's. Every person who is in my father's *parentela* is nearer to me than any person who can only claim kinship through some ancestor remoter from me than my father. For a moment and for the sake of simplicity we may speak as if there was but one ascendant line, as if the dead man had but one parent, one grand-parent and so forth, and we will call these progenitors father, grandfather and the like. The rule then becomes this: Exhaust the dead man's *parentela;* next exhaust his father's *parentela;* next his grandfather's; next his great-grandfather's. We see the family tree in some such shape as that pictured on the next page.

The remotest kinsman who stands in Parentela I is a nearer heir than the nearest kinsman of Parentela II. Between persons who stand in different *parentelae* there can be no competition. In a purely gradual scheme my great-great-grandfather, my great-uncle, my first cousin and my great-nephew are equally close to me. In a parentelic scheme my great-nephew, since he springs from my father, is nearer to me than my first cousin. We have here, it is said, not a "gradual" but a "lineal-gradual" scheme.

Within each *parentela* or line of issue the "grade" is of importance; but no computation of grades must induce us to jump from a nearer to a remoter line so long as the nearer line has a single representative.[50]

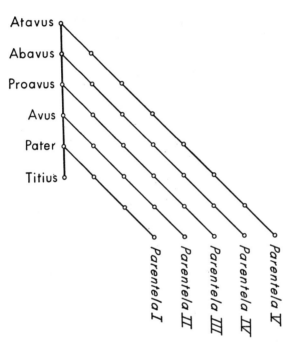

We have preferred to state the matter in this abstract, and in England unfamiliar, fashion rather than to repeat the rules that have been admirably expounded by Hale and Blackstone. English, Scottish and Norman law seem to afford the best specimens of the parentelic scheme. Whether this scheme is of extremely ancient date, or whether it is the outcome of feudalism, is a controverted question which cannot be decided by our English books and records. We can only say that in the thirteenth century it seems to be among Englishmen the only conceivable scheme. Our text-writers accept it as obvious, and this although they will copy from the civilians an elaborate *Arbor Consanguinitatis* and hardly

---

[50] Modern opinion seems to be inclining to the belief that the parentelic scheme was ancient and general.

know that the English law is radically different from the Roman.[51]

A good illustration is afforded by the careful pleadings of John Balliol in the great suit for the crown of Scotland. He traced the downward descent of the crown from David to the Maid of Norway. He himself had to go back to Henry, earl of Huntingdon, in order to find an ancestor common to him and the *proposita.* But he had to face the fact that William the Lion left daughters, and he could not get so far back as Henry without alleging that the lines of these daughters had become extinct. On the Maiden's death, "the right resorted" to William's *parentela,* but it found that *parentela* empty and so had to go back further.[52]

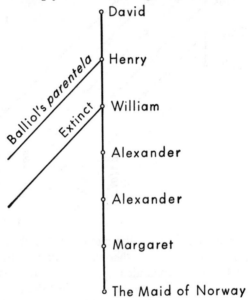

---

[51] The works of both Bracton and Fleta ought to have in them *arbores* borrowed from the civilians; such trees are found in several MSS. of Bracton's book. The *arbor* is given in Nichols's edition of Britton. The use of these trees is apt to perplex the writer's exposition of English law. Still the parentelic scheme comes out clearly enough in Bracton, Fleta, and Britton.

[52] Several of the competitors professed that they stood in a lower *parentela* than that represented by Balliol, Bruce and Hastings; but their claims seem to have been stained by illegitimacy and were withdrawn.

We have said that the *parentelae* or stocks are to be exhausted one by one. The method of exhausting them is that in accordance with which the descendants of the dead man are first exhausted. Suppose that it is the *parentela* of the dead man's father that is to be exhausted; we must apply to those who stand within it our six rules: (1) A living descendant excludes his or her own descendants. (2) A dead descendant is represented by his or her own descendants.[53] (3) Males exclude females of equal degree. (4) Among males of equal degree only the eldest inherits. (5) Females of equal degree inherit together. (6) The rule that a dead descendant is to be represented by his or her descendants overrides the preference for the male sex.

But of course we have as yet been treating the problem as though it were much simpler than really it is. The dead man does not stand at the end of a single line of ancestors. He must have had two parents, four grandparents, and so forth. Along which of the lines which met in him are we to move in search of those *parentelae* which are to be called to the inheritance? Our medieval lawyers, copying the pictures drawn by canonists and civilians, are guilty of the same unjustifiable simplification with which we can be charged. They represent "the ascending line" as a single line. In the first "cell" in it they write "*pater, mater,*" in the second "*avus, avia,*" in the third "*proavus, proavia*" and so on, apparently forgetting that every person has four grandparents, and that the English system is not one which can treat these four persons as sharing a single "cell." More instructive would it have been had they drawn their picture thus:

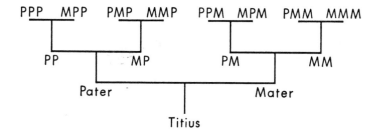

---

[53] The application of this principle gave Balliol the victory over Bruce.

Had they done this, they might have left us some clear principle for directing our choice between the various ascendant lines and have solved some problems which were still open in the nineteenth century.

As it is, we can see the rule that the heir must be one who is related by blood kinship not only to the *propositus* but to the purchaser. By "purchaser" is here meant the person who last acquired the estate otherwise than by inheritance. Now if the person whose heir we are seeking was himself the purchaser, our rule will admit every blood kinsman or kinswoman of his. But if he was not the purchaser, then our choice will be restricted. Suppose that his father was the purchaser, no one can be admitted who is not related by blood to that father. Suppose that his mother was the purchaser, any one who takes the inheritance must be related by blood to her. Suppose that his father's mother was the purchaser, a successful claimant must be her blood kinsman. We have here the rule that in foreign books is expressed by the proverb *Paterna paternis, materna maternis.*[54] Our English law does not merely postpone the *materni* or, as the case may be, the *paterni;* it absolutely excludes them. My father's brother can not inherit from me land that descended to me from my mother; my father's father's brother can not inherit from me land that descended to me from my father's mother. So far as we can see, this rule was in force in the thirteenth century. Attempts have been made to represent it as a specifically feudal rule, one which takes us back to a time when only the descendants of the original vassal could inherit; but such attempts seem to be unnecessary; a rule whose main effect is that of keeping a woman's land in her own family is not unnatural and may well be very ancient.[55] We see its naturalness when we apply it to the descent of a kingdom. When the Maid of Norway died, her father, King Eric, put in a claim to the throne of Scotland and sent learned Italian lawyers to argue his case in Edward's court; but no one seems to have

[54] Abroad this return of the inheritance to the side whence it came was known as *ius revolutionis, ius recadentiae, Fallrecht.* It is a widely distributed phenomenon.

[55] The common form which prevails now-a-days when a bride's personal property is to be settled bears witness to this desire that, if there be no children of the marriage, the wife's property shall in certain events come back to her own kinsfolk.

taken him or his claim very seriously. The ascending line along which the inheritance must return should obviously be the line of the Scottish kings; it is not to be tolerated that one who has no drop of their blood in his veins should fill their place. In the thirteenth century no wide gulf could be fixed between the inheritance of a kingdom and other impartible inheritances. John Balliol argued on the expressed assumption that the rules applicable to baronies were applicable to his case. If therefore at a later day we find the law of Scotland not merely rejecting the rule *Materna maternis,* but absolutely excluding all *materni* even when the inheritance has come from their side, we may suspect that it is no true witness to the ideas of the thirteenth century, and take to heart the lesson that a system that looks exceedingly "agnatic" and that refuses to trace inheritable blood through a female except in the descending line, is not of necessity very old. Those rules of inheritance which deal with unusual cases are often the outcome of no recondite causes, but of some superficial whim.

The rule *Paterna paternis, materna maternis* may exclude from our view certain of those ascending lines which go upwards from our *propositus;* it will not enable us to make a choice between the lines that are not thus excluded. Thus suppose that the person whose heir is wanted was himself the purchaser of the land, none of his kinsmen are excluded and we have to choose between many ascending lines. We think it certain that in the thirteenth century, as in later times, the line first chosen was that which we may call agnatic, the line, that is, in which there is an unbroken succession of male ancestors, and that so long as there was any one who could trace descent from a member of that line no other person could inherit. Such a rule is a natural part of a system which postpones females to males. Just as the inheritance will go down from father to son so long as the male line is unbroken, so when we look upwards we first look along the male line. The remotest person in the remotest *parentela* that comes down from an ancestor who stands in that line is preferable to the nearest person in the nearest *parentela* that does not start from a member of that line.[56]

---

[56] It is difficult to prove even this from the text-books. Glanvill, Bracton, Fleta, and Britton are apt to speak as though in ascending we might cross from line to line in order to find the nearest ancestor, so

Beyond this all is dark. We gravely doubt whether during the middle ages any clear canons were established to regulate the order of succession as between those *parentelae* which could trace their kinship to the *propositus* only through some female ancestor of his. That "the male blood is more worthy than the female" was indubitable; Adam was created before Eve; but a definite calculus which should balance worthiness of blood against proximity of degree was wanting. Our lawyers were not at pains to draw pictures of their own; they transplanted the trees of the Romanists, and these trees could not take firm root in English soil. In Elizabeth's day an exceedingly simple problem was treated as an open question for which the Year Books provided no obvious solution. A man purchases land and dies without issue; who shall inherit from him, his mother's brother or a cousin who is his father's mother's father's son's son? When this question had been decided in favour of the claimant who was of kin to the father of the *propositus,* it still left open a question about the order of precedence among the female ancestors upon the father's side, a question which was warmly debated and never really settled until a statute of 1833 rounded off our law of inheritance by declaring that the mother of the more remote male paternal ancestor is preferable to the mother of a less remote male paternal ancestor.[57] That in an age which allowed no testamentary disposition of freehold lands cases never happened which raised such problems as these is hardly to be believed; but, to all seeming, they did not happen with sufficient frequency to generate a body of established doctrine.[58]

Our law's treatment of "the half-blood" has been a favourite theme for historical speculators. We have been sent for its origin

that, *e.g.* we might prefer the father's mother's *parentela* to the father's father's father's *parentela*. But this we think due to the inadequate "arbores" that they had in their minds.

[57] Stat. 3–4 Will. IV c. 106. sec. 8. Hale, *Common Law,* 6th ed. p. 328, had taken one side in the dispute, Blackstone, *Comm.* ii. 238, the other. Blackstone's departure from Hale's rule gave rise to controversy of a kind that has been very rare in England, the academic discussion of a point of law that is of no practical importance.

[58] After looking through a large number of records of the thirteenth century we are much struck by the extreme rarity of cases in which any of the more recondite rules of inheritance are called into play.

back to a time when "feuds" were not yet hereditary; we have been sent to "the agnatic family." As a matter of fact we do not believe that the phenomenon which has to be explained is a very ancient one. It is this: Our common law utterly excludes "the half-blood." No one who is connected with the *propositus* only by the half-blood can inherit from him. A man buys land and dies without issue; his half-brother, whether consanguineous or uterine, can not inherit from him. If there is no kinsman or kinswoman of the whole blood forthcoming, the land will escheat to the lord. Of course all the descendants of a man or a woman are of kin to him or to her by the whole blood. A man leaves a daughter by his first wife, a son by his second wife; his son inherits from him. A man leaves no sons and no issue of sons, but five daughters, two by his first wife and three by his second wife; they will all inherit from him together and take equal shares. Any question about the half-blood can only arise when this man has ceased to be and one of his descendants has become the *propositus,* and no one of them, according to our law, will become the *propositus* until he obtains an actual seisin of the land. A man leaves a son and a daughter by a first wife, and a son by a second wife. His eldest son inherits and is entitled to seisin. If however he dies without issue before he has obtained seisin, then his father is still the *propositus.* That father has a daughter and a son. The son inherits before the daughter. He is not inheriting from his half-brother; he is inheriting from his father. On the other hand, if the elder son acquires seisin, all is altered. When he dies without issue he is the *propositus.* We have now to choose between a sister by the whole blood and a half-brother, and we hold, not merely that the sister is to be preferred, but that the land shall sooner escheat to the lord than go to the half-brother. *Possessio fratris de feodo simplici facit sororem esse heredem;* the entry of the eldest son has made his sister heir.

Now it seems clear that the law of Bracton's day had not yet taken this puzzling shape. Bracton holds that the half-blood can inherit, though it is postponed to the whole blood. First we take the case in which a man purchases land and dies without issue leaving a sister of the whole blood and a brother of the half-blood. The sister will inherit to the exclusion of her brother; but after her death and the failure of her heirs the brother will inherit;

he is merely postponed, not excluded for good and all. Next we take the case in which a man inherits land from his father and then dies without issue, leaving a sister of the whole blood and a consanguineous half-brother. Now some were for holding that the half-brother should in this case be preferred to the sister, and Bracton, though his mind may have fluctuated, probably shared this opinion. The distinction which turns on the question whether the eldest son has acquired seisin seems to be only just coming to the front. Fleta and Britton agree that if a man purchases land and dies without issue, his sister by the whole blood will be preferred to the half-brother. They do not affirm, as Bracton does, that in this case if there is no brother or sister of the whole blood, a brother or sister of the half-blood will be admitted; but neither do they deny this. As to the case in which the *propositus* has inherited land from his father, Fleta is for preferring the consanguineous half-brother to the sister of the whole blood, and this without reference to seisin; Britton is for preferring the sister by the whole blood, and this without reference to seisin. What is more, Britton holds that if a man has two wives and a son by each, one of those sons can inherit from his half-brother land that had descended to that half-brother from his mother; in other words, that I may on the death of my half-brother inherit land which belonged to my stepmother, though here of course I am not of the blood of the purchaser.

These are not speculative fancies. If we turn to the records of the time, we shall see much uncertainty; we shall see claims brought into court which the common law of a later day would not have tolerated for an instant, and juries declining to solve the simplest problems. Even Britton's doctrine that through my half-brother I can acquire the land of my stepfather or stepmother, does not seem ridiculous. In Edward I's reign the law seems to be setting its face against the claims of the half-blood; but even in Edward II's there is a great deal more doubt and disputation than we might have expected. It is clear that a sister will inherit from her brother of the whole blood a tenement that he purchased, and exclude a brother by the half-blood; but that the brother of the half-blood is utterly incapable of taking such a tenement is by no means so plain. When the tenement has descended from father or mother to the eldest son, the lawyers are beginning to make every thing turn on seisin, but they have not yet fully established the dogma that if once that eldest son is seised his half-brother will be incapable of inheriting from him.

Our persuasion is that the absolute exclusion of the half-blood, to which our law was in course of time committed, is neither a very ancient nor a very deep-seated phenomenon, that it tells us nothing of the original constitution of feuds nor of the agnatic family. In truth the problem that is put before us when there is talk of admitting the half-blood is a difficult one and our solution of it is likely to be capricious. We can not say now-a-days that there is any obviously proper place for the half-blood in a scheme of inheritance, especially in our "parentelic" scheme.[59] The lawyers of the thirteenth and fourteenth centuries had no ready solution, and we strongly suspect that the rule that was ultimately established had its origin in a few precedents. About such a matter it is desirable that there shall be a clear rule; the import of the rule is of no great moment. Our rule was one eminently favourable to the king; it gave him escheats; we are not sure that any profounder explanation of it would be true.[60]

---

[59] German and French customs afford a rich variety of rules. That the half-blood should be on an equality with the whole blood was rare; sometimes it took a smaller share; sometimes it was postponed; but the manner of postponing it varied from custom to custom. In 1279 it is alleged as a custom of Newcastle that the mother's inheritance will go to daughters by a first marriage in preference to a son by a second marriage. Such a custom, which has its parallel in Germany, should warn us that the rules of the common law were not the only rules that seemed natural to Englishmen.

[60] Maine: "In Agnation too is to be sought the explanation of that extraordinary rule of English Law, only recently repealed, which prohibited brothers of the half-blood from succeeding to one another's lands. In the Customs of Normandy, the rule applies to *uterine* brothers only, that is to brothers by the same mother but not by the same father; and limited in this way, it is a strict deduction from the system of Agnation, under which uterine brothers are no relations at all to one another. When it was transplanted to England, the English judges, who had no clue to its principle, interpreted it as a general prohibition against the succession of the half-blood." We have not been able to find any text of Norman Law which excludes the uterine but admits the consanguineous brother. The Grand Coutumier c. 25 B admits the consanguineous brother when the inheritance has descended from the father and the uterine brother when the inheritance has descended from the mother. As to land purchased by the *propositus,* we can see no words which declare the uterine brother incapable of inheriting. In the later custom (Art. 312) the uterine and

When an inheritance falls to the daughters of the dead man, each of these "parceners" (*participes*) is conceived as having a certain aliquot share in the as yet undivided land. This share is her "purparty" (*propars*); it will obey the ordinary rules of inheritance; it will descend to her issue, and, on failure of her issue, it will resort to her sisters or those who represent them. We may, as already noticed, see traces of an older scheme which would admit a right of accruer between sisters and the near descendants of sisters; but this was fast disappearing.[61] Once more we see the representative principle brought into play; the distribution of shares between the descendants of dead daughters is *per stirpes* not *per capita*. If we suppose the only issue of the *propositus* living at his death to be the two grand-daughters that have sprung from one of his daughters and the three that have sprung from another, the inheritance must first be halved, and then one half of it will be halved again while the other half will be divided into thirds. It would be a great mistake to suppose that our male-preferring and primogenitary system succeeded in keeping almost all of the great inheritances as unbroken wholes. Glanvill's own lands passed to three daughters. Twice within a few years the

---

consanguineous brothers can claim a share with the brothers of the whole blood. The strongholds of the distinction between the consanguineous and the uterine half-blood seem to be the Lombard law of feuds and the Scottish law. In the *Libri Feudorum* such a distinction is in its proper place and this without any reference to agnatic families. Except as an anomaly, no fief can descend to a woman or through a woman, for fiefs are the estates of a military class; and since it can not descend through a woman, it can not pass to a uterine brother. Scottish law postponed the consanguineous half-brother, and it utterly excluded the uterine half-brother, even when the land had descended from his mother. But we should like to see a proof that this is not due to the powerful influence which the *Libri Feudorum* exercised over the Scottish lawyers of the sixteenth and later centuries. Here in England and in the year 1234 it was argued that a uterine brother should exclude a sister of the whole blood from land which had descended to the *propositus* from his mother. When this was possible men were very far from "agnation." Again, for some time before 1855, Scottish law utterly excluded the mother and maternal kinsfolk even from the succession to movables; but it seems to be very doubtful whether this exclusion was ancient.

[61] So late as 1325 it is said that if a man dies leaving several daughters by different wives, and these daughters divide the inheritance, and one of them dies without issue, her share will go to her sisters of the half-blood as well as to her sisters of the whole blood.

inheritance of an Earl of Chester "fell among the spindles." The inheritance of William Marshall the regent was soon split into thirty-fifths, for one of his five daughters was represented by seven daughters.[62] For a male to get a share "by distaff right" was by no means uncommon. But generally when an estate, at all events when a great estate, became partible, it was soon physically partitioned. Any one of the parceners could demand a partition, and the days were past when a family would keep together after the death of its head. The young heiress did not long remain unespoused; her marriage was disposed of at the earliest possible moment; the rich widow generally found another husband, though the church would not bless her second union; it is rare therefore to find that any large mass of land long remains in the hands of a *feme sole.*

Germanic law seems to have set a limit to the reckoning of blood relationship, or "sib-ship." An inheritance can not be claimed by one who does not stand within a certain degree, or rather, a certain "joint" or generation, the fifth, the sixth or the seventh. The family was pictured not as a scale with degrees, nor as a tree with branches, but as a human body with joints. The parents, according to one scheme, stand in the head, brothers in the neck, first cousins at the shoulders, second cousins at the elbows, third cousins at the wrist, fourth, fifth and sixth cousins at the finger-joints; here the sib ends; seventh cousins would be "nail cousins" and there would be no legal relationship between them.[63] We may see traces of this idea in England and in Normandy.[64] The Norman custom held that the line of consanguinity did not extend beyond the seventh degree. Bracton refuses to draw the ascending line beyond the *tritavus,* the sixth ancestor of the *propositus;* beyond this point memory will not go. However, the rules for the limitation of actions that were in force in

---

[62] The annual value of a thirty-fifth share was reckoned at £217.

[63] The whole "family" which consists of parents and children stands "within the first joint," so that the reckoning by joints begins with first cousins. But a great deal is very obscure.

[64] An allusion to some such idea occurs in the Anglo-Saxon tract on Wergild. A certain payment is made only to those near relations of the slain who are within the joint (*binnan cneówe; infra genu*). In *Leg. Hen.* 70, § 20, the inheritance descends to males *in quintum geniculum;* but this is old Ripuarian law.

Bracton's day would in any ordinary case have made it impossible for even a fifth cousin to bring an action for an inheritance, for a demandant was obliged to allege that the common ancestor who connected him with the *propositus* had been seised since the coronation of Henry II.[65] The rule therefore against ascending beyond the *tritavus* fell into oblivion and then, owing to the spasmodic nature of our statutes of limitation, it becomes theoretically possible for a man to claim an inheritance from any kinsman however remote.

We turn to speak of an important episode which is intimately connected with the spread of primogeniture. In the thirteenth century the tenant in fee simple has a perfect right to disappoint his expectant heirs by conveying away the whole of his land by act *inter vivos*. Our law is grasping the maxim *Nemo est heres viventis*. Glanvill wrote just in time, though only just in time, to describe an older state of things.

Several distinctions must be taken. We must distinguish between military tenure and free socage; between land that has come to the dead man by descent ("heritage") and land that he has otherwise acquired ("conquest"); between the various purposes for which an alienation is made.[66] Without his expectant heir's consent the tenant may give reasonable marriage portions to his daughters, may bestow something on retainers by way of reward, and give something to the church. His power over his conquest is greater than his power over his heritage; but if he has only conquest he must not give the whole away; he must not utterly disinherit the expectant heir. Curiously enough, as it may seem to us, he has a much greater power of providing for daughters, churches and strangers than of providing for his own sons. Without the consent of his eldest son he can "hardly" give any part of his heritage to a younger son. The bastard therefore is better off than the legitimate younger son. Glanvill confesses that

---

[65] Not only must you take as your *propositus* one who died seised within the appointed period, but you may not "resort" to one who died beyond that period.

[66] Glanvill contrasts *hereditas* with *quaestus*. In borrowing from beyond the Tweed the words *heritage* and *conquest* we show that in England the distinction soon became unimportant. To express it we have no terms of our own less cumbrous than "lands which have come to a person by inheritance," "lands that have come to him by purchase."

this is a paradox; but it is law. As to the man who holds partible socage, he can give nothing, be it heritage, be it conquest, to any son, beyond the share that would fall to that son by inheritance. Glanvill however is far from defining an exact rule for every possible case; he nowhere tells us in terms of arithmetic what is that reasonable portion which the father may freely give away. We can see however that one main restraint has been the deeply rooted sentiment that a father ought not to give one of his sons a preference over the others; they are equals and should be treated as equals. In the case of partible socage land this sentiment still governs; but the introduction of primogeniture has raised a new problem. When Glanvill is writing the court is endeavoring to put the eldest son in the advantageous position that is occupied by each of the sokeman's expectant heirs; without his consent he should not be deprived by any gift made to his brothers of that which was to come to him upon his father's death. But under the new law what was to have come to him at his father's death was the whole of his father's land. Are we then to secure all this for him and that too in the name of a rule which has heretofore made for equality among sons? If so, then we come to the paradox that it is better to be a bastard than a legitimate younger son. This could not long be tolerated. Free alienation without the heir's consent will come in the wake of primogeniture. These two characteristics which distinguish our English law from her nearest of kin, the French customs, are closely connected. . . .

Part **V**

Law, Person,
and Corporation

Huebner's book on the history of German laws was introduced in translation to the English by Vinogradoff. In his writings, Huebner was linked to Vinogradoff and also to Maitland in many ways. Not only did he make use of information put forth by his colleagues in England, but they pursued the same ends: namely, to give social and historical depth to the law, and to use the law to gain insight into society. To the anthropologist Huebner is particularly important for his methodology. In the first part of his chapter, for instance, he asks the question: What is a person? and finds that in early German law merely to be born a human being was not enough to earn for a child the capacity for rights in society. The child had first to be received, or adopted, into the family of its father and its birth had to be validated.

The distinction between man's biological and social being is important in anthropology, particularly in the light of Bronislaw Malinowski's analyses of Trobriand Island society and Ralph Linton's theoretical work on social status and role, work done in the 1920's and '30's. Huebner in the last century was keenly aware of the underlying issues and submitted them to a thorough scrutiny.

231

A close analysis of the juristic and the corporate person is given in the second part of the chapter. Here Huebner makes common cause with Maitland on the origin of the association as first discussed by Gierke. The notion of the sib, or the self-perpetuating kinship group in general, as a corporation has been presented more recently by Lowie, Krader* and others. It is a juristic person insofar as it is repository of responsibilities: if it is answerable for the legal, e.g., criminal, acts of its members. Gierke, Huebner, Maitland, and others have shown how the form of the corporation as a social and legal person was molded by its early history.

The discussion of manor (*Mark*) rights and collective peasant associations should be read in conjunction with Vinogradoff's discussions of the organization of the Anglo-Saxon manor and rural community.

Huebner's work is of greater interest, however, than simply as a contribution to the early history of the idea of personality in society. The relationship of social, psychological, and legal personality still leaves much to be explored. Huebner's application of these relationships to early German society and law widens our knowledge of social processes and should lead to further examination of some of the basic principles of modern law and anthropology.

In the selection from Maitland, different kinds of early corporations are examined, in particular the church and the royal office, as well as the personality of the corporation and the king as a corporation sole. The notion of the corporation leads to the contemporary discussion of personality created by society, the persona ficta. Maitland believed that the king as a corporate (that is, perpetual) being in his office was a freak of English law, for the idea of the king's two bodies, the natural and the corporate, Maitland regarded as a bit of English sixteenth-century mysticism. Ernest Kantorowicz, in *The King's Two Bodies* (1957), has shown how this idea was developed on the European continent, and Meyer Fortes has generalized it in respect

---

* Robert H. Lowie, *Primitive Society* (New York: Liveright, 1947), Ch. VI. Lowie here refers to Philbrick, the translator, but the source is Huebner. Lawrence Krader, *Social Organization of the Mongol-Turkic Pastoral Nomads* (The Hague: Mouton & Co., 1963), Introduction.

to the ritual, status, and role of the king in Ashanti, West Africa.
Fortes conceived that at one time there was no clear-cut distinction between the king's official standing as king and that which
he held in his private capacity. Maitland's analysis of the socio-
legal nature of the corporate personality was based upon Maine's
theory of the corporation and on Gierke's work on the association.

The question of the corporation and the person created by law
and society is of the highest theoretical and practical importance,
both in law and in anthropology. A person is that aspect of the
human being whose existence has only a social derivation, structure, and function; his, her, or its legal existence is derived
therefrom. A natural person is a social person established on the
basis of a biological fact—the human being as a physical organ-
ism. From this point of departure, the fictive or artificial person
is treated within the legal and moral limitations of practice of
the society, as though it were the same as the natural person, both
having their social existence affirmed by due process of law and
of related social rules. The corporation is in this sense an artificial person. However, the process of affirming the existence and,
from this, the rights, obligations, duties, responsibilities, and
status of the person, natural or artificial, is not a simple one.
Society in its advanced and complex forms does not affirm the
existence of the social person directly as did the father in the
ancient and medieval Germanic practice; the state has taken over
this function and performs the act of affirmation through its
constituent agencies, the offices created within and under its jurisdiction. (There are other agencies which also act in this way on
behalf of the society as a whole, such as churches, or canonical
authorities in general; with these the state comes to terms. Thus
the question is far from simple.)

Corporate bodies within the state, created under the state, are
autonomous, but not sovereign in the way that the state is sovereign. The corporate bodies are autonomous in that they run
their own affairs, but are ultimately dependent upon the sovereign
organ of society, the state. As autonomous bodies within the
state, the corporations are thus shielded from the direct participation in and judgment of the social morality and are lacking in
social responsibility.

The liberty which corporations enjoy follows from the consideration that they are autonomous and therefore self-governing within the state; but they are not natural persons. For natural persons are members of society and therefore directly participate in its moral judgments; possibly they are also members of corporations, subject to the rules of the corporation, whereas the corporation is subject only to its rules, as approved by the law of the sovereignty as a social agency. However, the degree to which the social morality and corporate behavior coincide is controlled chiefly by negative factors: the interdiction of what the corporation does or may do in the light of the law and indirectly of the social morality. The corporation may therefore act in a way that is even contrary to the social morality, if it has not been specifically interdicted from doing so.

The matter of the social morality in those societies under the sovereignty of the state is complicated further: in a complex society different social classes may have different moralities, as different ethnic and religious groups, etc., within it. And even if many or all of these moralities may be seen ultimately as variations on one general moral system, they usually are sufficiently different and mutually opposed to cause conflict on moral issues. Under the state, one morality becomes official doctrine. Again, the state is a social and legal agency which adopts the moral view of that class or corporate body which is closest to it in interests and personnel—the ruling class. This fact serves to remove the corporation further from any answerability to even the most general social morality. Such questions have never been resolved in the judging of the actions of corporations. But within practical limits, to preserve the civil peace, the various social agencies which are (more or less) answerable to some significant segment of the social morality, however defined, will in fact retain a degree of control over the artificial persons created under the state and the law, so that, negatively, these agencies will act to prevent a continued divergence of the corporate bodies from the interest and morality of society.

The issues regarding the nature of the corporation and its relation to the society, which are raised by Huebner and Maitland in the selections incorporated in this part, are important issues of the present time. They are triply important, for they touch the social life of everyone, they have not been thoroughly explored, and still less have they been resolved. The closing part of this book is therefore devoted to the posing and documenting of open questions today, opened in the formative period of Western civilization, the period of its early law.

The most valuable historical contribution to the problems raised here, despite its outdated frame of reference, remains J. P. Davis, *Corporations* (2 vols.; New York: Putnam's, 1905). This work has been reprinted by Capricorn Books (New York: 1961), with an introduction by Abram Chayes. The introduction is an important contemporary statement of the legal side of the study of the corporation, pointing out the deficiency in its social scientific study; our study is pointed to the deficiency, not to fill out, but to indicate its derivation in Western culture history.*

L. K.

---

* For further discussion of the relation between the state and the corporation, see Lawrence Krader, *Formation of the State* (Englewood Cliffs, N.J.: Prentice-Hall, 1966), Chap. I.

§§ 10

MAN, RIGHT, AND ASSOCIATION

Rudolf Huebner

Man as Holder of Rights

CAPACITY FOR RIGHTS
(*Rechtsfähigkeit*)

Our present-day simple and perspicuous arrangement of the law of persons, based on a recognition of every human being as a holder of rights, belongs only to a modern period of civilization. German law, in its beginnings, like other systems, by no means treated all human beings as legally equal. To many classes it utterly denied all legal worth, to others it attributed only a partial worth. Only gradually was this primitive view overcome. With it there disappeared contrasts and distinctions which had once possessed profound significance in social life, above all that division into estates which characterized the medieval world. Even the Christian doctrine of the moral equality of men could not overcome this—albeit far-seeing spirits like Eike von Repgow recognized the legal equality of all men as a tenet of religion and morality, justifying this by the fact that God had created man in

From Rudolf Huebner, *A History of German Private Law*, tr. F. S. Philbrick, with an Introduction by Paul Vinogradoff (Boston: Little, Brown, 1918), pp. 41–52, 110–159.

his image and had given salvation to all equally through his martyrdom.

The doctrine of the Law of Nature first carried this view to final triumph. Under the dominance of its ideas serfdom was abolished, the feudal class divisions of society into estates were swept away, and the legal equality of different religious faiths established. The principle of the equality of men or of citizens, which found express adoption in many German constitutions in imitation of foreign models, was established without restriction within the field of private law: every man is a person in the legal sense, a subject of rights, *i.e.* "capable of appearing as the holder and bearer of rights." Hence the modern State, in Germany as elsewhere, banished slavery utterly from its soil, and in the more modern codifications it was explicitly provided that foreign slaves should become free the instant they should set foot within the boundaries of the State. The limitations in this respect still retained in the Prussian *Allgemeines Landrecht* of 1794 (II, 5, §§ 196–199) were abolished by a special statute in 1857.

In this case, therefore, development came, by way of exception, through statutory simplification. Yet it should not be forgotten that this realization of formal legal equality accompanied a steady deepening of economic contrasts, and that culture, particularly, has in most recent times created social divisions which at least equal in actual importance the one-time division between the free and the unfree—although perhaps this new contrast is itself about to lose its distinctness.

CAPACITY FOR LEGAL ACTION
(*Handlungsfähigkeit*)

In no stage of its development can the legal order ignore certain natural differences between persons. When it has so risen to a recognition of the equality, in principle, of all individuals, it must still treat minors and persons in tutelage otherwise than adults. Formerly sex also made a great difference, but modern times have established to an increasing extent the equality of man and woman in the private law. Sickness, also, was formerly of more widespread legal effect than it is to-day; though law must, under all circumstances, take into consideration diseased disturbances of mental capacity.

These differences in natural qualities and conditions do not destroy legal personality, the capacity for rights; but they do make more difficult any independent participation in legal transactions, or render this wholly impossible: they restrict or wholly do away with capacity for legal action.

Beginning of Capacity for Rights

BIRTH

Germanic law did not, generally speaking, recognize capacity for rights as beginning before one's appearance as an independent human being; in other words, not until after birth. Certain provisions, however, of the Frankish law would seem to indicate that its original theory attributed to the child in womb a capacity for rights in relation to property. Later, however, German law, like other systems, contented itself with holding open to such a child the acquisition of rights that would inhere in it in case it should be born alive, and especially the acquisition of a paternal inheritance—the actual distribution being delayed until the delivery of the decedent's pregnant widow. The medieval law thus realized an idea which the Roman system first formulated in principle; and though the modern codes adhered to the Roman system, they gave heed at the same time to native legal ideas. We find in them also the provision that a curator might be appointed for the *nasciturus* during gestation. On the other hand the moment of birth was decisive of its social status, nationality, and membership in the commune. However, in case a father lost his nobility during his wife's pregnancy, many legal systems did not let this affect the child.

ADOPTION

In the primitive law, unlike that of today, the natural fact of birth was by no means sufficient basis for the acquisition of full capacity for rights. Whether the child should be adopted into the family of its father, and thereby become a member of the legal community, depended, moreover, according to Germanic law, upon the father's will. He might expose it, *i.e.* disown it. "The newborn child lies on the floor until the father declares whether he will or will not let it live. If yes, he takes it up, or orders it taken up; it seems that the term for midwife (*Hebamme*) comes from this act (*Aufheben*)." This adoption (*Aufnahme*, "taking up") was the visible recognition of the child by its father.

The right of exposure was gone so soon as the first acts in care of the child had been done. "A child exposed must not yet have tasted anything whatever; a drop of milk or of honey assured it life." In cases of necessity, as *e.g.* after the father's death, the act of offering nourishment might stand in lieu of a formal recognition by the father. The first sprinkling or the first bathing of the child had a like effect according to primitive ideas.

The bestowal of a name, which was a necessary consequence of adopting the new-born child, was taken in hand among the Scandinavians immediately after birth, and among the other Germanic races (as among the Greeks and Romans) on the ninth day thereafter—with which fact seems to be connected the later jocular saying, with reference to the Swabians, that they remained blind for nine days after birth.

When the right of exposure disappeared, under the influence of Christianity, the necessity of a formal adoption of the child into the family disappeared with it.

PROOF OF BIRTH

Birth alive was a precondition to the origin of legal personality. In accord with the formalistic character of Germanic procedural law definite facts were required to be established when the birth of a living child was questioned. According to the South-Germanic systems the proof must be to the effect that the child had opened its eyes and seen the roof-ridge and four walls of the house. In North Germany emphasis was laid upon its filling with its cries the four walls. Often too, a cry of a particular character was required—*e.g.* in Westphalia one that could be heard through an oaken plank or a wall. It is Brunner's conjecture that this requirement of the child's cry, found in the whole body of Saxon, Frankish, and Anglo-Norman sources, is connected with the fact that the primitive law required the testimony of men, and in critical cases these could give proof of life only as ear, not as eye, witnesses; since for reasons of propriety men were not allowed to be present at the delivery.

Inasmuch as precisely these manifestations of life, and not any others one might choose, were regarded as proofs in the theory of the old law, the legal consequences attendant on a living birth did not follow when these exact facts could not be established, notwithstanding that the child might have lived without seeing or crying.

Only gradually did it become possible to establish the fact of life by other signs, until here too, with the abolishment of formal methods of proof, foothold was gained for an untrammelled judicial estimate of proof. Those manifestations of life that were once exclusively heeded retained thenceforth merely the importance of particularly reliable evidence, as *e.g.* still in the Prussian *Allgemeines Landrecht* (I, 1, § 13), which declared the birth of a child established "when reliable witnesses, present at the birth, shall have clearly heard its voice."

VIABILITY

Now when we consider that the older Germanic sources laid down the requirement of the child's cry; that the West-Gothic law required that a child, in order to inherit and leave property, must have lived ten days and been baptized; and that the bestowal of a name requisite to the acquisition of full capacity for rights must have taken place not earlier than nine days after birth—it becomes obvious that Germanic law attached legal consequences to the birth of such children only as proved capable of life. Those brought into the world in so premature a state that they could not maintain life, and monstrosities that showed no human form, were regarded as incapable of having rights. In this sense the *Sachsenspiegel,* for example, required (I, 33) that the child should be "large enough," *i.e.* born at such a stage of maturity, "that it should be capable of living" (*lifhaftich*).

Even after the Reception men held fast in the common law, under the influence of the Germanic legal ideas, to this requisite of vitality, interpreting in this sense the expressions of the Roman law, particularly law 2, Cod. *de postumis,* 6, 29. Savigny was the first to take the opposite view; nevertheless, in more recent years the older view has again found champions as against the common law. The modern Territorial systems did not adopt the requisite in question, and in this respect they were followed by the present

German and Swiss civil codes; only the *Code Civil* (§§ 725, 906) retained it.

REGISTRY OF BIRTH

The registry of births was in general ill cared for in the Middle Ages. The custom observed since the 400s by the clergy of keeping a register of baptisms died out, to reappear only in the 1400s in the practice of individual bishops, who aimed thereby to make possible the proof of disabilities for marriage. The Council of Trent made the Church's records, as registers of births and marriages, a general institution of Catholic countries, and the church ordinances of the evangelical church devised similar regulations. These church records were then recognized by the State as public documents. For all that these methods of authentication remained imperfect. Baptisms often took place only a long time after birth; the registers were confined to a definite diocese, were often ill kept, and imperfectly preserved; above all, all those persons who did not belong to the recognized Christian churches—the Dissidents, the Jews; in France, also the Protestants—were wholly excluded from them.

All these circumstances contributed powerfully to the introduction of governmental registers of personal status. Introduced first into individual Italian cities in the 1300s and 1400s, they received in France, through the legislation of the Revolution and the *Code Civil* (§§ 34 fg.), a universal application that served as a model for later times. Germany followed the French example in the imperial statute on personal status of February 6, 1875, which had been preceded by a Prussian statute, identical in content, of March 9, 1874. In the regions of the French law in Germany registers of civil status had already been introduced with the *Code Civil*, and had for the most part since then been maintained; only in a few regions, as *e.g.* in Hesse and Hamburg, had they been again displaced by reactionary legislation. Here, and in the other German States until the enactment of the imperial statute just referred to, men contented themselves with increasing the dependability of the church records, with the introduction of similar books in the synagogues for Jews, and with the intrustment to village magistrates or judges of the registration of dissidents and non-Christians.

Loss of Capacity for Rights

Natural death always involved, and in the law of to-day it alone involves, the end of capacity for rights. For purposes of record and for the proof of death, ecclesiastical records served in former times as they did for births; their place was later taken by civil registers.

With regard to the question whether, in case of the loss of several persons under circumstances of common peril, some should be regarded as having died before others—a question that may be of importance in the settlement of inheritances—no particular rule seems to have been adopted in most of the older Germanic sources. The modern State systems, with the exception of the *Code Civil* and a few Swiss statutes, rejected the presumption, taken over from the Roman into the common law, of the decease of certain persons before others—of parents before children beyond tutelary age, of children under tutelage before parents; on the contrary they generally established a presumption of the simultaneous death of those lost under circumstances of a common peril. To this principle the Civil Code has adhered. The Swiss Civil Code (§ 32) provides the same for all cases in which the time of death of the several persons is incapable of proof—*i.e.* it does not limit the presumption to death in a common disaster.

SOCIAL OUTLAWRY (*Friedlosigheit—* "PEACELESSNESS")

The primitive law was far from indissolubly associating capacity for legal rights with physical life, and therefore it could withdraw such capacity from a living person and thereby annihilate his jural existence, his legal personality. This was effected by putting him out of the peace, which was the central idea of Teutonic criminal law, and gave reality to the idea "that he who breaks the peace puts himself outside the peace." Outlawry in its extreme form constituted complete destruction of legal personality; the "peaceless" man lost his place in the circles of his fellows in the sib and folk; his wife became widow, his children were treated as orphans, his property was forfeited, his home destroyed. In time outlawry became less prominent. It retained its place longest in legal procedure, as the ultimate result of contumacy, in the form of judicial process.

CIVIL DEATH

While outlawry, even in the form of judicial process, finally disappeared from the law in Germany, there was developed from it elsewhere the legal institute known as civil death; particularly in France where the after effects of outlawry (*forbannito*) united the effects of the Roman *capitis diminutio* and *infamia* with those of Canonic excommunication. So late as in an ordinance of 1670 it was decreed as the consequence of contumacy, quite in the old-time manner; and during the 1700s it was involved in every condemnation to a capital penalty. And although it thereby became a punishment cruel in the extreme and was with justice violently attacked, it was employed freely against the Emigrants in the Revolution, and still found recognition in the *Code Civil* (§§ 22–23)—though not in the *Code Pénal*. In the form in which it appears in the *Code Civil*—according to which one condemned to civil death lost all his property rights and control of his heritable estate, became incapable of disposing of his property, saw his marriage *ipso facto* dissolved, and could enter into no future marriage—the institution was adopted in Germany in the regions of the French law. It was adopted, further, by the Baden *Landrecht* and the Bavarian criminal code. However, it had no long-lived authority in Germany. Modern ideas called for its abandonment. It was abolished in France by a statute of 1854, and was also done away with in Germany—in part even earlier than in France, as *e.g.* in Prussia by the Constitution (Art. 10). The present Imperial Criminal Code does not mention it, and has thus wholly done away with it for the entire Empire. English law still knows a "civil death"; it occurs, however, only with extreme infrequency, namely in cases of the still recognized penalty of civil *outlawry*.

CLAUSTRAL DEATH

In the Middle Ages those who entered a monastic order or sisterhood were, as the gloss to the *Sachsenspiegel* put it, "regarded by the world as dead" from the moment of taking vows.

An ecclesiastic "unburdened himself," to use again the expression of the *Sachsenspiegel* (I, 25, § 3), with his entry into the cloister, of the Territorial and feudal law. The English law as early as the 1100s, and later the French law, therefore explicitly designated him as civilly dead. It is true that this claustral death was a different thing from the institute discussed above, which arose out of the old outlawry. Monks were often enough immersed in worldly affairs, but in the view of the secular law they had no independent will; they were subjected to another's, "which as a matter of religion might be thought of as the divine will, but within the sphere of temporal law was represented by the will of the abbot." Entry into the cloister destroyed, therefore, proprietary capacity; and precisely herein lay the motive for the frequency of monastic vows: they were a favored means of avoiding the partition of family property. With the taking of his vows an ecclesiastic lost the power to dispose by testament of his property; this reverted at once, like the estate of a decedent, to his blood relations, or (as the case might be) to the heirs or legatees already by him appointed. Any further acquisition of property was for him impossible; nor could the cloister inherit for him. These rules of the medieval secular law were followed, among the modern codes, by the Prussian *Allgemeines Landrecht,* which declared (II, 11, §§ 1199, 1200) monks and nuns incapable of acquiring, possessing, or disposing of ownership and lesser rights in property. On the other hand the Canon law assumed a wholly different position: it did not in matters of property law nullify the personality of the ecclesiastic; rather, it transferred this to his cloister. This principle was accepted by the common law, and by the Territorial systems other than the Prussian. Limits were very generally set by modern statutes to property accumulations in a dead hand. The Civil Code, by recognizing (EG, 87) the limits placed upon such acquisitions in the State systems, has taken the same position.

ENSLAVEMENT

The older law recognized a voluntary enslavement (*obnoxiatio*), and enslavement might also be imposed as a punishment. There was likewise involved in this a destruction of legal personality during life; for persons in bondage were not originally regarded as subjects of rights. Thus *e.g.* Bracton, an English jurist of the 1200s, speaks explicitly of the *mors civilis* of slaves, since they are subjected to their lord precisely as the monks to the abbot. Inasmuch, however, as the harsh attitude of the old law was early abandoned and the legal personality of the unfree recognized, there remained in such cases thereafter only a mere restriction upon capacity for rights.

PRESUMPTIVE DEATH

In the Middle Ages it was a common occurrence that uncertainty prevailed at his home concerning the fate of one who had left his country; for travelling consumed much time and was dangerous, and the possibility of sending messages was slight. Especially one who was compelled to journey over sea as merchant, pilgrim, or crusader, often lost for a long period communication with his home. A prince of Mecklenburg, Henry I the Pilgrim, who had gone to the Holy Land, remained for six and twenty years (1271–1298) in captivity among the infidels; only four years after his capture did the news of it reach his people; afterward, rumors of his death were repeatedly circulated, and only his return finally put an end to uncertainty. In such cases of disappearance, as the Magdeburg and Lübeck laws show, the property of the missing person was delivered to his next heirs, although at first only provisionally; they were bound to give it back to one who returned, and to give security therefor in taking temporary possession. But if the missing person never returned, the possession was unchanged, and so became a definitive inheritance. At what moment the period of uncertainty should be taken to be ended and the death of the missing person to be certain, German law left open for judicial determination in each case, setting up no definite periods. The proof of death was not particularly difficult, because it could be made by the oath of him who averred it; for the medieval law of procedure permitted proof by oath even of those facts which the oath taker merely believed, without having independent knowledge thereof. Moreover, all definite proof of death could be wholly excused when missing persons, as the Magdeburg *Questions* put it (I, 7, D, 6), "could not in nature have lived longer," *i.e.* when they had already passed the years of a normal age. So long as death could neither be proved, nor assumed with full assurance on grounds of nature, the absent person was regarded as living. And so, for example, the son of the Mecklenburg prince above referred to, when he had attained majority and had taken over the regency for his father, always used the latter's seal in acts of government.

After the Reception the doctrine of unexplained disappearance received a more ordered form through the further development of older German legal ideas and their association with the results of Italian theory and practice. In the first place, fixed periods were introduced, and formal legal presumptions attached to them; and further, an ordered procedure was prescribed as a precondition to official declaration of death.

The classic Roman law knew, as little as did the older Germanic law, statutory presumptions of life and death; the judge was permitted to draw from the circumstances an inference of probable fact after an untrammelled weighing of the evidence. On the other hand, the Italian practice, "under the influence of the theory of formal proof," developed from the assumption (current among the Roman jurists as well) that a hundred years were to be regarded as the extreme age of man, the strong presumption being that the missing person should be taken to be living to the end of his 100th year of life ("presumption of life"), and from that moment on as dead ("presumption of death"). The former presumption was, however, rebuttable by proof, which in turn was facilitated by further presumptions.

These presumptions of life and of death were adopted in Germany. In the practice of the Saxon courts particularly, especially of the court of lay-judges at Leipzig, the attainment of a definite age was thus treated as decisive. The only change was that under the influence of Leipzig jurists, especially of Carpzow, the limit was lowered, in echo of the saying of the Psalmist, from the 100th to the 70th full year of life ("Saxon system"). This age then attained a common law authority.

A mode of calculating the necessary period, differing from the Saxon, evidences of which already occur occasionally in the Middle Ages, and which agrees also with the older French customary law, was prevalent in Silesia ("Silesian system"). This emphasized, not age, but the duration of absence, requiring for the assumption of death the passage of a definite period of time since the receipt of the last news, without regard to the age of the person missing. The expiration of thirty years was originally required; later, men were content with twenty, or more frequently with ten years. This method of reckoning was adopted by the Prussian *Allgemeines Landrecht* and by the Austrian Civil Code. Under certain circumstances the two systems were united; for when the missing person was of very great age a shorter period of absence was deemed sufficient—*e.g.* the Prussian law lowered it from ten to five years for persons above 65 years of age; or it was wholly waived—*e.g.* at 100 years according to the *Code Civil*, at 90 according to the Saxon Code. And according to many systems of law the requisite of advanced age was wholly disregarded in cases of exceedingly long absences; as *e.g.*, in Bavarian and French law, in case of an absence for 30 years.

All such periods were much shortened in case the missing person was proved to have been in jeopardy of life, as for example in a shipwreck or a theater fire. Notably after the great wars of 1864, 1866, and 1870–71, special statutes were enacted according to which the death of missing soldiers should be assumed after the running of a short period, or from a definite date in the future. The Swiss Civil Code (§ 34) has derived from these the new and general principle that the death of any person shall be regarded as proved, even though no one may have seen the corpse, whenever he disappeared under conditions that make his death seemingly certain.

The Saxon practice united in a peculiar way the imported presumptions of life and death with the native rules concerning provisional instatement in actual possession, transforming the latter, in analogy to the Roman *cura absentis,* into a so-called *cura anomala,* a peculiar guardianship of absent persons. A *curator absentis* was appointed at the instance of the next heirs for an absent person whose fate began to be doubtful, and thereupon the heritable estate was turned over to them with full powers of administration, subject to their giving security. The time reached to which was attached the presumption of death, the heir received back his security and acquired the inheritance definitively; moreover he was thenceforth treated as though the inheritance had fallen to him at the moment when the *cura* had been instituted (*successio ex tunc*). This antedating of the fact of inheritance was in harmony, however, with the older Germanic law, which knew no succession save in individual pieces of heritable property. It was only because men held fast to this view of the Germanic law, despite the theoretical reception of the principle of universal succession, that they did not at first remark the contradiction between the presumption of life and the antedating of the accrual of the heritage. But later the *successio ex tunc* was abandoned, being replaced by a *successio ex nunc;* that is, that moment was made decisive of definitive accrual of the heritage in which the [absolute] presumption of death took effect. This rule attained a common law authority. . . .

Juristic Persons and Other Associations

Associational Organization in Germanic Law[1]

SIGNIFICANCE OF THE ASSOCIATION

If we designate by the expression "association" (*Genossenschaft*), with entire generality, unions of several human beings into legal communities of narrower or wider scope, closer or laxer structure, such associations have at all times been numerous and of great importance in Germanic law. A strong associational quality is stamped upon Germanic law from the earliest times. It gives this a character distinct from that of the ancient Roman law. At the same time the fact is not to be overlooked that little is known respecting the actual development of the society and partnership law of antiquity: the scanty rules of the *Corpus Juris Civilis,* a meager final selection from a technical literature dealing with a practice that is lost to us, cannot be compared with the superabundant wealth of information that we possess respecting the actual legal practice, unaltered by scientific editing, of the Middle Ages. Nor should it be forgotten that this associational character is not, strictly speaking, a thing exclusively German. It is rather peculiar to all Germanic peoples; likely enough it had its richest development in England.

The political and economic conditions of the Middle Ages everywhere favored its development. While the omnipotence of

---

[1] Of fundamental importance are the great works of *Gierke* (see Introduction).

tic" or "group" (*Verbands-*) person beside the physical persons of its members, and increases by one their number as holders of legal rights.

Germanic and German law both attained to the development of these associational forms with independent legal personality, but this result was only gradually realized. It presupposes advanced cultural conditions, and a nicety of juristic technic that is not present in the youth-time of a race. The understanding of medieval legal development has, indeed, been made particularly difficult precisely at this point, because, with the reception of the Roman law, the fundamental concepts of its law of society and partnership acquired an unqualified ascendancy. Not only was the development of Germanic legal institutions interrupted, but a just scientific appreciation of them was made impossible. Modern research into Germanic origins has effected a change in this respect. It has discovered the ideas dominant in the historical evolution and in the present-day authority of the German law of associations; and above all, it has taught us to comprehend the characteristic differences that distinguish them from the Roman conceptions, which men long regarded as the only ones conceivable. In this connection it has appeared that, as contrasted with the rules of the Roman law, which were logically a perfectly consistent whole but for that very reason indigent in content, the medieval German law produced a great variety of legal communities, distinguished only by slight differences from one another; and maintained them, despite all romanistic attacks, down to the present day.

And so a general survey should here be given of the most important forms in which the Germanic associational type of organization found legal embodiment . . . In so doing the distinction already made between unions possessing independent legal personality and those lacking in such independence, is to be postulated as legally the most important—while remembering that only in the course of time did this distinction lead to their complete separation. In the case of some personal unions, nuclei for the development therefrom of independent juristic personalities were doubtless present from the beginning. But the legal institute of juristic personality attained perfection, as already remarked, only by degrees, and everywhere only in the second half of the Middle

Ages. Accordingly, juristic persons also became differentiated only in course of time, as a legally peculiar group among the numerous associations (*Genossenschaften*) of the German law, and consequently it is impossible in this place—where the problem is to give a general view of the historical development, and of the fundamental ideas reflected in it—to adopt the viewpoint appropriate to a dogmatic presentation of the positive law of to-day, or to direct attention exclusively to those unions which were, or have become, juristic persons. On the contrary, we must follow the method of treatment chosen by Gierke and Heusler, and consider here all types of the community (*Gemeinschafts-*) law, including those which in the scheme of Roman and modern law and in the new Civil Code find their place in the law of obligations.

Specific Types of Communities in Germanic Law

The Sib (*Sippe*)

ORIGIN

The oldest type of association, existing already in the primitive Germanic period, is the union of the blood-group (*Geschlechtsverband*), the sib. The sib is "the germ of all associational life." It developed at an early day out of the household community, the patriarchally administered "greater" family, in which the primalcell of all social evolution among Aryan races is discernible, in this way: that the younger members of household communities thus grown to independence, seceded, by stratification as it were, from the common household and set up their own economic establishments. Inasmuch, however, as these derivative separate families, each of which was under the rule of its founder, maintained intact the bond with the ancestral house, the sib remained beside the separate houses as a group embracing all.

ASSOCIATIONAL CHARACTER

The Germanic sib was constituted of a fixed circle of persons related by blood. Since the primitive Germans lived in father-sibs (*Vatersippen*), *i.e.* in sibs that based their kinship solely upon descent from a common tribal male ancestor, the Germanic sib was an agnatic union. Its solidarity depended on the fact that the women belonging to a foreign sib abandoned this by their marriage, and entered the sib of their husband, while no bond of relationship resulted for him and their children with the sib of the wife and mother. In contrast to the house-community, which was organized on a theory of patriarchal power, the sib of the primitive Germans, unlike *e.g.* the Roman *gentes,* was presumably from the beginning a union of equal fellows; all adult male members, but particularly the heads of the separate households, being thus regarded. A patriarchal head was foreign to the Germanic sib.

The sib stood at the center of all social and legal relations, played a great rôle in the military and judicial organization, assured its members internal peace, and protected them against attacks from without. It was also an agrarian union, and as such the prototype of the rural associations of the Middle Ages. Already in it we note a special form of collective real rights in land, similar to those developed in the mark-associations (below, pp. 255–257) and reflecting its legal solidarity under the law of persons. Thus, when Caesar reports (B. G., VI, 22) that the land had been distributed for cultivation *"gentibus cognationibusque hominum, qui tum una coierunt,"* the *gentes* stand for the agnatic sibs, to which the Gau assigned for common cultivation the land it occupied. Clear indications from a later time of a collective right of the sib in the mark-arable have also been preserved—for example, the dispute of the *genealogiae* over the limits of their districts which is treated of in the Almannic folk-law (81). And like the land, movables also seem to have been the object of collective rights, and indeed in early times of a collective ownership, in the sib.

DISINTEGRATION

The sib, as a solidary associational group, was bound to disintegrate when cognatic relatives, those connected through women, received legal recognition beside the agnatic. Many duties therefore incumbent upon the agnatic sib were then taken over by the kinship (*Verwandtschaft*). This last took a different form in every generation—in other words, it did not constitute a solidary and exclusive body—inasmuch as only brothers and sisters of equal birth have the same paternal and maternal kindred. Economic tasks, however, fell thenceforth upon the vicinage-groups based on bonds of locality, in place of the kinship unions of the sibs. A bond of neighborhood here replaced the bond of blood-relationship; the blood-mark was transformed into a vicinage-mark.

With this change there was associated a strong re-emergence of the house-community. The position of the individual households and of their heads became the more independent, the more the sphere contracted within which the sib was active. Within the unorganized and non-exclusive body of the kinship there developed, as the narrowest community determinant of legal and economic life, the household. Unlike the sib, this continued to retain in its *pater familias* (*Hausherr,* "house-master") a monarchical head; yet it might under certain circumstances perfectly well assume an associational character—namely, whenever the family-members who had been united under one authority continued their common life after the death of the *pater familias.*

Thus, the oldest associational group had already become subordinated to new growths at an early day. The further development of community organization from the principles already dominant, although not yet wholly distinct in the sib, took place first in the vicinage (*Orts-*) associations and in the communities of "collective hand" which were derivative from the house-community. Later progress was due primarily to urban life.

The Mark-Associations[2]

ORIGIN

When the land that had been originally assigned to the sibs by the Gau merely for temporary cultivation (above, p. 254) came

[2] Questions as to the age, originating causes, and nature of the mark-associations are still sharply debated. The view represented in the text, which is the older and as yet the predominant one, and which maintains the independent primitive origin of the mark-associations, is opposed by another that denies them such character. The former theory was accepted, among others, by Varrentrapp (at least before he allowed himself to be influenced by the assumptions of Schotte, which in my opinion are unsound), v. Schwerin, Thimme, Rörig, and in essentials also by Haff. Its most aggressive opponent is Dopsch; he contends that those marks of which there are reports in the sources of the Carolingian time were not the survivals of an undemonstrable agrarian communism of primitive

in time to be held in permanent possession, and finally in ownership, by them, they were thereby transformed into unions of
definite local limits which were united physically by the land
standing in their ownership—the mark (*Mark:* signifying originally boundary, or march, later the domain enclosed)—and
personally by the bond of neighborhood that had replaced blood-
relationship. These unions, which were the mark-associations,
ordinarily coincided with the village-communities wherever, as
was most commonly the case among the early Germans, settlement took place in that form; the village-communities were, so
to speak, the topographic projection of the sibs. In some cases,
however, the mark-association was greater in area than the
village-community because, for one thing, the Gau did not always
allot its whole domain among the blood-groups, but might retain
for itself parts of the same as a Gau-mark. These great collective-
marks—Gau-marks, and doubtless also hundred-marks—disappeared for the most part, it is true, in the course of the Middle
Ages; but in some regions, as *e.g.* in Allgäu, Upper Bavaria, and
North Tyrol, they have maintained themselves down to the
present day. Again, with the growth of population within the
territory of a village settlement, new derivative village communities arose, and this always led to a partition of the arable lands
among all such rural communes, but not always to a corresponding partition of the remaining land. In this case, therefore, as in
the other, the members of various village communities remained
united in one mark-association inclusive of their several individual
districts.

Although all the land was originally subjected, by its allotment among the neighborhood-unions as mark, to their collective
rights, a reduction of the mark was eventually caused by the
appearance and growth of individual ownership. All those parcels
which passed into the private ownership of individual mark
associates, ceased to be part of the mark; and also in the same
way isolated pieces of land assigned to individual usufruct. The
former included, at first, only house-plots with the yards and
gardens surrounding them, but later the arable fields as well.

Germanic times, but the result of the continued appropriation of forest
lands, originally lordless, either by manorial lords who were ever becoming more powerful or by free and independent landowners.

Thenceforth, the meadows and woods—the so-called *Allmende* (*Allgemein*, "commons")—constituted practically alone "the mark" or "the common (*gemeine*) mark."

Where settlement did not take place in villages, but by individual farms—as was the case in mountain valleys, and also in many regions of the lowlands, as *e.g.* along the Hellweg in Westphalia—the *Allmende*, in the indicated sense of meadow and woodland, was the sole basis from the beginning of the community constituted of the individual settlers. This was known in such localities as the "peasant"-community (*Bauerschaft*).

LEGAL NATURE

The origin of the mark-associations made them in their very nature economic unions, notwithstanding that their boundaries not infrequently coincided, in the earlier periods, with those of the political administrative districts, the Gaus and the hundreds, and that in consequence of this topographic coincidence there regularly resulted a complete fusion of the two into one communal entity, from one viewpoint political and from another purely economic. The mark-associations had for their exclusive end the advancement of the agricultural interests of the whole association and of each individual associate. These interests, however, were in no way contradictory, for the purposes of the whole were precisely the purposes of the individual associates. The individual associate needed the common land for any ordered prosecution of his own agriculture: he needed the right to pasture over and to cut wood upon it; and so on. And that these usufructuary rights should inure to each associate was for the benefit of all, and therefore of the group. It was these usufructuary rights that inured to each associate as an appurtenance to his individual ownership —originally in unrestricted measure, and later to an extent proportioned to that of his land (measured by the full-hide)— that embodied the practical value of membership in the association. Inasmuch, however, as no division of the common-mark took place incidentally to the usufruct thus enjoyed by each associate in the entire undivided common, such rights were *collective* rights of usufruct. To be sure, definite pieces of the common might be assigned to individual associates for individual usufruct; but in this case they ceased to be part of the common-mark. And when (as was still true in the Frankish period) the right of *Neubruch*—that is the authority to clear mark-land, especially woodland, and to appropriate its ownership—belonged to the associates, such land-breaks also became the separate property of the improver.

But who was the owner of the mark? To this much debated question no other answer can be given than this: that in the sense of the medieval law the associates in their *entirety* were *regarded* as the owners. This entirety, however, the association as such, was in medieval conceptions by no means opposed to the individual associates as a legally independent and distinct third person. On the contrary it was, as it were, "built up out of them as a personality uniting all: the associates stood as with one part of their personality in the group." The mark belonged to the totality of associates. And the same was true of "collective" chattels (*Gesamtfahrhabe*) such as implements, buildings, and breeding stock—which must always have existed, even though not always in great amount—and of the property accumulated out of taxes and penal fines. The associates as a body controlled the mark, they determined the economic plan for its exploitation. That this collective right of the association in the mark was a remnant of their one-time collective right in the whole domain, including the arable fields, was shown by the fact that it retained certain supreme powers over the arable that had passed into private ownership. Thus, for example, the individual was bound by the resolves of the commonalty in the cultivation of his arable land. This was the principle of compulsory regulation of the common fields (*Flurzwang*). Again, the whole body had the right to reclaim lands allowed to go to waste; and also a right of escheat in the hides left by heirless members. Indeed, under some circumstances even a new allotment of the arable (*Reebningsverfahren*) might be undertaken. With these powers over the mark that inured to and were exercised by the associates as a body, were united those of the individual associates. Nor were these in the nature of rights in *alieno solo*. They were simply derivative from the collective privileges that pertained to them as a body, and therefore also to each individual; not distinct and separate, but ideal, shares in a collective right, which were united by an associational principle. In the literature of modern Germanic studies this peculiar distribution of powers between the whole and the individual members is designated "associational collective-ownership" (*genossenschaftliches Gesamteigentum*). It was the counterpart in the law of things of that bond which united the associates themselves into a whole recognized by the law of persons, and which, while it did not as yet possess, unlike them, a legal independence, nevertheless at least did already represent an entity.

ORGANIZATION

That the associates were united in a legal entity was manifest in the fact that from the earliest times a definite organization was an essential of the mark-association. For without some organization, however simple, unions consisting of numerous members, such as the mark-associations were from the beginning, could not have continued to exist; though that is of course by no means to be regarded as proof of a legal personality inherent in them from their origin. Special officers of the mark-associations were necessary, however, only in those marks that belonged to a Gau or a hundred, since the officers of the Gaus and the hundreds exercised exclusively political powers. In the village communities the organs of the political commune served at the same time the village mark-association. The supreme administrative organ was the totality of associates gathered in the assembly of markmen, which sat under the presidency of the chief-markman (called woodward, *wald-grave,* village magistrate, etc.). It regulated the usufruct of the mark and the services imposed on the markmen; judged in cases of waste committed on the mark; elected the mark officials (foresters, field-guards, etc.); and doubtless chose a committee as a permanent supervisory organ. Originally all persons settled within the mark and possessing their own household—"flame and fire keepers (*Flammer und Feurer*) behind the mark"—ranked as "full" or "mark" associates, enjoying equal rights. Such were called *Märker, Erbexen, villani, vicini, commarcani.* However, it was a precondition to this that they should either have descended from a markman or should have been adopted by vote of the community. Inasmuch as the principle of majority rule was still quite foreign to the primitive law, so that resolutions could be taken only by unanimity in the assembly of associates, each associate might raise objections at any time within a year to the settlement of any stranger (as was laid down, for example, in the Salic folklaw).

FREE, MIXED, AND MANORIAL MARK-ASSOCIATIONS

The mark-association that corresponded to the Germanic agrarian system, consisting exclusively of free and equal fellows and endowed with far-reaching autonomy, lost ground following the Frankish period in consequence of the growth of manors. Fully free (*altfreie,* "primitive free") village and mark-communes maintained themselves only in Friesland, Ditmarsh, Switzerland, and in some regions of West Germany. On the other hand, wherever ecclesiastical and secular land-lords acquired the possession of numerous hides formerly subject to equal rights of vicinage, and remained at the same time within the union of the mark-associations, their rapidly expanding demesne lands and lands dependent thereon procured them a dominant position within such unions. And since usufructuary rights in the mark were measured by the extent of one's landed possessions, their supremacy was thereby continually strengthened, until finally it came to be an unqualified lordship over the mark and the mark-community, exercised through a bailiff. With this change the mark-community ceased to be free. It had still earlier become a so-called "mixed" mark-community, in which the land-lord became ever more prominent beside the free associates; and its development from that into an "unfree" community was due principally to the frequent entrustment of free hides to landed magnates and the abasement thereby brought about in the legal status of the tenants. From the beginning, moreover, unfree mark-associations resulted wherever village communes grew up under manorial law upon manorial estates that had either detached themselves from a union of free mark-associations or had never become part of such. These mark-associations of manorial law (*hofrechtliche Genossenschaften* or *grundherrschaftliche Hofmarkgenossenschaften*), which were especially numerous, and to which by far the most of the dooms refer, were exact replicas of the free communities save for the absence of personal freedom. Viewed from the standpoint of the Territorial law, it is true that their members enjoyed neither individual ownership in the plowland nor collective ownership in the mark set apart for them by the manorial lord, for the lord alone was owner of the whole domain. His will was therefore here decisive in a measure even greater than in the mixed associations, in matters concerning the mark; the more so because the office of a chief-markman was regularly conceded him by birth. The manorial law, however, which was being created within these limits assured to the associates a usufructuary ownership (*Eigen*) in the hide in the sense of *that* law, though not in that of the Territorial law, and a collective ownership of the mark; and it was also customary to concede them an autonomy, as concerned the mark, which was defined and protected by the manorial law. Of course these things remained in a flux of development, and development was possible in two different directions: it might lead to a gradual strengthening of the association's powers and to a repression of the power of the manorial lord, or it could lead to a complete absorption of the former into a fully developed, unqualified sole ownership of the lord. In the course of time there developed in connection with these manorial groups the conception of the *Anstalt* or "foundation"—a personified institution—as a wholly passive body of individuals who found in their lord a center of union (below, pp. 291 ff.).

TRANSFORMATIONS OF THE OLD MARK-ASSOCIATION

As already remarked, the tendency toward a differentiation of the group as distinguished from the associates was already growing in the Middle Ages. Nevertheless, the recognition of the aggregate of fellows as a distinct legal personality, that is as a corporate association in the sense of Germanic law (below, pp. 285 ff.), was first realized, not in the rural but in the city communes. These were similarly developing. "The economic as well as the legal status of a town commune was originally no different from that of the rural commune." It also generally had commons, though these lost their old importance in the larger cities the more agriculture and grazing diminished relatively to trade and industry. At the same time the singleness of ends characteristic of the rural commune disappeared. The varied problems, political, economic, and cultural in nature, whose solution the city was undertaking with the help of its new wealth built up out of the taxes of the residents (and no longer primarily destined, by any means, to the mere usufruct of the residents), made it appear as the instrument of an independent power and will that was plainly detached from the interests of the citizens considered individually. In this way the town grew into a corporately organized political commune with its own recognized legal personality. Now conditions were different in the rural communes in so far that a predominance was always retained in them by economic interests, relatively to which their political aspect was sharply subordinated. Yet in these also the individual began increasingly to feel a distinction between himself and the association quite in contrast with the views of the early Middle Ages. And this, in its turn, influenced the transformation of the village commune of the open country into an independent "corporate association," so that wherever the village commune and mark-association were united in the old way and so long as they remained so, the collective right in the mark inhering therefore in the commune, the collective ownership of the mark, which was formerly only "associational," became "corporate" in character. Here too, however, the economic association ultimately became completely separated from the political commune, so that the village commune and the mark-association appeared side by side as two independent *Körperschaften,* which were no longer necessarily of the same personal membership. This separation was connected with changes that took place in the membership of the mark-association.

Every person in independent possession of a hide who belonged to the association by birth or adoption was originally, as already stated, a "full" associate, and shared as such, by virtue of his right of membership, in the usufructuary rights in the common lands. The ordinary landless hired laborers (*Hintersassen*), the cotters, hovelers, cottagers and the like, settled on little plots without practicing true husbandry; the feudal tenants planted on the lands of others; and, finally, the landowners dwelling outside the mark (*Ausmärker*) were associated with the markmen solely for mutual defense (*Schutzgenosse*), and had shares in the mark only indirectly or by special favor. In time, the circle of "full" associates came more and more to exclude such communists of lesser privileges, in order to prevent a depreciation of the value of the right of fellowship through the increase in number of those entitled to defense. This was accomplished, in part, by abandoning the requirement of landholding, retaining unchanged only that of an independent household; while the adoption of strangers either took place no more, or only upon payment of high entrance dues. In this manner there originated within the village commune personal associations of families exclusively entitled to the usufruct of the common land, a "blooded village-patriciate." More commonly, however, landed ownership was maintained as a condition of membership, but with the new requirement that every member own either one of the old home-steads endowed with such rights of usufruct or a "full" peasant hide. There were thus formed within the village commune true "real" communes. Finally, in some regions—in Switzerland, Hesse, Ditmarsh—the right of usufruct in the common mark be-came an independent, heritable, alienable, partible, and accumu-lative ideal share-right, like a share of stock, which conferred full membership privileges in the usufructuary commune (*Rechtsame gemeinde* or *Nutzungsgemeinde*) that was constituted of the totality of such shareholders.

DISSOLUTION OF THE MARK-ASSOCIATIONS

Where the result was not the formation of such special agrarian corporate-associations as those just described, into whose collec-tive ownership the one-time common mark passed, this generally fell to the political commune, which by this time was independent. It thus became communal property, in which, however, the usu-fructuary rights of the communists theretofore entitled to such might continue. These rights were now commonly regarded simply as rights in the property of another, unless they were classed with rights in public streets and squares. Ownership of the commonties also frequently passed to the Territorial rulers, who had often laid claim to a commonty-regality already in the Middle Ages.

Finally, beginning with the end of the 1700s State legislation undertook a total dissolution of the few remaining remnants of the old mark-associations and the relations of collective owner-ship incident to them. On the one hand the common fields of arable and meadow, and therewith every restriction reminiscent of the old compulsory regulation of the common fields, were abolished by enclosures; and on the other hand, by the redemption of all statutory rights of usufruct in land, the usufructuary privileges of individuals in common lands were done away with. Above all, the so-called discommon ordinances (*Gemeinheitsteilungsordnungen*) that were issued in the different German States in the 1800s—*e.g.* the Prussian discommon ordinance of June 7, 1821, the Baden commune ordinance of 1831, the Saxon statute of redemptions and discommons of 1832, the Bavarian commune statute of 1834, etc.—swept away the community enjoyment of lands, apportioning the commonties on various principles as individual property among the landowners. In this manner most of the commonties disappeared, particularly in North Germany. In South and West Germany, where the commonties had become for the most part public communal property, and had been thereby subjected to far-reaching restraints on alienation, many old marks continued to exist; and so also in Switzerland. At the present day altered economic views are again more favorably inclined to commonties, and seek to hinder, especially, the partition of the woodlands.

Neighborhood Associations

Beside the mark-associations there originated in the Middle Ages many other associations which likewise had for their end the common usufruct of land, but in lesser measure.

AGRICULTURAL ASSOCIATIONS

Most nearly related to the mark-associations were associations for special agricultural purposes. They were distinguished from the former by this, that the land held in collective ownership was not a communal mark, and the associates were in no way united as members of a commune. These associations, like the mark-associations, very generally assumed a corporate-like character already in the Middle Ages. Some of these special agrarian associations have persisted down to the present day. Examples are:

The "*farm communities*" (*Gehöferschaften*) of the administrative district of Trier: agrarian associations which hold collective ownership over an arable mark. This is divided into a definite number of "lots," "shares," or "plows," which originally corresponded to the number of fully privileged associates. Such associations later denied membership to strangers, and the shares thereby became independent objects of commerce. The arable is periodically distributed anew by lot among the members, in the ratio of the share-holdings. These farm communities have played a great rôle in the investigation of economic and legal history, for Hanssen thought to identify in them the last remnants of the primitive Germanic system of common fields and allotment of arable described by Tacitus. Lamprecht has shown, however, in opposition to this view, that they originated much later. In his opinion, which Hanssen has accepted, they owed their origin to the manorial organization of the 900s to 1300s, and go back to the assarts made with the services of manorial serfs—*i.e.* to manorial tiller-unions (*Betriebsgenossenschaften*) on assarts (*Beunden*); associations of cultivators which then, after the decay of the manors, had retained ownership of the fields originally cultivated by them in the service of their lord. It is true, this view has itself since been controverted. In modern times woodland and meadow have become predominant over the arable, and the modern farm communities (of which in 1878 there were still 20 in the administrative district of Trier) have thus become very similar to the *Allmende* corporations alluded to above (p. 263).

The "*Hauberg*" *associations* of the region of Siegen in Westphalia are woodland associations whose property includes so-called *Hauberge,* or leafwood copses on the mountain sides. Every *Hauberg* is subjected to a rotation period of sixteen or eighteen years; the district is therefore divided into sixteen or eighteen "hews" or "fellings"—*i.e.* rotation parcels—of which one is cut over yearly, while the others are meanwhile wholly enclosed or used for grazing or as arable. The "hews" or "fellings" vary in area and productive value. All the "hews" of the same *Hauberg* are divided into an equal number of subdivisions called *Jähne* ("strips"). These strips are measured in terms of an imaginary unit, which furnishes the basis for the allotment of the hews among the associates. The strips are therefore mere quota rights, to which, however, there correspond definite pieces of land in the hew. The number of strips into which the hew is divided is identical with the number of persons having rights in the *Hauberg* as it existed at the time of the introduction of the strip system. By subsequent alienation or inheritance complicated subdivisions were formed. The *Hauberg* system of woodland management has been regulated in recent years by special "Hauberg ordinances" applicable to the Circles in which such woodlands still exist— Siegen, Dill, Oberwesterwald, and Altenkirchen. A Nassau ordinance of 1804 still serves for the administrative district of Wiesbaden.

The *Alp associations* in Switzerland are to-day purely private associations which, especially in the canton of Unterwalden, practice a community agriculture of the Alps. An Alp is terraced into a certain number of share-rights ("cow-rights," "cow-feeds"), which in turn may be divided down to "quarter-cows" or "hoofs."

In the Middle Ages *vineyard associations* were common which practiced a common cultivation of vineyards, and possessed for this end a corporate-associational organization. Supervision of the vineyards, the police of roads and boundaries, the setting of the slips, and the regulation of the vintage, were the chief objects of associate action.

ASSOCIATIONS DEVELOPED UNDER THE LAW OF WATERS AND MINING

[These] were similar to the mark-associations, although no definite piece of land constituted their material basis. [They] included fishery, dike, and sluice fellowships, and mining associations (*Gewerkschaften*). . . .

TRANSPORTATION ASSOCIATIONS

Finally, mention may be made of the transportation unions that arose in the Middle Ages and endured well into modern times. To these belonged the so-called "road-associations" (*Rottgenossenschaften*—"roaders' union") of Bavaria and the Tyrol, as well as the frontier "port-associations" of eastern Switzerland; companies of entrepreneurs which on one hand attended to the maintenance of the Alpine passes, and on the other hand claimed a more or less extensive monopoly of transportation. In the communes having rights of "road" those villagers were members of the road-association, who also shared as markmen in the usufruct of the commonty. The purpose of such roaders' unions was to attend to the transport of goods upon the great roads (*auf der Rod zu fertigen*) that led from Ulm through Landeck, Meran, and Trient, and from Augsburg through Innsbruck and Toblach, to Venice. Ports were maintained on the Septimer-road between Chur and Chiavenna (four); on the Splügen-road between Chur and Chiavenna; and on the St. Bernhard-road between Chur and Bellinzona (six). All the "ports" of each highway were organized, and held regular sessions under the presidency of port-magistrates. The roaders' unions were also organized.

The Craft Gilds

ORIGIN

The craft gilds owed their origin to the increasing prosperity of the medieval cities. They are therefore of considerably later origin than the rural mark-associations, the oldest reports of them being of the 1100s. And in their case the legal independence of the association as such, and its corporate-like organization, were from the beginning more sharply and more consistently realized.

The opinion, formerly widespread, that the craft gilds were derived from unions of unfree manorial craftsmen ("the manorial theory") is to-day generally abandoned. As little can their origin be traced to the dissolution of a "greater gild" that preceded them. For general *gilds merchant* (*Kaufmannsgilden*) of the kind that existed in the Netherlands, Flanders, England, and elsewhere, have, it seems, not been provable in Germany. Yet undoubtedly there existed there also, and at an early day, special gilds of merchants, who traded either in certain wares or with certain foreign market-towns. These gilds of merchants and itinerant traders became less important when increasing security of intercourse made less imperative the need of alliance. Nevertheless, gilds of merchants trading to foreign parts maintained themselves for a very long time—for example the Association of Herring Fishers in Lübeck; and along with these there were unions of German merchants in foreign lands, such as the Hanse of German merchants in Nowgorod, Bergen, Brügge, and London.

Contrary to the above theory, the development of the crafts seems to have had its starting point in official market regulations issued by local governmental authorities (Keutgen's theory).

From the Carolingian time the control of markets was included among the powers of public officials, or later among those of the city lords, especially the bishops, and they assigned the administration of the trade police and the jurisdiction of the market court either to the regular town magistrate or to a special administrative official (*Kämmerer,* "chamberlain," "custodian"). In order to exercise an effective control of the market the sellers were divided into groups of single traders, and separate stands (*Stände*) were assigned to them. These groups of artisans and tradesmen were the *craft-companies* (*Ämter* or *magisteria*). They were based exclusively upon the market ordinances issued by the municipal authorities. The local government soon came to restrict itself to a general oversight; it set over the gilds masters taken from the unions, who held the court and (often aided by a committee) exercised the police power.

The essential characteristic of free association, which marked the later craft gilds but was still lacking in the craft companies, made progress in the craftsmen's unions as soon as the artisans, united for industrial purposes in the companies created by the market authorities, extended the purposes of those unions beyond industrial matters to social, charitable, and religious ends. This was the more natural because it gave expression to an old Germanic idea, afterward strengthened by Christianity, that those with whom one stands in close relationship, even though not one of blood, are brothers, and that such brotherhood should be employed in a common cultivation of spiritual interests—which in those times ordinarily found primary expression in religious and churchly communion. The old Germanic brotherhood was a community of board (hence Mid. Low G. *matschap,* Mod. Dutch *maatschapij*), a community of bread (*Kompagnie* from *panis*), a community of the bowl (*convivium*), a gild—in short "a gathering for festive eating and drinking." Further, it was a fellowship of covenanters (*coniuratio*). The craftsmen started from these old ideas and institutions, and the brotherhood (*fraternitas*) offered them the institutional type by which to pass from the position of a branch of the municipal administration to that of a free society. The immediate result was an intimate fusion of the very diverse elements that had been brought together in the companies—freemen and men formerly unfree, native townsmen and immigrants; and which had theretofore wholly lacked all coherence, such as resulted in the mark-association from the earlier relationship of blood. And although, as is readily understood, the local governmental authorities were in no wise friendly disposed to any endeavors of the city population toward union, such tendencies toward religious and ecclesiastical unity must nevertheless have been least unwelcome to them, especially to the clerical authorities. Indeed, they owed their origin, to a great extent, precisely to clerical incitement. Their churchly ends, like their commercial purposes, being of a public nature, the establishment of craft gilds that were to be at the same time fraternities required the authorization of ecclesiastical authority. Moreover, it was not true that every craft gild of later times had necessarily originated in a company: freedom of association was the basis of many of the later crafts from the beginning. Nevertheless, the craft gild as a special type of association is to be conceived of as having originated in a coalescence of company and fraternity.

ESSENTIAL NATURE

Principle of "Gild-coercion" (Zunftzwang) The craft (*Zunft,* from *ziemen,* to be fit), a name which was used exclusively in South Germany down into the 1500s for what were ordinarily called in North Germany "gilds" (*Gilden*), was a union that affected the entire personality of the gildmen, being therein akin to the mark-association. It concerned itself with all their relations, under both private and public law, those that were social and those merely human. For this reason the whole family of an associate, not merely himself alone, belonged to the craft gild. But in the crafts, as in the mark-association, the economic purpose was primary; they were essentially economic associations. From this aspect their most important characteristic was the principle of "gild-coercion," which was already essential in the administrative "companies." "Gild-coercion" meant that definite handiwork or industrial tasks (*Werk*) were assigned to each union as its peculiar field of activity and production; and that only its members had the right to exercise these callings and perform such work within the town-limits or the surrounding *banlieue,* and to offer there the products of their labor for sale. At the same time, the question was not one merely of handiwork in the true sense;

on the contrary the trades of fishermen, tilers, vintagers, and inn-keepers were frequently organized as crafts; and various classes of merchants, money-changers, etc., formed gilds, for the most part of great prestige. The medieval view did not distinguish between tradesmen (*Händler*) and industrials (*Gewerbetrei-bende*), but included both under the common conception of the merchant (*mercator, Kaufmann*).

The right to prosecute their respective handiwork or industries inured to the gildsmen collectively; but it was imposed upon them, also, as a collective duty. Especially in the flowerage period of gild and city life the artisans regarded themselves on that ac-count as officials, and men looked upon the craft as an office to be administered with the utmost possible fidelity and con-science. Consequently, not alone the public authorities but the gild itself protected the interests of the public through associa-tional oversight, by means of penalties, price-tariffs, and other-wise. On the other hand, the craft was supposed, from its begin-ning, to guard and further the interests of its members and realize equality and fraternity among the gild fellowship, to the end that none might sink to the position of a dependent wage-earner, nor raise himself above his fellows by an undue extension of his busi-ness. Above all, it should preclude the competition of workers not included in the gild—who were later known as *Bönhasen* (bunglers).

Organization From the beginning the gilds possessed a regular organization which was, in substance, always the same. In earlier times it rested upon the craft privileges conferred by the public authorities; later it was recorded in the gild rolls and further developed as a result of the autonomy conceded to the crafts.

Since the essence of the craft gild was an organized community of labor, and since every worker was obliged by the principle of "gild coercion" to enter that organization which corresponded to his calling, the rules concerning memberships constituted the most important part of the gild law. And though even at an early date special circumstances might make the gild a closed corpora-tion—as *e.g.* when all the stalls or shops assigned to a particular industry were occupied, to the last place—nevertheless acquisition of membership was generally little impeded in early times. Whoever had gone through the preparatory schooling of apprentice and journeyman, had passed his master's examination, and had completed his master-work, and paid certain fees, was taken in, provided he had also become a burgher of the city. For men at first regarded the increase of members as an advantageous strengthening of the gild, economically and politically, not as an unwelcome lessening of their share in the labor market. Only toward the end of the Middle Ages did an increasing exclusiveness come to be dominant.

The organs of the gild were those that everywhere recur in German corporations: the assembly of members and the directorate. The former—which, on account of the hour at which it originally always met was also called the morning parley (*Morgensprache*) or "breakfast" parley—exercised the rights of autonomy granted to the gild, making decrees relative to the gild-property, and when necessary establishing new by-laws. At the same time it was subject to the oversight of the public authorities—that is, the town-council; which in Lübeck, for example, was exercised by delegating two councilmen (so-called "morning-parley men") to the gild-assemblies, notice of whose sessions was given to the council. One or several "masters" (*Zunft-, Amts-, Gilde-meister*) constituted the directorate: they too were subordinated in a definite way to the council, and must take oath to it to take care that the gild should do nothing prejudicial to the common weal of the city. The gild-masters exercised the right of autonomous judicature which, like that of legislation, belonged to the gild: gildsmen who violated the gild ordinances were punished by them, acting as the gild-court, or the wrongdoers were expelled from the craft. Civil controversies of lesser import between fellow craftsmen must be brought before the gild judges for settlement; if outsiders desired to make complaint against gildsmen they must, before applying to the public court, apply to gild masters for an adjustment. Above the gild-court stood, as a court of second instance, the council or the court of the city's lord.

Corporate Character From the beginning the entire body of gild members, as such, stood opposed to the individual associate in an independence far more pronounced than was originally the case in the mark-associations, and this is explained by the fact, already adverted to, that there was not in the case of the crafts, as there was in the case of those associations, a complete coincidence of the purposes of the group with those of the members. The craft was not from the beginning designed to further merely the interests of individuals; we have seen that it was precisely the older period when the idea was vital that it had ends to fulfill in the interest of the association, the city, and the purchasing public. But though it was thus, as a body, distinct from its members—possessing, for example, in the seal it used an external sign of this independence—nevertheless, there was no more realized in it than in the mark-association a total separation of the association, as such, from the physical persons of the members who composed it. In particular, the gild property was not the property of an independent third person; it could not have seemed to the gild fellows a thing wholly alien to themselves. The gild-chambers, the gild-furniture, the capital accumulated by contributions, entrance fees, and penalties, and gifts, served not alone the ends of the association, but also the economic, social, and other purposes of the members. Every associate might, for example, use the gild-houses for his convivial pleasures; each could demand support or loans from the capital of the gild; and so on. These benefits were not, however, indispensable to the gild members in the same way that the usufruct of the commonty was to the markmen; the gild-property was devoted in far greater degree to the whole body as such. It was not merely an associational but a corporate-like associational collective property.

DECLINE AND DISAPPEARANCE OF THE CRAFTS

The organization of industries in crafts continued to flourish, speaking generally, down into the 1500s, notwithstanding that some abuses manifested themselves earlier. From that period onward the craft system fell into an increasing torpidity and renitence which, in conjunction with the general decline of intellectual culture and material civilization, led finally to complete decay. From remotest times the regulation of entrance conditions to the gild had been, as already remarked, essential to the gild-organization and with good reason, since the crafts were supposed to be responsible for good workmanship. Hence the requirement of the master's examination, and the exhaustive regulation of apprenticeship and journeyman's service. But these institutions were now made over in uncompromisingly monopolistic fashion. "Egoism became supreme in place of public spirit." Membership in the crafts came to be a purchasable thing; members of the gild families were shown preferences formerly unheard of over strangers; the journeyman system, instead of being used to broaden the workers' views, as was so necessary, was developed into a most oppressive fetter. Above all, the requirement of stainless civil honor (*Ehre*) was overemphasized to a most unreasonable degree. Illegitimate birth constituted an absolute cause for exclusion, not to be avoided even by legitimation; which must have seemed the stranger because the other social estates tolerated in this same period decidedly free ideas on that point. It could justly be said that the 1700s saw bastards climb to the highest honors in State and army, but cobblers and tailors they could not have become in a German town. And equally extravagant was the extension given to the concept of dishonorable industries.

Thus, precisely because of the craft organization German handicraft continuously declined. In place of seeking the introduction of fresh blood, it timidly shut the way to this. From the proud burgher who had once defended his city in arms, there sprang the jibe-provoking *Spiessbürger* ("piddle burghers"—of parochial outlook and cheese-paring policies) or philistines. The word "gild-spirit" (*Zunftgeist*) acquired at that time its unpleasant secondary meaning.

The abuses of the old gild system, which nevertheless found a warm defender only shortly before its complete disappearance in so perspicacious a man as Justus Möser, demanded ever more insistently a remedy. The municipal authorities being too weak to achieve reforms, the imperial and Territorial governments finally intervened. But the endeavors made by these in the 1700s —the decree of the Imperial Diet in 1731, and the Territorial statutes associated with that—failed to bring about any lasting improvement. And thus men finally found themselves compelled in Germany, following the example of France, to do away completely with the crafts in their character of involuntary organizations of city artisans endowed with exclusive industrial privileges. This was done in Prussia by the edict of Nov. 2, 1810, and the statute of Sept. 7, 1811; and the Imperial Industrial Code (*Reichsgewerbeordnung*) of June 21, 1869, accomplished as much for all Germany. In more recent years imperial legislation has again abandoned the principle of unqualified industrial freedom, and introduced anew gild-like organizations. Supplements to the Industrial Code, particularly the statutes of July 18, 1881, and July 26, 1897, once more conferred upon trade unions (*Handwerkerinnungen*) a compulsory character, subject to definite preconditions. These unions of the present-day law are juristic persons—societies (*Vereine*) in the sense of the Civil Code—and indeed public corporations (*öffentliche Körperschaften*).

Other Associations without the Bond of Vicinage

Just as there developed alongside of the mark-associations other groups bound together by interests connected in some way with landholding, so the craft-gilds were accompanied by numerous other associations which in part pursued industrial ends and in part other purposes, without, however, being consolidated by bonds of vicinage.

INDUSTRIAL ASSOCIATIONS

To these belonged, among others, the *minters' associations*. In the Middle Ages the *Münzherr,* that is the holder of the regality of coinage, was accustomed to entrust the care of the mint to a corporate association endowed with various privileges known as the *Hausgenossen* (mint fellows), at whose head was a mint-master whom they freely chose. The *Hausgenossen* were originally unfree artisans of the city lord, and the mint-master was chosen from his household servitors. Later both attained a respected position, for in time the indispensable precondition to membership in the minters' association came to be the possession of a fortune, instead of technical skill, its chief task having become the procurement of the necessary minting metal at its own cost and risk. The technical labor was left to servile workers. Thus the minters' association came to imply membership in a corporation of high repute; it obligated the associates merely to a money contribution and secured them in exchange a share in the profits of coinage.

This was employed by them principally in the business of money changing.

The minters' association already shows the type—not yet, to be sure, fully developed—of a *capitalistic association* (*Kapitalgenossenschaft*). This type has attained in modern legal and economic life an importance far exceeding that of all other personal unions. Modern capitalistic associations are imaginary unions (*begriffliche Vereine*) in which a social fund divided into numerical shares constitutes the essential *raison d'être* of a group of persons possessed individually of complete legal independence. According to their form they are in part share companies, in part coöperative (*Erwerbs-*) and economic associations, in part mutual insurance companies. Inasmuch, however, as they have been developed, primarily, as products of or in connection with commercial law, it would be superfluous to go further into their nature in this place.

CONVIVIAL, RELIGIOUS, AND SCIENTIFIC ASSOCIATIONS

As mentioned above (p. 269), the medieval crafts, in addition to their industrial purposes, pursued as brotherhoods religious, convivial, and social ends. There were also at that time many associations that existed exclusively for such purposes. It was precisely the oldest personal unions, based not upon kinship or neighborhood but upon voluntary agreement, that belonged to this category. This was true of the Frankish gilds of Carolingian times, which, like all Germanic gilds based upon the idea of brotherhood, united within a peculiar communal life the religious end of spiritual welfare with the temporal ends of fraternal support and a common table (whence their other name of *convivia*). Then there were the later fraternities founded for special religious or secular ends. The religious were closely connected with the church, their members being admitted without regard to family or social status, and obligated to the practice of pious works and performance of churchly services that they might be assured eternal salvation; the secular secured to their members mutual support and legal aid. Both classes, however, merged easily in each other. Secular gilds for mutual defense (*Schutzgilden*) did not play in Germany the same rôle as, for example, in England,

Denmark, France, and the Netherlands. The merchant gilds above mentioned (p. 267) may be reckoned among these. On the other hand ecclesiastical brotherhoods were similarly widespread in Germany, at the end of the Middle Ages. In many German cities there were as many as a hundred and more of them—*e.g.* in Cologne, Lübeck, and Hamburg. The calends-gilds or "calends," so called after the custom of the priests to assemble on the first of the month, were exclusively of the ecclesiastical class. The societies of Beguins or Beghards, which spread to Germany from Belgium and were at times pursued as heretical, were very popular, particularly in North Germany. Originally intended only for women, but later also for men, they often included both in a common household and community of goods, like the kindred monastic associations of brothers living a communal life. Their members devoted themselves, without monastic vows, to industrial labors and pious and useful works.

Among associations for idealistic ends were the universities. That these go back for their origin to Germanic legal ideas clearly appears from the beginnings of Bologna and Padua, the two type-universities of the Occident. In Bologna the "scholars," *i.e.* the students, grouped themselves in free associations (*universitates*), each of which was divided into a number of compatriotic unions called *nationes*. Among these the one of greatest power and prestige was the *natio teutonica,* the German student colony. Its archaic, purely Germanic organization shows all the essential characteristics of a Christianized, Germanic frith-gild; this shows us that it was a phenomenon allied to the mercantile hansas, the protective gilds founded by German traders in foreign lands. In Paris the academic union was not composed of the "scholars" alone, but embraced also all the holders of learned degrees— bachelors, masters, and doctors—much as is still the case at Oxford and Cambridge; so that there existed there a union comparable to the gilds. The principle of an industrial union (*Innung*), also, was reflected in the fact that the Parisian *studium generale* was divided, at the beginning, not into "nations," but into four "faculties," corresponding to the four learned professions. Later, however, the Italian model was accepted also at Paris, and the entire body of scholars, inclusive of the *magistri* of the Faculty of Arts (our modern Philosophical Faculty), were divided into four nations, at whose heads stood the rector chosen by the masters of arts. To him the masters of the three higher faculties were compelled finally to bow. The *studium generale* itself, the "University" in the specialized modern sense, thus became a centralized association, and the rector its head. "In this stage of development Paris became the model of the universities established on German soil." The oldest German universities constituted, therefore, "voluntary, self-perpetuating corporate-associations. They possessed, as entities, a quantity of special rights and duties, but above all the usual rights of associations; particularly—besides the right of public instruction and its consequences—autonomy, judicature, and self-government, the free determination of their own organization and choice of directors and organs, the admission and exclusion of members, and the capacity to carry on trade and to hold property under the private law." Their branches, the individual faculties, formed separate corporations. The associations of the students—the colleges and students' gilds (*Kollegien, Bursen*)—early lost importance in Germany, as compared with England.

POLITICAL ASSOCIATIONS

Finally, political ends—which were important even in the case of many of the associations already referred to, especially the craft gilds—might be the essential incentive to union. For example, there appeared in many medieval towns so-called gilds of "ancient burghers" (*Altbürgergilden*), "tavern clubs" (*Stubengesellschaften*), "round-tables" (*Artushöfe*), "Junker clubs" (*Junkerkompagnien*), and commensal and drinking fellowships (*Konstaffeln*); all of which, though dedicated incidentally to the promotion of good fellowship and piety, were chiefly intended to assure to their members, as a body, a prominent share in the town government. Here belongs, for example, the much debated magistrates' club (*Richterzeche*) of Cologne, an association of the wealthy persons of the whole city which originated in the second half of the 1100s. It was composed of three classes of members: the two actual burgomasters, ex-burgomasters (*verdienten*), and the officials from whom that office was still to be filled (*unverdienten, Anwärter*). Their functions consisted in an oversight over the crafts, the administration of the municipal police of trade and industry, oversight of the wine trade, and the conferment of rights of citizenship—in short, political privileges, whose oppressive exercise drew upon the gild the hatred of the artisans. The public (Cathedral) scales were included among their property. The great town leagues, also, the Hansa and the Rhenish City League, were of associational character. The knightage was organized in numerous unions of corporate character. These associations of knightly covenanters (*Eidgenossenschaften*), such as the widespread Order of the Lion, the Order of the Mace in Swabia, and the Stellmeiser of the Mark of Brandenburg, played an important rôle, particularly in the 1300s. While all these political associations possessed only transient importance and sooner or later fell apart, the various alliances, compacts, and treaties of peace out of which the Swiss *Eidgenossenschaft* arose developed into a unitary political community (*Gemeinwesen*). Finally, the estates represented in the imperial Diets—usually the clergy, the nobles, and the cities—were organized in the Territories into corporate estates of the realm.

Not only the individual estates (*Ständekorpora*) or *curiae* (*Kurien*) as such, but also all of them collectively (the *Landschaft*). possessed such corporate character. These corporations were inconsistent with the conception of the modern State: only in few Territories were they able to withstand, down into modern times, the advance of that idea. The Empire, in its old form, also recognized political corporations of the same kind: unions (*Vereine*) of the electoral princes, princes, and counts of the Empire; the colleges, *curiae,* and benches of the imperial Diet; the corporately organized imperial knights of Swabia, Franconia, and the Rhine Province—who did not enjoy the privileges of estates of the Empire; the corporations of the Catholic and Evangelical estates of the Empire; and the Circles of the Empire.

The Communities "of Collective Hand"

NATURE

Besides the associations that were by their very nature so organized as to confer upon the entire body of members, as such, more or less independence apart from the individual members, the medieval law also knew personal unions which, because they included and were calculated for only a relatively limited number of members, showed no such corporal independence. Nevertheless, in their case also there was equally recognized a sphere of common rights distinct from the spheres of individual rights of the persons interested, and the holder of those common rights, namely the associated individuals as a body, constituted a legal entity. In their case also, therefore, a community will was operative within the union, and the aggregate membership appeared to the world as an entity endowed with capacity for rights and action. That this entity, however, was not at all regarded as something different from the members individually, was shown in the fact that it was active only through the *collective* action of all the co-holders of the rights held by the community. The associates (*Genossen*) or commoners (*Gemeinder,* the term usual in this connection) must clasp hands, and then, as with collective hand (*zu gesamter Hand, communi, communicata manu*), perfect the juristic act. Only so, in unison, could they exercise the right pertaining to them collectively. The individual could not in any way exercise it alone, not even with limitation to the partial interest pertaining to him individually. From this form of common action this species of personal union derived its name. "The unitary nature of action by collective hand lies in this, that rights and duties are realized only through common action, action by one without coöperation of the others being impossible." It was not impossible, it is true, under given circumstances, to grant to one of the "commoners" authority to act at the same time for the rest. And therefore there was quite possible, in the case even of these personal unions, a certain internal organization that corresponded to the apparent solidarity which they presented externally; they showed what we are accustomed to call a certain "corporate" element.

ORIGIN

The communities of collective hand had their roots in the Germanic law of the family. Their point of origin was the Indogermanic institution of the household-community (above, p. 253). Just as the family-members united under the *potestas* of the house-father constituted a community of which he was the representative, to which community belonged the allotted lands as the collective property of the house, so among the primitive Germans it was a widespread practice that the grown sons, instead of dividing the heritage after the death of their father, should continue to hold the inherited estate "in collective hand," that is in a common household, in order, by thus living together, to maintain the family estate in as compact a form as possible. Such greater "house associations" (*Hausgenossenschaften*) or associations of commoners (*Gemeinderschaften*), which might include even grandchildren or more remote descendants, are explicitly attested in the folk-laws of the Lombards, Alamanians, Bavarians, and Franks. The Saxons, Frisians, and Anglo-Saxons knew them, also, as did the original East Germans (Burgundians), and equally the Scandinavians. The Latin texts designate the commoners as *coheredes, comparticipes, consortes;* an old German translation of a Carolingian capitulary that is preserved to us already uses the common medieval expression *Ganerben,* that is co-heirs. These communities of collective hand of the family law persisted down to the end of the Middle Ages, and locally down even to present times—though of course not everywhere as an institute occurring, as it once did, equally throughout all classes of society, but only as one occurring in sporadic forms.

SPECIFIC TYPES

Within the *peasant* estate communities of collective hand were widely spread throughout the Middle Ages in South and West Germany. Though they have even to-day by no means wholly died out in these regions, they have nevertheless gradually grown rarer, for the most part retreating into Switzerland. They played a great rôle there in the 1500s and 1600s, as well in the Burgundian as in the Alamanian districts. Even to-day they are there still alive in the popular consciousness. In the Zürich Code of 1853–55 they were capitally regulated. The new Swiss Civil Code, continuing the traditional development of the law, classifies them exhaustively from a socio-political viewpoint. These peasant communities existed for the most part among brothers and sisters and their descendants, but almost always among individuals of equal rights, and consequently not among parents and children. The last, at any rate, was only exceptionally the case, and was explicitly excluded in the legal systems of many regions because inconsistent with parental powers. Such communities were marked, throughout, by the old characteristics of the family law. However, they did not originate solely by force of statute as a consequence of the death of the heritor but might be also established by contract. The latter was the case, particularly, with the very numerous communities that existed among serfs, especially among those of ecclesiastical houses, which were formed for the purpose of avoiding the necessity of paying the tribute due on the death of every serf; tribute being paid only on the death of the eldest commoner, who represented the community. The commoners or share-holders (*Geteilten*) usually lived in communal household, in joint profit and loss; in the words of the sources, they lived "*in einem Mus und Brot*" ("with common pap and bread"). The community generally extended to the entire heritage; in addition to which the individual members might of course possess separate estates—the property of the wife a man took was, for example, so regarded. Shares existed only in the ideal sense; any separate disposition of the same was impossible. Externally the community of collective hand appeared, as of old, only in the common act of all its members. But the eldest male member was usually, nevertheless, the representative of the community: as it is put in a doom of Einsiedeln, the eldest brother might "undertake to attend the courts, and to represent the other brothers who remain at home" ("*zu den gerichten gan und die anndern brüder, so daheimen beliben, versprechen*"); and so too the eldest was alone liable to death duties. If a commoner died, his children took his place *ipso facto;* if he died without descendants, there was originally benefit of survivorship in favor of the remaining commoners, to the consequent exclusion of such heirs of the decedent, whether equally near or more distant, as did not belong to the community. In some legal systems, however, such benefit of survivorship was in time weakened in favor of the heirs. The community was readily dissolvable; in particular, dissolution could be demanded in case of the loss (*Wegfall*) of any members. Indeed, in some places the commoners possessed a right, exercisable at any time, to give notice of withdrawal. The dissolution of a community in consequence of the complete partition and consequent satisfaction of the rights of the individual commoners out of the family estate theretofore held in common (*Tod-, Grund-, Real-*

and of advowson, as well as the common seigniories of the old Swiss Confederation of the Thirteen Places.

Finally, a form of community of collective hand that appears in all Germanic lands and in all classes of society, was the *marital community of collective hand* (*Eheliche Gesamthand*), which controlled the legal relation of husband and wife wherever the idea of the husband's guardianship was supplemented in the field of property law by the idea of the *Genossenschaft,* and the law of marital community of property built up upon that double basis. The community of collective hand between the spouses was often extended to the recognition of a community of goods between the surviving spouse and children. . . .

THE MODERN DEVELOPMENT

Personal unions of collective hand either remained or became of great importance for modern German law, and even for the law of today. It is indeed true, as already remarked, that the peasant communities of collective hand have disappeared in Germany save for scanty vestiges: the co-heir communities of knights have wholly disappeared, and the herital fraternities have been completely divested of their slight content of private law. On the other hand the marital community and the "continued" marital community of goods have persisted in various legal systems. Some, as *e.g.* the Prussian *Landrecht,* regulated the herital communities (*Erbengemeinschaften*) as communities of collective hand. Others, as *e.g.* here again the Prussian *Landrecht,* gave effect to the same principle—either unconsciously or under the influence of conceptions of the Law of Nature—in regulating the *general* law of societies or partnerships (*Gesellschaftsrecht*). But it was of still greater importance that the principle remained (or again became) dominant in commercial law. . . . not only the commandite partnership, and in peculiar degree the ship partnership (*Reederei*), but above all that particular form of mercantile partnership which is recognized in our law to-day as the typical form, namely the mercantile partnership of unlimited liability, are based upon the principle of collective hand. The question may be left unanswered whether the unlimited partnership goes back in origin—as many reasons indicate to be at least probable—to co-heir communities of collective hand in which the sons of a merchant continued the business of their father. Equally without discussion must the question (variously answered) remain, whether in medieval Germany, and especially in the world of trade dominated by the Hansa, the unlimited partnership had already been adopted to any considerable extent before contact with the law of Southern and Western Europe. At all events, the Germanic principles of collective hand were adopted in the Italian and French legislation of the 1500s and 1600s, which regulated the unlimited partnership in a sense which, especially in France, was decisive of its later development. They were thence brought back, through the old Commercial Code, to Germany, thereby acquiring importance as models for the law of the present Civil Code.

Practical and Theoretical Results of German Legal Development

General Principles of the German Law of Associations

If one takes a general view of the legal ideas that have controlled the development of associational organization in German law, one notes first of all a contrast, which was present from the beginning, between associations proper (*Genossenschaften*), which included a great number of members, and communities dominated by the principle of the collective hand (*Gemeinderschaften*), whose organization was adapted to a smaller number of participants.

ASSOCIATIONS PROPER AND CORPORATE ASSOCIATIONS

These unions [associations], which were ordinarily relatively large, went through an evolution that gradually brought to full development certain nuclear principles which, though already present in them from the beginning, were at first undeveloped. In the oldest form of such unions that can be denominated associations in the strict sense (*Genossenschaften*)—namely in the sib, and especially in the mark-associations of the early Middle Ages —there was, indeed, already recognized a certain independence of the entire body, as distinguished from its members; but it was one of which contemporaries were as yet scarcely conscious. It gradually became manifest, however, and with increasing definiteness. It found clearest expression in those localities where the commune appeared, in contrast with its members and their separate economic interests, as a group impelled by its own political purposes. This was earliest true of the urban communes. But the rural communes followed the same development, and likewise the purely economic unions; and this was true of these last alike when they had existed independently from the beginning beside the village commune as a complex of mark-associations, and when they were only gradually differentiated, in varied forms, from the political communes.

Wherever such a process of differentiation took place, and a group-entity as such made its appearance in legal life as the locus of an independently active will, the *Genossenschaft* (association) had developed into a *Körperschaft* (corporate association). It was characteristic of such corporate associations of Germanic law that the group (*Verband*) was on one hand regarded as an independent entity endowed with its own legal personality—a collective person composed of the physical persons of the associates, and possessing a collective will, which was formed through the formal fusion of all individual wills; but, on the other hand, the abstraction which men already needed for the mere *conception* of a collective personality unembodied in a definite physical being, was not carried so far in medieval law that men would have recognized in this entity to which independence was so far attributed, a subject of rights wholly distinct from the individual associates, and into legal relations with which the associates could have entered only as with a wholly alien person. Therefore, and in particular, the usufructuary rights of the associates in the property belonging to the group were not regarded as rights in the property of another. On the contrary all possible rights in the association property appeared as apportioned between the group and the individuals, and this in such manner that the right of disposing thereof inhered essentially in the whole body, but the rights of usufruct therein inhered in the individuals. This view reflected the peculiarity of the German concept of ownership. A corporate collective personality behind which the plurality of associates is in no way hidden, found its counterpart in the law of things in a corporate collective property.

As collective personalities, an organization was essential to the corporate associations; but no other or greater organization than the older associations already possessed. In this way it became possible to conceive of a unitary will, although in the constitution of this the majority principle, by which the greater body of persons was enabled to bind the lesser, did not find absolute recognition until a late day. The corporate organs, through which it exercised its autonomy in enactments, judicature, and administration, were everywhere the general assembly of members and a directorate consisting of one or several persons. The directorate represented the *Körperschaft* (the corporation of Germanic law) in its external relations; but it sometimes happened that in certain cases special representatives were named, as for example in lawsuits. Here again, however, the old view long made itself felt that the group, that is all the members together, must appear before the court, in order to bring complaint, be impleaded, take oath, and so on; and special privileges were besought and granted by which representation by a few members was recognized as sufficient. So, for example, in a lawsuit which the city of Göttingen prosecuted in 1383, 278 burghers were obliged to appear before the Territorial Court; only in 1385 was it provided by charter that two councilmen and four or five worthy burghers should thenceforth act as representatives of the city. In 1443 the town of Lauingen was similarly summoned before the Veme in the person of her 88 burghers above 20 years of age.

In consequence of the legal personality of the corporation it was regarded as capable of holding property, and therefore also as possessing capacity to inherit. All the varieties of medieval corporations that have been discussed, and equally the still older types of association, were owners alike of immoveable and of moveable property: commonties, herds, agricultural and industrial implements, buildings in town and country, food supplies, stocks of goods, capital funds, etc. And they might equally well possess, as corporations, real rights of all kinds, and obligational claims.

From the corporation's capacity for rights and action the medieval law logically deduced the rule that it might also commit torts; in other words, it had delictual capacity. But here again the characteristic regard shown at once for the group and for the individuals composing it, found clear expression. For the consequences of a violation of law committed by a corporation—*e.g.* the pronouncement of an unjust doom, the choice of an inefficient official, the breaking of a contract, the punishment of alien subjects contrary to law, etc.—might fall either upon the corporation as such or upon the individual associates, and either in the form of an obligation to give damages or as a penalty. It was not rarely the case, in the medieval period, that villages, cities, communes, whole countries, as well as other corporations were proscribed by vehmic right outlawed, or excommunicated; that their corporate property was confiscated, and their corporate rights taken away. And such punishments—as outlawry, ban, proscription, razure of the town—came home to every individual in a very near way. But aside from that, when the city was bound to pay damages execution was possible, in case of necessity, against the persons and private property of all the burghers. That is, although men found it possible to distinguish between city or village and the citizens or villagers, and to conceive of the council or local governing authority as an *organ* of the commune, nevertheless, in cases of *obligations* of the commune under the property law, not only the communal property but also all the commune members, or at least the councilors, were regarded as liable. Not infrequently, in the establishment of city schools, the council expressly made the individual burghers co-obligors. Conversely, the whole association was originally liable for the delinquencies and contractual obligations of the individual associates; though this view, it is true, was more and more abandoned, speaking generally, even in the Middle Ages. At least the cities thenceforth admitted their liability for the contractual obligations and delictual liabilities of their burghers only when the city denied the creditors of these a legal hearing, or otherwise protected the wrongdoers, thereby making their debt its own.

Most of the corporations of the Middle Ages originated as a product of customary law. Mark-associations and communes existed from the earliest times, and gradually assumed associational and corporate character quite in the natural course of development. Other corporations, however, originated in consciously creative acts. Such acts often proceeded from the State or from the local superior authority; manorial lords formed manorial communes and mark-associations; kings and princes established cities or conferred the privileges of town-law upon older settlements; city lords called craft companies into being and consented to their conversion into gilds; and so on. Many other associations, however, owed their existence to voluntary union, that is, to an establishment by virtue of compact, as was true of the protective gilds and brotherhoods—and indeed the impulse of voluntary union was essential to the craft gilds. As these varied modes of origin show, the Middle Ages knew no general, invariant legal rules that applied in all cases to the process by which associations and corporations were formed. As a matter of fact the principles of voluntary corporate organization was of wide prevalence. It is true that the local authorities claimed the right to dissolve personal unions that appeared to them dangerous, and that general prohibitions of gilds and fraternities were consequently repeatedly resorted to from the Carolingian period onward for political reasons, although without lasting effect. But at all events the view was unknown that an existing personal union, recognized as such, needed any special act of the State as a prerequisite to the acquisition of legal personality. On the contrary this was inherent in all corporate, and in lesser degree in all other, associations.

THE COMMUNITIES OF COLLECTIVE HAND

The *Gemeinderschaften,* unlike associations proper (*Genossenschaften*), originated in the house community, and not in the sib, and they continued to the end without independent legal personality. The principle of collective hand by which they were controlled always remained distinct from the associational and corporate bond. It is true, however, that this contrast first appeared in full clarity when the corporate association had everywhere been developed out of the older and looser association. Thenceforth, the community of collective hand could be contrasted, as a type of union lacking legal personality, with the corporation as a personal union endowed with individual legal personality. But despite this fundamental and principal unlikeness, there was no sharp division between the two types in actual life, so that under some circumstances the one might pass over into the other—as was the case, for example, with many co-heir communities of knights that gradually acquired a corporate character (above, p. 282). The reason for this fact, peculiar to medieval law and springing from its scant liking for clean-cut and exclusive formulas, lay in the following qualities (already mentioned) of those two varieties of personal unions. The corporate association involved as little as the association proper a complete absorption of the individual associate in the entity of the union: on the contrary the right of the whole was restricted by the individual rights of the associates. There resulted from this, despite the recognition of the totality as an independent legal personality, an approach to the principle of collective hand, to which was essential an *exclusive* regard for the individual commoners and the absence of any fully developed entity embracing them. On the other hand, in the case also of the community of collective hand, although this remained a mere legal relation among several individuals, it was nevertheless possible to unite these participants into a group recognized by the law of persons and to bind their separate wills "associationally." For the principle of collective hand merely signified that the united commoners were the holders of the collective right; that no one of them possessed even a distributive power of disposition, in proportion to his share, over the community property. In that respect, however, the community of collective hand approximated a corporate organization, although without passing over into it. Moreover, a certain organization, and notably the conferment upon one of the commoners of representative power, was also by no means impossible in its case.

In these forms of association, corporate association, and community of collective hand, the medieval law had devised a regulation of associational unions which was closely adjusted to the rich expression of the social life of the time, and excellently adapted to its needs, and one which rested throughout upon sound and simple conceptions. Undoubtedly it was susceptible of further development, and would have presented no difficulties to a thorough scientific elaboration and systematic treatment. But the reception of the alien law made all that impossible.

Reception of the Alien Law and Renascence of Germanic Law

CORPORATION THEORY OF THE ALIEN LAW

With the Reception the romanistic corporation theory, as it had been constructed in medieval Italy upon the basis of the rather barren Roman sources by the Civilians, Glossators, Post-Glossators, and Canonists—an elaborate structure of ideas influenced in many parts by Germanic legal conceptions—attained a dominance at first unlimited. Unfortunately, the Roman-schooled jurists of Germany lacked understanding for the Germanic elements of that theory, and the native law was in danger of dying in the bonds of alien legal concepts. For the fundamental concepts of the alien law were diametrically opposed to those of the Germanic law. Its distinction between juristic persons and other forms of personal unions, as well as its classification of juristic persons, contradicted theretofore familiar conditions and conceptions.

Universitas and Societas   The Roman-Italian law arranged personal unions under two categories that were in the sharpest contrast, notionally, with each other:[3] that of the "universitas" and that of the "societas."

The *universitas,* or corporation in the narrow sense (*Korporation*), is a collective person, or group entity, endowed with legal personality. It is entirely independent of, and is sharply distinguished from, the members of the corporation. The property of the corporation is not the property of the corporation members; these can have rights in it only as in an alien thing, but no distributive or share rights therein based upon such membership. The claims and obligations of the corporation are not claims and

---

[3] For the contrary view see *Mitteis, Römisches Privatrecht bis auf die Zeit Diokletians,* I (1908), 342–47. He attempts to establish the existence in the Roman *universitas* of traces of the associational idea, declaring it possible "that the inflexible corporation concept of the classical period was merely the result of a long evolutional process which may perhaps have started with a group-concept quite as full of germinal vitality as that of the Germanic law."

debts of its members.[4] In a lawsuit the corporation is an independent litigant party; its members are not parties. Acts of the members neither give rights to nor impose obligations upon the corporation as such, unless when those members are formally empowered to act as its representatives. The corporation is organized for all time; a change in the content of its membership has no effect upon the existence of the corporation. In Roman law, the Roman State and, particularly, the commune were regarded as such *universitates.* Private societies (*Vereine*), though many such existed, played only a subordinate rôle.

Unlike the *universitas,* the *societas* or partnership (*Gesellschaft*) was no subject of rights, but merely a legal relation between the partners. The partnership is therefore, as such, without capacity either for rights or action, and consequently is incapable of holding property. There is therefore no partnership property that can be distinguished in any manner from the private property of the partners. If the partners accumulate property through contributions or otherwise, it belongs in shares, distributively, to the individual partners. Each partner can at any time require the dissolution of the partnership relation, and has a claim, then, to his share as a partner. The partnership is a legal relation that exists exclusively between the persons who join in the partnership contract; every change in the membership theoretically dissolves the partnership. Moreover, the Roman *societas* exacted of the individual not even the slightest sacrifice of his existence as a separate personality.

Nature and Species of Juristic Persons   Under the influence of Christianity, the later Roman law came to recognize as corporations, besides group-persons (*universitates personarum*), so-called *universitates bonorum.* That is to say, it assumed that property segregated by juristic acts *inter vivos* or *mortis causa,* and dedicated as an "endowment" (*Stiftung*) to a pious or charitable purpose (*pia causa, pium corpus*), could itself be an inde-

---

[4] According to *Mitteis,* 345, this principle, ascribed by dominant legal theory to the Roman law, is also not in point: "Expressions such as '*quod universitati debetur singulis non debetur*' express merely the formal unity of corporations in relations with third parties, and leave quite untouched the question as to the nature of the internal bond."

pendent holder of rights and duties. But it was not from the scanty rules of the Roman law that the Canon law developed the doctrine—dominant in medieval and in modern times—of the "foundation" (*Anstalt*) and the endowment as independent legal personalities. The conception of the "foundation" as an immortal person, endowed with special property, created for special ends, and subjected to an external will, found a prototype in the ecclesiastical theory of the Church, which men conceived of as an establishment ordained of God, organized from above, and endowed as an independent holder of rights. The legal concepts of foundation and endowment passed, however, from the Canon into the German law. The latter had developed in the localized property of the proprietary church, or in certain parts thereof— namely the benefice, the church lights, and the church-buildings (*Fabrikvermögen*)—a peculiar ecclesiastical type of a special estate (*Sondervermögen*). And though the statutes of the Church relating to advowsons later swept away the element of ownership which was the basis of this, they nevertheless recognized this special estate as an independent endowment. "It was not out of the endowment of the old Roman law, with which connections had for centuries been broken, but from Germanic roots, that the personality of the foundations and endowments of the ecclesiastical law directly grew—and mediately, the foundations and endowments of the private law. But of course this development was furthered by the revival of legal science." Finally, as regards the nature of the juristic person or corporation, the fiction-theory, only suggested in the Roman sources, attained complete elaboration and undisputed dominance. Men were agreed that the *universitas* was, indeed, a person; but equally that its personality rested on a legal fiction, that it was an insensible and invisible thing without body or soul, cognizable by reason only. True, men remained uncertain as to the relation between conception of this *persona ficta* and that of the aggregate of individuals. The idea appeared that an artificial holder of rights had been created out of nothing. This idea was opposed to the other and more Germanic idea, according to which the fiction consisted only in regarding the aggregate of individuals as a personal entity separate from the members.

RECEPTION OF THE
ALIEN DOCTRINES

After attempts had been made from the 1300s onward to interpret the German law of associations in terms of the doctrine of the alien law, this was finally adopted by German jurisprudence at the beginning of the 1500s. In this movement the Imperial Chamber of Justice took the lead, and the judicial-opinions of the university law faculties, and the counsel-practice of individual scholars powerfully coöperated. Legislation next passed under the same influence. But at first, of course, the influence of native conditions and ideas continued to be felt at many points, and even in the final elaboration of the common law they retained a not unimportant influence.

In particular, the conception of the foundation was now for the first time put forward in contrast to the Roman concept of the corporation (*Korporation*). And it was just here that connection could be made with old Germanic conditions. For the German law too, as above pointed out (p. 260), had known from the earliest times relations of power and dependence in which a mass of dependent persons were united about a lord who was their common superior. Above all, the growth of national sovereignty and of the modern State that sprang therefrom became of decisive importance. Men came to regard the national sovereign, as such—the ideal entity, outliving changes of dynasties and time, of a governing group (*obrigkeitlicher Verband*) ruling over a particular country and attached to a particular ruling house—as the bearer of supreme governmental rights and duties; as an invisible person, although, indeed, without other physical embodiment than the person of the Territorial ruler, and therefore identified with him, or at least with the ruling house. These were theories of secular content which harmonized with the above-cited Canonistic theories, and which eventually found additional and important support in the political theory of the antique world with which men were then making acquaintance. There was thus developed, within both State and Church, a like conception of the foundation. And this was now applied, following the Canon law, to endowments established by private persons, which were left unconnected with State and Church save that to both of these there was attributed a general power of oversight over such endowments. The contrast between *Anstalt* and *Körperschaft* thenceforth retained fundamental importance. The corporate association represented an aggregate of persons (*Personengesamtheit*) conceived of as a holder of rights directed by the collective will resultant from the formal fusion, in prescribed manner, of the several individual wills. On the other hand, the "foundation," was not based upon the will of a majority, but was subjected to an external will from above, be it that of a ruler or superior in whom the foundation is integrated, or that of the founder, who remains permanently active in his private endowment. In the development of the concept of the foundation and in the classification under it of the State, of ecclesiastical establishments (*Institute*), and of endowments, one may well recognize an extension, reasonable enough from the standpoint of Germanic law, of the doctrine of collective personality.

The same cannot be said of the extension to corporate associations of "foundational" elements, and the transformation of many corporate associations—for example, universities—into "foundations." But this reflects the growing tendency of the time to break down the self-imperium (*Selbstherrlichkeit*) of the medieval *Körperschaft;* a tendency which ultimately, under the lead of the law of nature, united politics and jurisprudence in an endeavor to destroy all independent corporate life, and to set in its place an all-powerful State, sweeping away the corporate-concept along with that of the foundation.

The *Körperschaften* of the German law were treated outright as *Korporationen* in the sense of the common law theory. They were regarded, therefore, as fictitious persons. Accordingly, since as non-existent beings they could not act, representatives must be appointed for them. And so men came, in Germany also, to class juristic persons with infants and insane persons, who can likewise participate in legal transactions only through representatives recognized by the statutory law. This arrangement passed over into modern codes. True, capacity to hold property was conceded them as a matter of course; but delictual capacity, in the strict sense of the Roman law, was denied them. The sharp division between juristic persons as such and their members—a division which was flatly contradictory of the native law—was advocated as at least the sole institute that satisfied the needs of theory; but of course this could not be fully established by statute. Similarly, the Romanists demanded the introduction of the Roman concession theory of incorporation. In fact most of the Territorial systems of law took this view, and associated the attainment of juristic personality with an express act of recognition by the State. Whether this principle also acquired a common law authority remained, it is true, in dispute. At all events, it was in complete contradiction to the native tradition. Moreover, men were constrained to do away with it as regarded certain classes of corporations and to introduce for these the freer principle of normative preconditions.

As the *Körperschaft* was subjected to the corporation-concept of the alien law, so the principles of the Roman *societas* were applied without qualification to the relationships of collective hand of the German law; and there was doubtless involved in this a violence to the native law still more incomprehensible. Precisely here, however, the alien doctrine proved incapable of forcing into its categories the forms of the living German law. The types of partnership of the commercial law, particularly, escaped from its control at a comparatively early date; and in the regulation of partnership law the legislation of the 1700s was compelled to make many concessions to Germanic ideas (above p. 285).

RENASCENCE OF NATIVE LAW

In Legal Theory So long as the associational (*Vereins*) life of Germany was prostrate in consequence of its general political and economic decline, and so long as the literary and legislative activity of the jurists was directed, in more or less naïvely rationalistic manner and with an entire lack of historical discernment, toward an adjustment of legal theory to the needs of practical life without much regard to logic or principle, the unsatisfactory state of the law of associations was not urgently apparent. But it was bound to become so when the associational type of organization wakened to new life at the beginning of the 1800s, and modern historical and doctrinal research showed that the existing law was neither in agreement with the Roman sources nor itself presented a consistent system. The more zealous the

Romanists were to establish the principles of the pure Roman law as the only ones entitled to recognition, the more insistent was the opposition thereto on the part of the Germanists. It was the great achievement of the associational theory—as this was first formulated by Beseler, and then elaborated, in particular, by Gierke, who chose this in a special sense as his life work— that it finally cleared the way for an understanding of the German law, taught men to realize the peculiar genius of this, and helped it to a revived authority.

The "association-theory" (*Genossenschaftstheorie*) in the ultimate form given it essentially by Gierke, showed that the two Roman categories of *universitas* and *societas* did not suffice to make intelligible the types of the Germanic law of associations. It offered in their place the contrast developed in the sources between corporate association and association in communities of collective hand in the senses above explained, and proved that the wealth of forms in German law was explicable only by the possibility which it afforded of assimilating the corporate association to the community of collective hand through a recognition of the separate rights of the members, and the community of collective hand to the corporate association by regarding the commoners collectively as constituting a composite entity recognized by the law of persons, and by the recognition of a special social property (*Gesellschaftsvermögen*). It showed that the German law had developed in the *Körperschaft* its own peculiar conception of a collective person (*Gesamtperson*) distinct from the physical members. This collective person of German law is not, like the Roman *corporatio* (*Korporation*), a fictitious person; nor can it be understood through the principles of appointed funds for special purposes (*Zweckvermögen*), or by making the beneficiaries (*Destinatären*) collectively the subjects of the common rights—nor did these theories even fit the Roman law itself.

The *Genossenschaftstheorie* pointed decisively toward the conclusion that the collective person possessed an actual existence in all the forms in which it was manifested; hence it necessarily sought to deduce from general principles of legal philosophy a solution of the difficult problems of the nature of juristic persons and the possibility of a collective will. Granting that it may, in this endeavor, have fallen to some extent into all too abstract

and nebulous refinements; granting also that it may well have
left unduly in the background the indisputable fact that such
collective person, through its very lack of a natural basis, must
always remain essentially different from the separate individuals
composing it, and that after all it is the individual human beings
for whose sake all human unions exist, not vice versa—still, it
sharpened our sight for discernment of the fact that juristic persons, even though not sensible to sight and handling, share this
lack of physical existence with *all other* juristic facts and concepts. And as we nevertheless ascribe reality to property or to
an obligational relation, so too the State, the commune, the
society, the endowment, are real; not merely fictional. We are
compelled in our juristic thinking to group together certain phe-
nomena and processes of social life under the category of juristic
persons—that is of legal personalities—that correspond to no
individual human beings. The discernment of this fact of legal
theory, which became of essential importance in the theory of
the State, was an achievement of ideas developed in Germanic
law.

In Positive Law   After the *Genossenschaftstheorie* had won
increasing influence in the administration of justice and had received recognition in many imperial statutes, notably those of the
commercial law, it was adopted by the present Civil Code as the
basis of the law of the society (*Verein*) and of the partnership
(*Gesellschaft*). The Civil Code no longer knows a *persona ficta;*
it concedes to juristic persons not merely capacity for holding
property, but also—as it does to physical persons—situs, name,
civil honor, etc.; it ascribes to them capacity for action, and also
—here again like the old Germanic law—delictual capacity. It
is true, however, that because of political misgivings a general
introduction of the principle of free association, such as is realized
in the English law for example, has not been ventured; the con-
cession-system being retained to a considerable extent beside
that of normative requisites. On the other hand, the Swiss Civil
Code has adopted the principle of complete freedom of association and endowment. Societies (*Vereine*—"*associations*" in the
French text of the Code) with economic ends do require registration in the commercial register (§ 61); but the steps to such
registration, "instead of leading through strict normative condi-

tions expressive of anxiety and distrust, are completely free": so soon as the corporation is organized it is empowered to demand registration. And "societies that are devoted to an end neither political, religious, scientific, artistic, charitable, social, or otherwise non-economic, attain personality so soon as the will to exist *as* a corporation (*Körperschaft*) is discernible in their bylaws" (§ 60). As species of juristic persons, the German Civil Code (which, be it remembered, regulates only those of private law) sets beside the society (*Verein*)—which corresponds to the corporate association (*Körperschaft*) of the old German law— the endowment (*Stiftung*); that is, a "foundation" (*Anstalt*) with a legal personality that is created by the will of a private person. Finally, the principle of collective hand has been made by the Code the basis, not only of the marital and continued marital community of goods and the community of heirs, but also—what is most important—of the ordinary partnership of the private law (§§ 705–40). In so doing it assimilated this to the unlimited mercantile partnership, following the example of the Prussian *Landrecht*. The ordinary mercantile partnership of the private law of today constitutes, like the old community of collective hand, an entity in which are bound together the individual associates, and which, without actually possessing independent legal personality, has the appearance, particularly in relations with third parties, of a solidary and self-sufficient body. It can have its own social property, which, as a separate estate distinct from the private estates of the partners, belongs to these in collective hand. Similarly, partnership obligations are possible that are not at the same time private debts of the members, and for which these are liable in collective hand.

Thus, within the law of associations, a triumph great almost beyond expectation has been vouchsafed to Germanic legal science, both in theory and in positive law.

11

CORPORATION AND PERSON

Frederick Pollock
Frederic W. Maitland

Corporations and Churches

Every system of law that has attained a certain degree of
maturity seems compelled by the ever-increasing complexity of
human affairs to create persons who are not men, or rather (for
this may be a truer statement) to recognize that such persons
have come and are coming into existence, and to regulate their
rights and duties. In the history of medieval Europe we have to
watch on the one hand the evolution of groups (in particular,
religious groups and groups of burgesses) which in our eyes
seem to display all or many of the characteristics of corporations,
and on the other hand the play of thought around that idea of
an *universitas* which was being slowly discovered in the Roman
law books.

We have become so familiar with the idea of "a corporation
aggregate of many" that we have ceased to wonder at it. When
we are told by statute that the word "person" is to include "body
politic," that seems to us a very natural rule. Nevertheless, this
idea was gradually fashioned, and when we attempt to analyze it

From Frederick Pollock and Frederic W. Maitland, *The History of
English Law before the Time of Edward I*, 2nd ed., vol. I (Cambridge,
1899), pp. 486–526.

we find that it is an elastic because it is, if we may so say, a very
contentless idea, a blank form of legal thought. Little enough in
common have the divers corporations known to English law: for
example, the Ecclesiastical Commissioners for England; the Dean
and Chapter of Ely; the Chancellor, Masters and Scholars of the
University of Oxford; the Mayor, Aldermen and Burgesses of the
Borough of Cambridge; the Governor and Company of the Bank
of England; the Great Northern Railway Company; Styles, Nokes
and Company (Limited). Among "natural persons" the law for
a long time past has been able to single out one class as being
normal or typical and to treat other classes as exceptional; and
to this we may add that in course of time some of the exceptional
classes disappear; the noble class disappears, the unfree class
disappears. Far otherwise is it with the "artificial persons" or
"group-persons"; we can hardly call one corporation more
normal than another and modern legislation is constantly supply-
ing us with new kinds. Thus we are not likely to find the essence
of a corporation in any one rule of law. If, for example, an English lawyer would make all turn on the common seal, he would
be setting up a merely English rule as a necessary maxim of
jurisprudence; nor only so, for he would be begging an important
question about the early history of corporations in England.
Some again may feel inclined to say that a corporation must have
its origin in a special act of the State, for example, in England
a royal charter; but they again will be in danger of begging a
question about ancient history, while they will have difficulty in
squaring their opinion with the modern history of joint-stock
companies. Modern legislation enables a small group of private
men to engender a corporation by registration, and to urge that
this is the effect of "statute" and not of "common law" is to
insist upon a distinction which we hardly dare carry beyond the
four seas. Or, to come to a more vital point, shall we demand
that an individual corporator shall not be liable for the debts of
the corporation? "*Si quid universitati debetur singulis non debetur;
nec quod debet universitas singuli debent*"—is not this the very
core of the matter? Once more modern legislation bids us pause:
there is no reason why a statute should not say that a judgment
obtained against a corporation can be enforced against all the
lands and all the goods of every single corporator, and this al-

though the corporation still exists—in ordering that this be so, the legislature does not contradict itself.[1] Nor again is it only from modern statute that we receive this warning; our ancient common law gives us the same warning in unmistakable terms. If we insist that common law can not hold the *singuli* liable for the debt of the *universitas,* we shall find little to say about corporations in any century earlier than the fifteenth.

Hitherto the lesson that we have been taking to ourselves is that we are not to deny the presence of the idea of a corporation merely because it is not producing all of what we consider its natural effects. The warning is equally necessary that in remote times we may somewhat easily discover corporations that never existed. The history of the earlier part of our own century proves that large commercial enterprises may be conducted and much done in the way of subordinate government by aggregates of men that are not incorporated. The law of tenancy in common and joint tenancy, the law of partnership, these have been found equal to many heavy and novel demands. And when we turn to a far-off past we may be in great danger of too readily seeing a corporation in some group of landholders, which, if modern distinctions are to be applied at all, would be better classed as a group of joint tenants than as a corporation.

The core of the matter seems to be that for more or less numerous purposes some organized group of men[2] is treated as a unit which has rights and duties other than the rights and duties of all or any of its members. What is true of this whole need not be true of the sum of its parts, and what is true of the sum of the parts need not be true of the whole. The corporation, for example, can own land and its land will not be owned by the sum of the corporators; and, on the other hand, if all the corporators are co-owners of a thing, then that thing is not owned by the corporation. This being so, lawyers from the thirteenth century onwards have been wont to attribute to the corporation a "personality" that is "fictitious" or "artificial." Now "person" and "personality" seem to be appropriate words, and, if they were

---

[1] In the first half of this century our parliament tried many experiments of this kind.

[2] We neglect for a while that unhappy freak of English law the corporation sole.

not at our disposal, we should be driven to coin others of a similar import.[3] The corporate unit has become a subject of rights and duties. On the other hand, the adjectives which are often used to qualify this personality are open to serious objection, since they seem to speak to us of some trick or exploit performed by lawyers and to suggest a wide departure of legal theory from fact and common opinion. It may at least be plausibly maintained that the subject of those rights and duties which we ascribe to the corporation is no figment but the organized group of men, though this group is treated as pure unit. Unless all social and political organization deserves to be called fictitious, a contract between a municipal corporation and a joint-stock company is not a relationship between two fictions; it is a relationship between two groups, but between two groups each of which is so organized that for the purpose of the matter in hand, and for many other purposes, it can be treated as an indivisible unit and compared to a man.

One of the difficulties that beset us at this point is that we are tempted or compelled to seek the aid of those inadequate analogies that are supplied to us by the objects which we see and handle. First we picture to ourselves a body made up of men as a man's body is made up of members. Then we find ourselves rejecting some of the inferences which this similitude, this crude anthropomorphism, might suggest. For instance, we have to admit that every "member" may be injured while the whole "body" suffers no injury. And then perhaps we say in our haste that the corporation which has rights and duties can be no better than fiction or artifice. But all that is proved by the collapse of such analogical reasoning is that social organization differs from, if it also resembles, that organization which the biologist studies; and this should hardly need proof.

Were we to digress to modern times, we might be able to show that the theory which speaks of the corporation's personality as fictitious, a theory which English lawyers borrowed from medieval canonists, has never suited our English law very well. It should at all events be known that on the continent of Europe this doctrine no longer enjoys an undisputed orthodoxy either among the students of the Roman *universitas* or among the

---

[3] Such as the German *Rechtssubject, Rechtssubjectivität*.

students of medieval and modern corporations. But here we are
dealing with a time when in our own country the need for any
idea of a corporation, whether as *persona ficta* or as "group-
person," has hardly become evident.

Now if for a moment we take our stand in Edward IV's reign,
when the middle ages are nearing their end, we can say that the
idea of a corporation is already in the minds of our lawyers; it
may trouble them—this is shown by their frequent discussions
about its nature—but still it is there.[4] First we notice that they
already have a term for it, namely, *corporacion,* for which *corps
corporat* and *corps politik* are equivalents. Then under this term
several entities which have little in common have been brought:
in particular, abbot and convent, dean and chapter, mayor and
commonalty. With such "incorporated bodies" they contrast aggregates of men that are not incorporated, townships, parishes,
gilds. They demand that incorporatedness shall have some definite
and authoritative commencement; the corporation does not grow
by nature; it must be made, by the act of parliament, or of the
king, or of the pope,[5] though prescription may be equivalent to
royal charter. The rule that the corporation can do no act save
by a writing under its common seal they enforce with severity;
it is an anomaly, a concession to practical necessities, that the
commands of the corporation about petty affairs can come to its
servants through less formal channels. The corporation is invisible, incorporeal, immortal; it can not be assaulted, or beaten
or imprisoned; it can not commit treason; a doubt has occurred
as to whether it can commit a trespass, but this doubt (though
it will give trouble so late as the year 1842) has been rejected
by practice, if not removed by any consistent theory. We even
find it said that the corporation is but a name. On the other
hand, it is a person. It is at once a person and yet but a name;
in short, it is *persona ficta.*

The main difficulty that the lawyers have in manipulating this
idea is occasioned by the fact that almost every corporation has

---

[4] See the Year Books of Edward IV in general.

[5] Dean and chapter, mayor and commonalty are incorporated by the
king; the mendicant friars by the pope; abbot and convent by both king
and pope.

a "head," which head is separately and expressly designated by the formal title of the juristic person. It is regarded as an anomaly that at Ripon there should be a corporation of canons without a head; normally there is a head; the ideal person is not the Convent of St. Albans, the Chapter of Lincoln, the Commonalty of Norwich, but the Abbot and Convent of St. Albans, the Dean and Chapter of Lincoln, the Mayor, Sheriffs and Commonalty of Norwich. This keeps alive the anthropomorphic idea. In 1481 a puzzling question arose as to whether when a dean and chapter brought an action, a juror might be challenged on the ground that he was brother to one of the canons. An advocate who urges that the juror is "a stranger to the chapter, for it is a body of such a nature that it can have neither brother nor cousin," none the less concedes that peradventure it might have been otherwise had the juror been brother to the dean. Elsewhere the relation between dean and chapter is compared to that between husband and wife; "the chapter is *covert* by the dean as the wife is *coverte* by her husband." From the same year, 1481, we get one of the most interesting cases in all the Year Books: The Abbot of Hulme sued the Mayor, Sheriffs and Commonalty of Norwich on a bond, and they pleaded that when the bond was made the then abbot had got the then mayor in prison and extorted the bond by duress. The lawyers very generally admit that the corporation itself can not be in prison or suffer duress, and that it would be no defence to urge that when the bond was made some few of the citizens of Norwich were (as they generally would be) in gaol. But then in this case "the head" of the corporation was incarcerated. "I tell you, Sir," says counsel for the city, "that every body politic is made up of natural men. And as regards what has been said touching its inseverability, I do not admit that; for they allow that mayor, sheriffs and commonalty make up a single body; here then are members, namely, the mayor is one member . . . the sheriffs another member . . . the third is the commonalty . . . In this case there is an alleged imprisonment of one of the distinct members named in the title of the corporation, to wit, the mayor, who is the head and (as in a body natural) the principal member . . . and if one member of the body natural be restrained or beaten, that is a restraint or battery of the whole body." This idea that a corporation consists of head and members, that every act of the corporation requires the assent of its head, that, if for a while it is headless, it is capable of no act save that of electing a new head, has given trouble in more recent times and is perhaps capable of giving trouble even at the present day; it is a relic of what we have called anthropomorphism. In Edward IV's day we are told that the Mayor and Commonalty of Newcastle gave a bond to the person who happened to be mayor, naming him by his personal name. It was held void, for a man can not be bound to himself. So long as such a decision for such a reason is possible, the modern idea of a corporation is not secure; at any rate it is hampered by an inconsistent and older idea. Still in the Year Books of Edward IV that idea is present, nay, prominent, and some important rules of law in which it is implied have already been settled. In particular it is established that if the corporation becomes liable upon contract or for tort, this does not give a remedy against the persons, lands or goods of the corporators; the corporation itself is liable; execution will be done only on its lands and its goods.

We go back but a little way in the Year Books and the idea that we have been watching begins to disappear. The figure of the ideal person vanishes, or rather it seems at times to become a mere mass of natural persons. One instance will serve to illustrate this change. So late as 1429 an action of trespass was brought against the Mayor, Bailiffs and Commonalty of Ipswich and one J. Jabe. The defendants pleaded the marvellous plea that Jabe was one of the commonalty and therefore was named twice over. If the defendants are found guilty, then (it was urged) Jabe will be charged twice over; besides he may be found not guilty and the commonalty guilty: that is to say, he may be found both guilty and not guilty. We do not know how the case was decided; but it was twice discussed. Incidentally a fundamental question of corporation law was raised. Suppose that judgment is given against the commonalty, can the goods of the members be taken in execution? On the whole the judges think that they can not, but are not very sure. They make an admission of great importance to us, namely, that it is the common course in the King's Bench that if a community be amerced, the amercement shall be levied from all the goods of the members of the community.[6] The obvious tendency of this admission they seek to avoid by saying that there is a great difference between the king and anyone else. As we shall hereafter see this admission was unavoidable; the goods of the members of municipal communities were constantly treated as liable to satisfy the king for debts due by the community as a whole. And a mere doubt about the general principle of corporate liability occurring at so late a date as 1429 is remarkable.[7] We have indeed observed before now that the non-liability of individual corporators for the debts of the corporation can not be regarded as of the essence of a corporation. Still unless such non-liability had been common, the modern idea of a corporation would hardly have been formed.

In all this there is nothing to surprise us. Surprising it would have been had the English lawyers of Bracton's day obtained a firm hold of the notion of an *universitas*. In that case they would have been ahead of their Italian contemporaries, who had Code and Digest to set them thinking. It would be a mistake to suppose that what we are wont to consider the true theory of *universitates* lay so plainly written on the face of the Roman law-books that no one could read them attentively without grasping it. The glossators did not grasp it. Bracton's master Azo had not grasped it. They were by no means certain about the difference between the *universitas* and the *societas* or partnership. The canonists of the thirteenth century were just beginning to proclaim that the *universitas* is a *persona* and a *persona ficta*. Bracton's contemporary, Pope Innocent IV (Sinibaldus Fliscus), has been called the father of the modern theory of corporations. We now begin to hear the dogma (of which all English lawyers know a vulgar version) that the *universitas* can be punished neither in this world nor in the next, for that it has nor soul nor body. And

---

[6] The words are "*sera levie de touts biens,* etc."; it is clear from the context that this means "shall be levied from all the goods of the members."

[7] In 1437 it is said that if a man recovers debt or damages against a commonalty he shall only have execution against the goods that they have in common.

yet, when these steps had been taken, many an elementary question lay open for the civilians and canonists.[8]

This premised, we turn to the law of Henry III's day, for the purpose of hearing what it has to say (1) of corporations in general, and (2) of the more important kinds into which corporations may be divided. But at once we discover that of corporations in general little is said, and the law is not dividing corporations into various kinds, thus proceeding from the abstract to the concrete; rather it is slowly coming to the idea of a corporation by dealing with corporations (if so we may call them) of very different kinds.

In the first place we can find in our law-books no such terms as *corporation, body corporate, body politic,* though we may read much of *convents, chapters,* and *communities.* The largest term in general use is *community, commonalty,* or *commune,* in Latin *communitas* or *communa.* It is a large, vague word; in the fourteenth century it is often applied to the English nation, "the community" or "the commune of the land"; it is applied to the Cistercian order; it is applied to the University of Cambridge, for "in the vill of Cambridge there are two communes, one of clerks and one of lay men"; it can be applied to "the community of merchants who hold the king's staple of wools"; it was applied to the "bachelors" of England who in 1259 had joined together to obtain concessions from the king. But we dare not translate it by *corporation,* for if on the one hand it is describing cities and boroughs which already are, or at least are on their way to become, corporations, it will stand equally well for counties, hundreds and townships, which in the end have failed to acquire a corporate character, and we should be unwilling to suppose that the corporate character once definitely acquired was afterwards lost. One term there was (so it may seem to us) capable of binding together all the groups of men that were personified, namely, the word *universitas.* But its fate has been curious and instructive. In our modern languages the Roman

---

8 Innocent says, "*cum collegium in causa universitatis fingatur una persona.*" Johannes Andreae says, "*universitas non est capax poenae capitalis, corporalis, spiritualis. . . . cum corpus animatum non habeat ad hoc aptum.*" The amusing question was discussed whether a corporation could be a godmother.

term that most nearly answered to our *corporation* stands for the corporations of one small class, the learned corporations that were founded in the twelfth and thirteenth centuries and others that in later days were fashioned after their likeness. These were in the middle ages the corporations by preeminence, and if the universities of Oxford and Cambridge cared to assert that they are the oldest of English corporations something might be said in favour of their claim. For the rest, the word *universitas* is of common use in legal documents; but only in one context, and one which shows how vague a term it could be. The maker of a charter salutes "All the faithful in Christ," or "All the sons of Holy Church," and then requests their attention by *Noverit universitas vestra*. Now the idea of the Church as the mystical body of Christ has had an important influence on the growth of the law of corporations; it did much towards fashioning for us the anthropomorphic picture of the many members in one body. Still in days when the word *universitas* was put to its commonest use in describing a world-wide, divinely created organization, it could be of small service to lawyers as an accurate word of art.

Bracton has a little to say about *universitates;* it is meagre, it is vague, it is for the more part borrowed from Azo, but none the less it is instructive. In the first place, the cities and boroughs are the only examples of *universitates* which occur to him. In the second place, following the Institutes, he admits that there are *res universitatis* which are to be contrasted with *res singulorum*. Thirdly, no definite examples of *res universitatis* does he give save those that are given by the Institutes, namely, the *theatrum* and *stadium*. The inference is obvious that, though he allowed the possibility of an *universitas* holding land, he knew little of the English city or borough as a landowner; it is not in his manner to give Roman examples when he can give English, while as to our medieval boroughs having *stadia et theatra,* that is nonsense. Fourthly, he knows that if the English *universitas,* the city or borough, has but little land and few goods, it has magnificent *libertates,* franchises, governmental powers and immunities, and these are a common subject of litigation. Fifthly, when he speaks of such litigation he speaks vaguely, and hardly distinguishes between the *universitas* and the aggregate of *singuli*. Sixthly, he nowhere makes an act of royal or public power necessary to the existence of an *universitas*. Lastly, he does not bring any ecclesiastical bodies under this heading; they fall within another form of thought.

Being unable to find any theory about corporations in general, we are obliged to descend to the various kinds of corporations: to consider, that is, the manner in which the law of the thirteenth century treated those various groups of men which seem to us to have a more or less corporate existence. They are either ecclesiastical or temporal.

For many centuries before Bracton's day there have been in England what we may call "church lands." In some sort or another they have "belonged" to "churches." But to fashion a satisfactory theory as to the ownership of these lands has been a task beset by practical and intellectual difficulties. The scheme of church-property-law which had prevailed in the Roman world before the German deluge had been a system of centralized and official administration. All the ecclesiastical property within a diocese was under the control and at the disposal of a single officer, the bishop of the *civitas*. His powers were very large; his subordinates, the diocesan clergy, received the stipends that he allowed them. Such a scheme was adapted only to an age that was far advanced in commerce and orderly government, and we may doubt whether it served even as an ideal in England where the thread of ecclesiastical tradition had been broken. It implies an easy transmission of wealth and messages from place to place; it was thoroughly civic and could not be maintained in a world of villages and manors inhabited by rude barbarians. If there is to be much Christianity in the land, not only must there be village churches, but the village church must be a proprietary centre, an economically self-sufficing institution.

Then, as we are beginning to understand, the German has brought with him into the Roman and Christian world the notion that, if he builds a church upon his land, it is his church. If in the days of heathenry he had built a god-house on his land, it would have been his god-house, and he would have made profit out of it. This is the origin of ecclesiastical patronage. The right which from the twelfth century onwards appears as a mere right

of patronage, an *advocatio* or advowson, is in origin an ownership of the soil upon which the church stands and an ownership
of any lands or goods that have been set apart for the sustenance
of a priest who offers sacrifice at the shrine. By slow degrees,
which are now being traced, this church-founder and his heirs
have to be taught that they can not do just what they like with
their own; and, for example, that they can not have their church
worked for them by ordained slaves. The bishop will not con-
secrate the altar unless a sufficient provision of worldly goods is
secured for the priest. The owner or patron, whichever we call
him, must hand over the church and an appurtenant glebe to the
priest by way of "loan." In modern England it is in this context
and this context only that we still know, though only in name,
the "land-loan" of the old Frankish world: the parson still has a
"benefice," a *beneficium*. It is long before the founder's ownership is whittled down to patronage. We may be fairly sure that
the famous ceorl who throve to thegn-right by "having" five
hides of his own land, "church and kitchen, bell-house and
burhgeat," was conceived to "have" the church in no very different sense from that in which he "had" the bell-house and the
kitchen. In Domesday Book the village church is apt to appear
as an owned thing if also as an owning person: "There are here
a church and seven serfs and one mill": "There are here a
chapel and three serfs and one mill": "There is one chapel
which renders eight shillings": "Culling the burgess has a church
of St. Mary of 26 acres, Leofstan the priest has a church of St.
Augustin of 11 acres, Leoflet a free woman had a church of St.
Laurence of 12 acres." Even Bracton must complain that the
layman will talk of giving a church when he means that he is
giving an advowson. Hence the strongly proprietary element that
there is in the right of patronage, an element of which the
"religious" take full advantage when they engulf the parish
churches in the property of their minsters. Modern ecclesiastical
reformers who would curtail such rights as the patron still enjoys
may fairly say that they are consummating the work of a thou-
sand years; but they should not talk of "restoration."[9]

---

[9] It is not contended that as regards every parish church this is the
history of its advowson. The *Eigenkirche* (the owned church) begins to
affect the whole system of law, and the bishop's power over churches that

The early history of church-property in England has never yet been written, and we can not aspire to write it. We do not, for example, know how the parish church became an owning unit with rights distinct from those of the bishop and his cathedral church on the one hand and from those of the founder or patron on the other. But there is a supernatural element in the story. Great changes take place behind a mystic veil. At least for the purposes of popular thought and speech, God and the saints become the subjects of legal rights, if not of legal duties. "God's property and the church's twelve fold"—such were the first written words of English law. In the old land-books this notion is put before us in many striking phrases. In the oldest of them the newly converted Æthelbert says, "To thee Saint Andrew and to thy church at Rochester where Justus the Bishop presides do I give a portion of my land." The saint is the owner; his church at this place or that is mentioned because it is necessary to show of which of his many estates the gift is to form part. If a man will give land to the chief of the Apostles he should give it to St. Peter and his church at Gloucester, or to St. Peter and his church at Westminster; Justinian himself had been obliged to establish a rule for the interpretation of testaments by which the Saviour or some archangel or martyr was nominated heir and no church or monastery was named. The Anglo-Saxon charters and Domesday Book seem to suppose even a physical connexion between the land given to a saint and the particular church with which it is, or is to be, legally connected; geography must yield to law; the acres may be remote from the hallowed spot, nevertheless they "lie in the church." Just as the earl or thegn may have many manors and a piece of land remote from the manorial centre may "lie in" or "be of" one of those manors, so the saint will have many churches each with land belonging to it. Gradually (if we may so speak) the saint retires behind his churches; the church rather than the saint is thought of as the holder of lands and chattels. When it comes to precise legal thinking the saint is an impracticable person, for if we ascribe rightful we may also

---

perhaps had never been owned now begins to look proprietary; they are "his" churches. So too kings assert a patronage over ancient cathedrals, and the emperor may even wish to treat the church of Rome as "his" church.

have to ascribe wrongful possession to him, and from this we shrink, though Domesday Book courageously charges St. Paul with an "invasion" of land that is not his own. But how is the church conceived? In the first instance very grossly as a structure of wood and stone. Land belongs to a church, is an appurtenance of a church, just as other land belongs to or is appurtenant to some hall or dwelling-house. But, as the saint retires, the idea of the church is spiritualized; it becomes a person and, we may say, an ideal, juristic person.

All this while there are human beings who are directing the affairs of the saint and the church, receiving, distributing, enjoying the produce of the land. They are the saint's administrators; they are the *rectores* of his church. Some of them, notably the bishops, since their powers of administration are very large, may be spoken of as landholders; but still the land which the bishop has as bishop is hardly his own; when he demands it, he demands it not *ut ius suum,* but *ut ius ecclesiae suae.*

Very often in Domesday Book the saint is the landowner; Saint Paul holds land, Saint Constantine holds land, the Count of Mortain holds land of Saint Petroc. Leofstan held land under "the glorious king Edmund." Often a particular *ecclesia,* or an *abbatia,* holds land. Sometimes the land is described as that of the saint, but the church is said to hold it; sometimes this relation is reversed, the land is the land of the church but the saint holds it. Often, again, the land is spoken of as that of the ruler of the church; this is frequently the case when a bishop is concerned: the land is the land of the Bishop of Exeter and the Bishop of Exeter holds it. Still this is no invariable rule; the church of Worcester, an episcopal church, has lands and St. Mary of Worcester holds them; and it is not the Bishop of Rome, but the Roman church of St. Peter the Apostle who holds land in Somerset. Sometimes the abbey holds land, sometimes the abbot; sometimes a distinction is drawn between abbey and abbot; the demesne manors are held by the church itself, but the manors given to knights are held of the abbot. These are cases (not very many) in which groups of canons are said to hold lands, to hold them in common.

We have said that the "church" becomes a person. If, however, we ask how the "church" is to be conceived, we obtain very various answers from canonists, divines and philosophers. Materialism and mysticism are closely allied. At one moment a theorist will maintain that between the death of a parish priest and the induction of his successor the possession of the glebe is being held and retained by the walls of the church; at the next moment we hear of the body or the bride of the Redeemer. With the more exalted of such doctrines the lawyer has little concern; but he should notice that the *ecclesia particularis* which stands on a certain spot is conceived as a part and member of the *ecclesia universalis,* for this theory leaves a strong mark on that notion of a corporation, an *universitas,* which the canonist propagates. He is by the law of his being a centralizer, and perhaps will not shrink from the conclusion that, if analysis be carried to its logical limit, the *dominium* of all church-property is in the pope. At any rate the will of the *ecclesia particularis,* the episcopal or parochial church, is not to be found wholly within it. It lives a life that is not its own; the life of a "member."

Meanwhile the legists, exploring Code and Digest, were slowly discovering the *universitas* and endeavouring to mark it off from the partnership and the group of co-proprietors. The canonists seized this new learning and carried it further. The greater churches had about them a certain collegiateness; there was a group composed of bishop and canons, or abbot and monks. Here then was an idea that they wanted. The *ecclesia* is an *universitas,* and the *universitas* is a *persona.* That they should go on to add (as Innocent IV did) that it is *persona ficta* was not unnatural. The organized group was distinct from the "church"; its will might not be the church's will. To this we must add that the canonist's law aspired to deal not only with wrong and crime, reparation and punishment, but also with sin and damnation. In his eyes a person who can not sin and can not be damned can only be *persona ficta.* So the *universitas* is not the organized group, but a feigned substratum for rights. This theory will easily lead to a denial that a corporation can commit either crime or wrong, and Innocent went this length; but both practice and theory rejected his doctrine.[10] The relationship between the group

---

[10] Why the law should create "fictions" which commit torts and crimes must always be a difficult question, though when once breach of contract or wrongful possession has been attributed to a corporation the plunge

and the feigned substratum could never be fully explained. The leading idea, however, was that the group was not, but only represented, and at times (if we may so speak) misrepresented, the corporation. How little of corporateness, of collegiateness, there is in the canonical idea of a corporation is shown by the ease with which this same idea is extended to a case in which there is no plurality, no group. Our curious phrase "corporation sole" only appears late in the day and seems to be exclusively English; but the canonists had come very near to it in their treatment of the cases in which an *ecclesia* had but one cleric connected with it; the *dignitas* or the *sedes* or the like could be personified.[11] Here, as in the case of a "corporation aggregate," there is "fictitious" personality. So the canonist's corporation is rather a personified institution than a unified group of men.

With the evolution of these ideas the English temporal courts of the thirteenth century were not concerned. The canonical theory of the *persona ficta* was to bear fruit, some good, some bad, in the English common law of later days; but the internal affairs of the ecclesiastical groups could seldom or never be brought before the lay tribunals, and at the time of which we speak municipal growth had hardly reached that stage at which there would be a crying need for some theory or another of a town's personality. As yet we hear nothing in the secular courts of corporations whether aggregate or sole, and though we hear much of "churches" the lawyers at Westminster have no occasion to analyze the idea that they are employing.

---

has been made. If, however, wrong-doing was to be ascribed to an *ecclesia,* there was convenience in the theory that *this* "church" was only *nomen iuris* or an intellectual device and not a member of the body of Christ.

11 Gierke says that this personification of the *sedes* or *dignitas* did not introduce a second and independent category of juristic persons beside the corporation; rather the canonist's idea of a corporation was already so much the idea of an institution [not of an organized body of men] that the corporate element in it might disappear altogether without any essential change becoming necessary. True, he continues, the personified *dignitas* was not directly subsumed under the title of a corporation [this is just what did happen in England], but it was regarded as a phenomenon analogous to a corporation, and to some extent as a variation on the same theme. So far as we are aware the "corporation sole" begins to appear *eo nomine* only in the later Year Books.

From their point of view we may look at the churches, and first at the parish church. When the rector dies or resigns his post there is no breach in the ownership or even in the possession. It is common to find a rector pleading, "I found my church seised of that land." The theory is well stated in a judgment of 1307: A church is always under age and is to be treated as an infant, and it is not according to law that infants should be disinherited by the negligence of their guardians or be barred of an action in case they would complain of things wrongfully done by their guardians while they are under age. Here we have a juristic person, the church, with a natural person as its guardian, and with the patron and the ordinary to check that guardian in his administrative acts, for some things the rector can not do without the consent of patron and ordinary. Had this principle been held fast our later law books would have been relieved of some cumbrous disputations about "the kind of fee" that a parson has.

The case of an abbey was less simple in theory, though the monarchical character of abbatial rule deprived some speculative questions of their importance. The *ecclesia* or *abbatia* succeeded the saint as the subject of proprietary rights. But, at least in the view of the king's courts, the abbot's power was almost that of an absolute owner. Already in Domesday Book we see that it matters little whether one says that the land is held by the church of Ely, the abbey of Ely, or the abbot of Ely. True that when lands are given to an abbey it is rare to find no mention of "the convent" or "the monks" as well as of God, the saint and the abbot. True also that when the abbey lands are alienated the feoffment is usually said to be made either by the abbot and convent, or by the abbot with the consent of the convent. For all this, the temporal courts are apt to treat the abbot as the one and only natural person who has anything to do with the proprietary rights of the abbey. To the complete exclusion of convent or monks he fully represents the abbey before the law; he sues and is sued alone.[12] A rule of ecclesiastical law forbidding prelates to dissipate the lands of their churches was so far

---

[12] The same is true of an independent priory; the prior is its representative before the law.

enforced by the temporal courts that they would give to an abbot an action for recovering lands that had been alienated by his predecessor without the consent of the convent. But this action was given to the successor, not to the convent. Had the convent raised its voice, it would have been told that all its members were dead in law; and even the succeeding abbot could not get back the land without a law-suit; the alienation was voidable, not void. And so with obligations: the question commonly takes the form "when and how can an abbot bind his successors?" rather than "when and how can an abbot bind his church or the convent?" In short, owing to the legal deadness of the monks, the abbey property seems to be administered by, and represented by (and we may easily pass thence to possessed by and owned by), the series of successive abbots. In the hands of the king's justices even this series is apt to break up into a set of disconnected links, each of which is a man. Each successive abbot might sue for lands of which the church had been dispossessed during the abbacy of one of his predecessors; but if a claim for compensation in respect of some unlawful act, such as an abstraction of the church's goods, accrued to one abbot, it died with him and was not competent to his successor. *Actio personalis moritur cum persona*, and here the person wronged is dead, for he was a natural person and could die. To make the law otherwise, a clause in the statute of 1267 was necessary.[13] Thus, though even in the legal notion of an abbey there is an element that we may call "communal," an element which is recognized by the ordinary forms of conveyances and obligations, and sanctioned by the rule that alienations of land are voidable if made without the consent of the convent, still this element is by no means prominent, and the abbot's powers of dealing with property and of binding the abbey (that is his successors) by contract are limited much rather by the idea of the church itself as the true subject of rights and duties, than by any principle that would make him but one among a number of corporators.

The case of a bishop is not essentially unlike that of an abbot. True that the lands of the see are very often, from Domesday Book downwards, spoken of simply as the lands of the bishop;

---

[13] This came of our having no "real" action for movables.

the fact that they constituted a barony made such language the more natural; none the less they were the lands of his church.[14] And in the bishop's case it is at least necessary to distinguish the man from the bishop. All the abbot's lands are the abbey lands, but a bishop may hold lands and goods which in no wise belong to his see; he will have "heirs" as well as official "successors" and may make a will; occasionally he has a great private fortune. In recognizing the possibility of one man having, as we should say, two capacities, a natural and a politic or official capacity, the law made an important step; there are signs that it was not easily made; but the idea of the church as the true owner of the episcopal lands made this step the easier, for in one of his two capacities the bishop was no owner but merely a *rector* or *custos*. Again, there was a communal element to be considered. The lands of the see, if they were the lands of the bishop, were also in some sort the lands of the cathedral convent or chapter, and this, though it might be a group of monks dead to the law, might also be a group of secular canons, each of whom was a fully competent legal person. To a small extent the law recognized the interest of this group; without its consent the bishop could make no alienation of the church's lands that would not be voidable by his successor. Still the members of the chapter had no action if the bishop without their consent dissipated the wealth of the see, and this shows us that the person wronged by such dissipation was not a community of which the bishop was the head, but rather the church, an ideal person, whose guardian he was. He might do nothing to the disherison of his ward without the advice of his council, his constitutional advisers.

There is, however, within the ecclesiastical sphere a well marked movement towards individualism; it goes on from century to century. The clerical groups begin to divide their property. As a first stage we may notice the permanent allotment of lands to specific wants of the group; one manor supplies the monks with food, another with clothing, one in some sort belongs to the cellarer, another to the almoner, sacrist, vestiary. Such arrange-

---

[14] The usual form of a royal charter makes this clear; the grant is "to God and the church of St. Mary and the bishop of Salisbury and his successors"; "to God and the church of SS. Mary and Ethelbert of Hereford and Giles bishop of the said church and his successors."

ments, though they seem to have been regarded as solemn and permanent, were matters of internal economy and, at least as regards the outside world, had no legal effect: the abbot still represented all the lands and all the affairs of the abbey before the law. But sometimes, even in a monastic society, the process went further; often when a bishop's church was monastic, as for example at Canterbury, Durham and Worcester, a partition of lands was made between the bishop and the monks, and even the temporal law took notice of such a partition; the Prior of Canterbury became the legal representative of one section, if we may so speak, of the now divided *ecclesia* of Canterbury.[15] Even in the case of an abbey such partitions were sometimes made, and the Prior of Westminster sued the Abbot. When the group was not monastic but secular the process often went much further; prebends were created; the bishop held lands in right of his bishopric, the dean in right of his deanery, the prebendary in right of his prebend. Though for ecclesiastical purposes the group might be organic, it as a unit had little to do within the sphere of lay justice, and, if we may use the terms of a later day, the "corporation aggregate" was almost resolved into a mere collection of "corporations sole."

Still throughout the middle ages there were groups of ecclesiastics which, as we should say, were corporations aggregate and which, being composed of seculars, were not subject to the monarchical rule of an abbot. The number and wealth of such bodies, and therefore their importance in the history of our law, might easily be exaggerated, but still they existed, and took part in litigation; suits, for example, are said to be brought by and against the canons or the dean and canons of a church. In these cases we seem to see all the elements of a corporation aggregate. In the first place, there is personality; the lands, the affairs, administered by dean and canons, master and brethren, are the lands, the affairs, of a church or a hospital. In the second place, the administrators for the time being are a legally organized body,

---

15 The *Epistolae Cantuarienses* contain a long account from the twelfth century of the litigation between the Archbishop and the monks of Christ Church touching a partition of their territory. In this case even Domesday Book shows a partition; the Archbishop has land and "the monks of the Archbishop" have other land.

a body which perdures while its members come and go.[16] In the third place, this body transacts business as a body by means of meetings and votings and resolutions; the motive power is not (as it is in the case of an abbey) the will of a single man. Our lawyers, however, learnt from the ecclesiastical groups fewer valuable lessons than we might have expected. The groups which were compact were despotically ruled, and the groups which were not despotically ruled were not very numerous nor very wealthy and seldom came before the courts as organized bodies.

As regards the internal economy of the ecclesiastical groups, our common law of the thirteenth century had little to say. Not only was this a matter for ecclesiastical law, but a deep-seated reverence for a seal served to adjourn some difficult questions which otherwise must have come before the king's courts. A natural person is bound by his seal; he has himself to blame if some one else, at all events some one whom he has trusted, puts his seal to a bad use. So with the church. If Brother Walter, the sacrist of St. Edmunds, gets hold of the seal which usually hangs beside the holy bier and therewith seals a bond for forty marks to Benedict the Jew of Norwich, there is nothing for an enraged abbot to do but to depose Brother Walter. It would seem that normally the abbot kept the seal and thus could bind the house. In 1321 it was said that many a priory in England had no common seal; the prior's seal served all purposes. A remarkable attempt was made by Edward I and his barons to protect the house against the abbot, not so much in the interest of the monks, as in the interest of pious founders, who saw their good intentions

---

[16] Bracton's best passage about this matter runs as follows: "If an abbot, prior, or other collegiate men demand land or an advowson or the like in the name of their church on the seisin of their predecessors, they say, 'And whereof such an abbot was seised in his demesne etc.' They do not in their count trace a descent from abbot to abbot, or prior to prior, nor do they mention the abbots or priors intermediate [between themselves and him on whose seisin they rely], *for in colleges and chapters the same body endures for ever,* although all may die one after the other, and others may be placed in their stead; just as with flocks of sheep, the flock remains the same though the sheep die; nor does one succeed to another by right of succession as when a right descends heritably, *for the right always belongs to the church and the church is permanent:* and this one sees in charters, where the gift is made first and foremost to God and such a church, and only in a secondary way to the monks or canons.

brought to naught and the fruits of their donations sent across the sea to the profit of the alien. The common seal, said the Statute of Carlisle (1307), was to remain in the custody of the prior and four discreet inmates of the house and be laid up in safety under the privy seal of the abbot. This statute should be famous, for it was one of the very few illustrations that Coke could give of his doctrine that a statute may be void for unreasonableness; and certainly it would seem that in 1449 the court took upon itself to call this statute void, partly because it was self-contradictory (for how can one use a seal at all if it is always locked up?) but also "because if the statute were observed every common seal might be defeated by a mere surmise which could not be the subject of a trial." From this we may gather that the statute had little effect.

The canonists had by this time much to say about the manner in which legal acts can be done by or on behalf of corporations aggregate. They had a theory of duly convened meetings, and a theory of the powers of majorities. The most noticeable point in their doctrine is that the will of the *universitas* was expressed, not necessarily by the *maior pars conventus,* but by the *maior et sanior pars.* Presumably the major was also the saner part, but an opening was given for dissentients to represent to the rulers of the church (for after all an *ecclesia particularis* was but a member of the *ecclesia universalis*) that the resolution of the majority was not the will of the church. Much of this learning about corporate acts must have been fairly well known to many educated Englishmen, including some of the king's judges, and must have been frequently discussed in the chapterhouses, for chapters were quarrelsome and the last word about their quarrels could be said by Italian lawyers. But the influence of all this doctrine upon English temporal law was as yet indirect and subtle and we have not the knowledge that would enable us to trace it.

It is in no wise strange that the English lawyers of this age had not as yet brought the ecclesiastical and the temporal corporations under one heading; so different were they. This we see at once when we have asked the question "What temporal groups of men are there which can have any claim to be corporate?" and have answered it by saying "Chiefly counties, hundreds, townships, manors, cities and boroughs, in a word (since we can coin

no better term) *land communities*." The church, the religious
order, the hospital, exists for a definite purpose: for the honour
of a patron saint, the defence of the Holy Land, the relief of
lepers. The ideal person has a permanent ideal will expressed in
the rule of St. Benedict or in some foundation charter. But for
what purpose do townships and boroughs exist? Where is the
permanent will of a city to be found? Again, the group of monks
or canons is a voluntary society; of their own free choice and by
a definite act men become members of chapters or convents; but,
at least normally, the member of a township can hardly be said to
have chosen to be a member; it may be that he has inherited a
tenement; it may be that he has bought one; but even in the latter
case the main thing that he bought was a tenement, not a place
in a community. In these respects the chapters and convents
stood nearer to our modern joint-stock companies than to the
medieval boroughs. The company is a voluntary society and has
a definite aim expressed in its memorandum and articles. But the
township or the borough has come into being no one knows
when, and exists no one knows why.

Bracton seems to feel—to feel perhaps rather than to know—
that among these communities a line should be drawn, that cities
and boroughs display some phenomenon, some degree of organic
unity, that is not to be found in the open country, that the civic
or burghal community is no mere community but an *universitas
civium vel burgensium*. But at this point we must for a while
break off our discussion. The question whether and in what sense
these land communities or some of them deserve to be called
corporate units can only be approached after we have examined
their structure and functions, and to this examination we must
devote another chapter. Only at its end and, it is to be feared,
after many digressions, can we return to the person who is not a
man. That person, if he exists, is implicated in a system of local
self-government.

The King and the Crown

The legal position of the king has been fully discussed by
historians of our constitution, and on the province which they
have made their own we do not intend to trespass. Nor do we

think that a chapter on the law of persons is the proper place in which to collect all or nearly all that can be said of the king. Still there is a question concerning him to which we are naturally led by what we have recently said about "fictitious" persons: Is the king merely a natural person, or does the law see beside or behind the natural Henry or Edward some non-natural, ideal person, some "corporation sole"?

In the sixteenth century our lawyers will use mystical language of the king. At times they will seem bent on elaborating a creed of royalty which shall take no shame if set beside the Athanasian symbol. The king has a body corporate in a body natural and a body natural in a body corporate. They can dispute as to whether certain attributes which belong to the king belong to him in his natural or in his politic capacity. Some of their grandiose phrases may be due to nothing better than a desire to stand well with the reigning prince; some of their subtle distinctions may be due to that love of mystery which is natural to us all; nevertheless we must allow that there were real difficulties to be solved, and that the personification of the kingly office in the guise of a corporation sole was in the then state of the law an almost necessary expedient for the solution of those difficulties. Also we might show that if, on the one hand, this lawyerly doctrine was apt to flatter the vanity of kings, it was, on the other hand, a not very clumsy expression of those limits which had gradually been set to the king's lawful power and that it served to harmonize modern with ancient law. But we are now to deal with ancient times, in particular with the thirteenth century. The metaphysical king, the corporation sole, does not yet exist; the difficulties which are met by his creation are only beginning to arise.

In the first place, let us notice that a great deal can be done without any personification of the kingly office. The mere amount of the business that is performed in the king's name but without his knowledge does not demand any such feat of jurisprudence as the creation of a new person. The ordinary law of agency is equal to the occasion. To this we may add that the gulf between the king and the greatest of his subjects is by no means so wide as it will afterwards become. A great prelate or a palatine earl will like the king have many high placed officers, stewards, chancellors, treasurers and the like, who will do many acts in his name, judicial acts and governmental acts, of which in all probability he will hear no word.

Then again, the rights of the king are conceived as differing from the rights of other men rather in degree than in kind. At the beginning of Edward I's reign this is expressed by lawyers in their common saying, "The king is prerogative." As yet the term *prerogative* is hardly used except in this adjectival manner. It suggests to us that the king has the rights which are given to others by the ordinary law, but that we are likely to find that each particular right is intensified when it is the king's; the usual definition of it is exceeded, "for the king is prerogative." For example, he has the rights of a feudal lord to wardships and marriages, but in his case these rights are augmented. If the whole law were written down, we should not be sent to one great chapter of it to learn the law of the kingship; rather we should see at the end of every proposition of private law or procedural law some note to the effect that this proposition must be modified before it is applied to the king's case. "Prerogativity" is exceptionality.[17]

Such is the general conception; and, turning to particulars, we shall usually see that the king's rights can be brought under it. He has hardly a power for which an analogy can not be found elsewhere. If he holds a court of his tenants in chief, his barons will do the like; if he asks an aid from them, they will ask an aid from their knights; if he tallages his demesne land, they can exercise a similar right. It is with difficulty that they are restrained from declaring war. If he prosecutes criminals, this is because his peace has been broken, and other lords are often proceeding against offenders who have done them "shame and damage" by breaking their peace. In pardoning a criminal, the king only waives his rights, and he can not waive the rights of others; he cannot prevent a private prosecutor from urging an appeal of felony.

The kingly power is a mode of *dominium;* the ownership of

---

[17] Year Book 20–21 Edw. I p. 57: "*Mes yl ne tendy nul averement pur le Roy, pur coe ke le Roy sy est prerogatyf*"; p. 69 "*Le Roy est prerogatif; par quey nul prescripcion de tens ne court encontre ly*"; p. 112 "You can not, in this writ of right, demand on the seisin of Kings Richard and John and Henry, in such wise that if one fail, you may hold to the others." "Sir, we can, for the king is prerogative." . . .

a chattel, the lordship, the tenancy, of lands, these also are modes of *dominium*. We may argue backwards and forwards between the kingly right and the rights of private landholders. This is the more remarkable in the case of inheritance, for, as is well known, the notion that the kingship is in some sort elective is but slowly dying. For all this, the king is conceived to hold his lands by a strict hereditary right, and between his lands and the kingship it would be hard to distinguish. This is the way in which King Edward asserts his title to land in Lincolnshire: "Richard my ancestor was seised thereof in his demesne as of fee, and from the said Richard, because he died without an heir of his body, the right descended to a certain King John as his brother and heir, and from him to King Henry as his son and heir, and from the said Henry to me as his son and heir." Such a declaration may seem strange, for nothing is said of Arthur, and in Edward I's day the ordinary law of inheritance would have preferred Arthur to John. But this brings out another point: We may argue from the whole kingdom to each acre of land. The problem which was opened by the death of Richard was at that time an unsolved question—primogenitary rules were as yet new—Glanvill did not know how it should be answered. John obtained the crown. This was a precedent in favour of the uncle against the nephew, and as such it was treated by Bracton in the case of private inheritances. The nephew may have the better right, but if the uncle is the first to take possession, the nephew can not succeed in an action "because of the king's case." In Edward I's day lawyers know that there is something odd in the king's pedigree: we must not argue about it. Still the descent of the crown was not so unique a phenomenon then as it is now-a-days. No one, it may be, would have proposed to divide England among several co-heiresses, and we can not say with certainty that a woman could have inherited the crown; but the question whether the county of Chester was partible had lately been treated as open, while in Scotland not only was the crown claimed for the Maid of Norway, but Bruce and Hastings urged that the kingdom was divisible and should be divided between them and Balliol.[18]

---

[18] Bruce at one turn in the argument asserted "*quod mulier regnare non debt, quia officium regiminis exercere non potest.*" The theory that the kingdom was partible was but the second string to his bow. At another

Even if we find that the king has some unique rights, rights for which analogies will be sought in vain, still they are rights that a natural person can exercise. Thus the royal lawyers are bent on establishing the doctrine that all justiciary powers are derived from the king. In terms made familiar by the canonists, they assert that the king is the "judge ordinary" of the whole realm and that all others who administer justice are "judges delegate." They have difficulty enough in making good this assertion in the teeth of feudal claims; but, when it is made, it does not attribute justiciary powers to a fictitious person, it attributes them to a real Henry or Edward. Bracton is in earnest when he says that, were the king strong enough, he would do all justice in person. Far distant is the thought that the king may not sit as the active president of his own court. King Henry sits there and important cases will be adjourned if he be not present. Justices have been fined for proceeding in the king's absence. There is something anomalous in the ascription to a king of powers that he may not lawfully exercise in person, something which may suggest that our "king" is rather a figment of the law than a man; but that a man should be able to do by delegate what he may do himself if he pleases—there is nothing strange in that. Then again, the doctrine that the king's will can only be expressed by formal documents, sealed, or signed and countersigned, does not belong to the twelfth or thirteenth centuries. On the contrary, the king's will expressed by word of mouth is more potent than any writ.

The rule which in later times will be expressed by the phrase "The king can do no wrong" causes no difficulty. That you can neither sue nor prosecute the king is a simple fact, which does not require that we shall invest the king with any non-natural attributes or make him other than the sinful man that he is. The king can do wrong; he can break the law; he is below the law, though he is below no man and below no court of law. It is quite conceivable that he should be below a court of law. In the second half of the century some lawyers are already arguing that this is or ought to be the case. What is more, a pious legend of Westminster Hall tells how "in ancient times every writ of right

---

turn he asserted that the ordinary rules of inheritance were inapplicable and that the canons for the inheritance of a kingdom should be found in "the law of nature."

droiturel or possessory lay against the king." The lawyer who said this in Edward I's day was careful to leave the ancient times indefinite; probably he was referring to the good old days of the Confessor and, like Blackstone after him, saw "our Saxon ancestors" impleading each other by writs of entry. But the legend grew, and, as legends will, became more definite. In the middle of the fourteenth century the common belief was that down to the time of Edward I the king could be sued like a private person, and a judge said that he had seen a writ beginning with *Praecipe Henrico Regi Angliae*. If he had seen anything of the kind, it was some joke, some forgery, or possibly some relic of the Barons' War. About this matter there should be no doubt at all. Bracton, no mere text writer, but an experienced judge of the highest court, says plainly that writs do not run against the king. "Our lord the king can not be summoned or receive a command from any one"—this comes from a judgment of the king's court in 1234. "Our court is not above us and can not summon nor compel us against our will"—this comes from a writ tested by Hubert de Burgh in 1223. This positive evidence is strong; the negative evidence is overwhelming. If Henry III had been capable of being sued, he would have passed his life as a defendant. In the opinion of many of his subjects he was for ever breaking the law. Plea rolls from his reign there are plenty, and in the seventeenth century they were jealously scanned by eyes which did not look kindly upon kings. Where are the records of cases in which King Henry issued writs against himself? We can not but believe that *Praecipe Henrico Regi* is what Francis Bacon called it, an old fable. To this must be added that the king has power to shield those who do unlawful acts in his name, and can withdraw from the ordinary course of justice cases in which he has any concern. If the king disseises *A* and transfers the land to *X*, then *X* when he is sued will say that he can not answer without the king, and the action will be stayed until the king orders that it shall proceed. So if the king's bailiff is charged with a disseisin done in the king's name, the justices will indeed take a verdict about the facts, but they will give no judgment *Rege inconsulto*. Still all this "prerogativity" is compatible with humanity, and when the king appears as a plaintiff or submits to be treated as a defendant the difference between him and a private person is less marked in the thirteenth century then it is in later times. When he is a plaintiff he will often employ one of the ordinary writs. A defendant, instead of using what even in Bracton's day was becoming the proper formula "I can not answer without the king," will sometimes boldly say "I vouch the king to warranty." "In the pleadings and proceedings of the king's suits," exclaims Bacon, "what a garland of prerogatives doth the law put upon them!" This garland is not woven all at once and some of its flowers were but buds in the days of Henry III. But our main point must be that there is as yet little in the law of procedure to suggest that the king is other than a natural person, nothing to suggest that he has two capacities. He enjoys the same privileges whether the matter under discussion is what we should call "an act of state" or whether it is a private bargain. And, after all, the grandest of his immunities is no anomaly. He can not be compelled to answer in his own court, but this is true of every petty lord of every petty manor; that there happens to be in this world no court above his court is, we may say, an accident.

Then again, no line is drawn, at least no marked line, between those proprietary rights which the king has as king and those which he has in his private capacity. The nation, the state, is not personified; there are no lands which belong to the nation or to the state. The king's lands are the king's lands; the king's treasure is the king's treasure: there is no more to be said. True that a distinction is made between "the ancient demesne of the crown" and lands that have come to the king by modern title. The main import of this distinction is to be found in the strong sentiment— it is rather a sentiment than a rule of law—that the ancient demesne should not be given away, and that, if it be given away, some future king may resume it. But even here private law affords or has afforded an analogy. It is only of late years, only since Glanvill wrote, that a tenant in fee simple has been able utterly to disappoint his expectant heirs by alienating his land; his power over land which he himself has purchased has been greater than his power over lands which have descended to him and which constitute the ancient demesne of his family. The king, who asserts a right to revoke the improvident grants of his ancestors, is relying on an antique rule of family law, rather than upon any such doctrine as that kings are trustees for the nation. The idea that a man may hold land or goods in two different capacities is not easily formed.

We may see this even in the ecclesiastical region. Though here the personality of the saint or of the church makes the distinction easier, still in age after age people find much difficulty in marking off office from property, and in separating the lands and goods which a man enjoys or uses because he is the ruler of a church from those which, as we should say, belong to him in his private capacity. On the one hand, it is hard to prevent the ecclesiastical benefice from becoming hereditary. On the other hand, it is not readily admitted that a bishop or a parson can have property which is in no sense the property of his church. This difficulty it is which provides an excuse for that interference by the king with the goods of dead bishops, which historians are too apt to treat as sufficiently explained by mere rapacity. An abuse we are willing to call it, but there is an excuse for it. On the death of the bishop, the king is guardian of the temporalities of the church; the dead bishop's goods are the goods of the church.[19] This idea is well brought out by what is told of St. Hugh of Lincoln. He did not approve the new custom that bishops should make wills. Still he consented to make one lest otherwise his goods should be seized by the king. Evidently the saintly bishop thought that his goods were his church's goods; he made a will in order to defeat, if possible, the all too logical, if impious, deduction which kings were ready to draw from this pious doctrine. King Stephen had to promise that he would not interfere with the testaments of the bishops, and that, on the death of a bishop intestate, his goods should be distributed for the benefit of his soul by the counsel of the church; but then he was also making something very like a renunciation of his right to a profitable guardianship of the temporalities of the vacant see. His successors seize the goods of intestate bishops and expect bishops to apply for a licence if they want to make wills. When Archbishop Roger of York died in 1182, Henry II enjoyed a windfall of £11,000, to say nothing of the spoons and salt-cellars. A very just retribution, says the dean of St. Paul's, and quotes from his Digest "*quod quisque*

---

[19] This notion begets the *ius spolii, droit de dépouilles,* of continental law.

iuris in alterum statuerit, uti debet eodem iure," for this Roger had obtained a papal bull enabling him to seize the goods of any clerk in his diocese who, even though he made a testament, did not before his death distribute his goods with his own hands. The pope was just as bad as the king in this matter. In 1246 he proclaimed that the goods of all intestate clerks belonged to him, though in the next year he retired from an indefensible position. No doubt the canonists could distinguish well enough between the property of the church and the property of the prelate; still we can see that this is a lawyerly distinction; a saintly bishop, like Hugh of Lincoln, will scout it in the interest of his church, a covetous bishop will make light of it in the interest of himself and his kinsfolk, a needy king will know how and when it can be profitably ignored.

If these things be done without the ecclesiastical sphere where dead saints still are active, where the canon law with its Roman traditions prevails, what may we not expect in the temporal sphere? Far easier for us is it to personify a church which actually holds the body, and is guarded by the soul, of the saint, than to personify a nation, a state. No medieval king is tempted to say "I am the state," for *"Ego sum status"* would be nonsense. On the other hand, no one will say to him "This land, though it may be called your land, is really the land of the state." And so the king's land is the king's land and there is no more to be said about it. It should be remembered that in our fully developed common law the king, or crown, is the only corporation sole of a lay kind. The temporal law of the thirteenth century will aid us with no analogy if we would distinguish between the king's private property and his official property. Often enough has office become property, or rather (for this we believe to be nearer the truth) rights which older and vaguer law had regarded as half official, half proprietary, have become definitely proprietary. Earldoms and serjeanties belong to this category; but we can not distinguish between the lands which the earl has as earl and those which he has as man. On the other hand, those offices which have not fallen into this category do not comprise or carry with them any proprietary rights of any kind. The shrievalty is an office, but the sheriff as sheriff has no lands, no goods.[20] What is more, trusteeship, at all events a permanent trusteeship, is as yet unknown to the law and can supply us with no analogy. No form of legal thought that is at our disposal will enable us to separate the lands of the nation from the lands of the king.

But at least, it will be urged, the king can not devise the kingdom by his will. No, but the general law is that a landowner can not devise his land by his will: only God can make an heir, not man. And, after all, this impotence of the king has not been very clearly demonstrated. If standing in the thirteenth century we ask why on the Conqueror's death Rufus became king of the English, while Robert became duke of the Normans, it is not plain that there is any better answer forthcoming than that the Conqueror, like other lords who had lands on both sides of the sea, partitioned his estates among his sons. But, as already said, the fact that land can not be devised by testament is a sufficient reply to any who would draw distinctions between kingdoms and other estates. Moreover in the middle of the thirteenth century it is by no means so clear as a patriotic Englishman might wish it to be that the king of England does not hold his kingdom of the pope at an annual rent by virtue of John's surrender and Innocent's regrant. And, as we saw above, if the king ought to consult his barons before he grants away any large tract of his kingdom, common opinion has expected that a great baron will consult his men, or at least profess to consult them, before he makes large grants out of his honour. As to the king's treasure, it is the king's treasure and he may do what he pleases with it, though very likely his successor may find an excuse for disregarding some or all of his bequests. Edward III, in his will, draws a marked distinction between the debts that he owes as a private person and the debts that he owes as a king; his executors are to pay the former, while the latter will fall upon his heir and successor. We shall hardly find such a distinction in earlier times.

---

20 We make our nearest approach to the personification of a temporal office when some officer attempts to prescribe for fees or perquisites. In 7 Edw. I a castellan of Bamborough is charged with holding certain pleas which, according to general law, belong to the sheriff. He replies, "I found the said castle seised of this custom." Here Bamborough castle is personified. But this is not a fruitful idea.

As yet no king has succeeded to another without there being an interregnum. In the case that is just happening when we make our survey this interregnum is very short. Edward I far away in the Holy Land began to reign on the day, not of his father's death, but of his father's funeral.[21] But there is here no legal fiction, nothing that demands any mysterious phrase about the king's immortality. Edward I really reigns, before he is crowned, and Edward II will really reign so soon as his father has ceased to breathe. There is less excuse here for a fiction than there is in the case of a bishop; also there are fewer materials ready to the hand of the constructive lawyer. The bishop's throne must be vacant at least for a few days, and meanwhile the eternally infant church has other guardians, a guardian of its temporalities, a guardian of its spiritualities. But looking back a little way to cases in which there has been an interregnum of considerable duration, we see that lawyers have not been prepared to stop the gap with a metaphysical king, the personified kingship. When the king dies, his peace dies, and there is no king's peace until another king is crowned. The king then who has a peace is a mortal man. The evil consequences of this principle may have been somewhat lessened by a proclamation of the peace of one who, though he is not yet king of England, is by hereditary right lord of England. Still such a shift tells us that the only king known to the law is a natural person.[22]

A case has lately occurred which, so we may think, must have put the old theory of the kingship to a severe strain. A child but nine years old was crowned. The coronation of Henry III was an important event. It was, if we may so speak, a two-edged event. On the one hand, it confirmed the doctrine of pure hereditary right; it applied to the kingship the common land law. On the other hand, it showed that a king capable of ruling was no necessity; all that a king could do might be done by a regent and

---

[21] Henry died late on Wednesday. Edward's peace was proclaimed in Westminster Hall early on Thursday. But he dates his reign from the next Sunday, on which day his father was buried and the magnates took the oath of fealty.

[22] In John's day an appellor alleges a crime committed during the late interregnum but after "the peace of the King then Duke of Normandy and Lord of England" had been sworn.

a council in the name of an infant. How William Marshall became "*rector regis et regni*" is in this context a question of no great interest. There was a grave national crisis; there was civil war; a foreign enemy was in the land. Those barons who had not rejected John did the obvious thing, chose the obvious man as their leader. It was not a time for constitutional dissertations. What happened during Henry's minority is of greater significance. In litigation which touches royal rights the ordinary rule of private law is applied. An action for land is brought; the person in possession alleges that the king is his warrantor; the action must remain in suspense until the king is of full age. Then, when Henry was of full age, he insisted that all charters granted in his name during his minority required confirmation, even the Great Charter and the Forest Charter. He did this we are told by the advice of Hubert de Burgh. To exclaim against his faithlessness, his greed, his imprudence, is far easier than to discover any then admitted principle of law which would condemn him. Suppose that his guardians have improvidently alienated some piece of his demesne land, is he not to have the ordinary right which every infant enjoys on attaining his majority?[23] Donations, we might say, are one thing, laws another, and *Magna Carta* is a code of laws. But where and how could the line be drawn? In form the Great Charter was a charter, and between it and the mere gift of single knight's fee there was a long and gently graduated series of charters granting "liberties" of various kinds to individuals and to larger or smaller classes of men. A claim to revoke what is in fact a body of general laws is one which will set men thinking, and may lead them in the end to some mystical dogma such as that the king is never under age; but no such dogma has as yet been fashioned. The king of the thirteenth century is a natural person and may be "under disability."

In course of time we see the beginnings of a doctrine of public or official capacities. Lanfranc hints at it when he suggests that the Conquerer, though he may not arrest the bishop of Bayeux,

---

[23] The king of Scots petitions for a wardship, urging in his favour something that happened during the minority. Henry's council replies that this happened "*tempore Huberti de Burgo Comitis Kantiae qui amicus fuit et familiaris ipsi Regi Scotiae et qui regnum Angliae habuit in manu sua.*" Therefore it is of no avail.

may lawfully arrest the earl of Kent. Some progress has been
made before the end of the thirteenth century. In a carefully
worded judgment our king's court declares that the bishop of
Durham "has a double status, to wit, a temporal and a spiritual
status." The archbishop of York has excommunicated the bishop
for imprisoning some of his metropolitan's men. But to imprison
men belongs to the bishop's temporal status. Therefore the archbishop has excommunicated not his suffragan bishop but the
king's tenant in chief and must pay a fine. A still more interesting
case concerns King Edward himself. He in his father's lifetime
was holding the vill of Stamford and was exercising in it the
franchise known as the return of writs. He granted the vill to the
earl of Warenne. Having become king, he demanded by what
warrant the earl claimed the franchise. The earl replied "By your
own gift; you gave me all that you had in Stamford." The king's
counsel then pleads that Edward himself had no title to the
franchise, and that, being king, he is bound to resume all rights
unlawfully detached from the crown, even though he himself,
while as yet no king, was the guilty person. "He is now of another estate than he was then and is *quasi* another person." The
earl combats this theory—"He is one and the same person that
he was when he made the gift." Judgment is given for the king.
Thus the idea of dual personality may already prevail when the
king relies upon it. To enforce it when it would tell against his
interests would be a harder task. And as yet this idea looks very
new. If there is to be a personification, something material, something as visible as a church, must be personified.

We can see the beginnings, but only the beginnings, of a process which personifies the king's "crown." And here it may be
remarked that even in our own day this process has never gone
so far as to modify the formal language of our law. Of course
lawyers and judges and even statutes have now for a long time
spoken of the rights of the Crown, have spoken of the Crown
as doing this, that, and the other act. Still in the strictest language of the law, the language of pleading, the Crown does nothing; it does not sue, it does not prosecute; the king or queen does
it all. A personification of the crown has been required, not so
much by any purely "juristic necessities," as by constitutional
doctrines which, though they may now-a-days be as well observed

as any laws could be, are none the less no laws. Under the cover of the crown—that "metaphor kept in the Tower," as Tom Paine called it—our slow revolution is accomplishing itself. In the thirteenth century this golden circlet is beginning to be useful. We first hear talk of it when crimes are committed, not only against the king's peace, but also against "his crown and dignity." Then we hear of rights which are inseverably annexed to the crown; they indeed make the crown, for the king's crown is to do justice and keep the peace. This is pleasant doctrine for the king, if it is also a sound doctrine for the state; it enables him to resume "liberties" which have been alienated from the crown and check the growth of seignorial justice. In the fourteenth century it is possible to say that the crown, like a church, is always under age and that no lapse of time will bar the demands of this *quasi* infant. But as yet to distinguish between the crown and the king, between the king and the man, is to teach a treasonable doctrine. In Edward II's day that doctrine becomes prominent and charges of holding it are bandied to and fro. The barons who are leagued against one of the king's favourites, Piers Gaveston, are said to hold that allegiance is due rather to the crown than to the person of the king. A few years afterwards the barons who are leagued against another of the king's favourites, the younger Despenser, accuse him of having held this very doctrine, and, owing to their success, it becomes for all time, to use Coke's phrase, "a damnable and damned opinion." But all this lies in the future.

We are not contending that the proprietary theory of the kingship—if we may give that name to the doctrine which we have been endeavouring to expound—is the most ancient theory, or that it ever fully expresses all the facts and thoughts and feelings which determine what a king shall be and what a king shall do. Probably there has been a one-sided development of those elements in the ancient ideas which have been found capable of legal treatment, while other elements have been forgotten or extruded from the sphere of law. The Conquest of England, the strong monarchy, the tyranny (if we please to call it so) which was founded by the Norman kings, have favoured those and only those notions which exalt the king and give him a property in his kingdom. Still the phenomenon in question is not purely English and can not be explained without reference to the history of jurisprudence. The elements in the old tribal kingship which survived in the struggle for existence were those which in the then state of legal thought were capable of being accurately expressed and defined. For vague thoughts, for half thoughts, the lawyer can find no place. What, for example, is he to make of a title to the crown which is partly hereditary, partly elective? The elective element can not be developed, for no one can define who are the electors, no one as yet has rules about the powers of majorities. Therefore the elective element must perish or become a mere form. And so with the king's lands. Either they belong to him or they belong to some other person or persons. Say for a moment that they belong to the nation, how can such a doctrine be enforced when as yet we have no idea, or but the vaguest idea of official capacities, of trusteeship, or corporations aggregate and corporations sole? We do not wish to prejudge any debatable questions of early English history, but that men had clear ideas about these matters in the tenth century and lost them during the twelfth and thirteenth, those ages of brilliant intellectual progress, is not easily to be believed. The one general result to which we come at the end of this long and variegated chapter is that even in Bracton's day the number of legal ideas is very small and public law has hardly an idea of its own.

BIOGRAPHICAL NOTES

RUDOLF HUEBNER (1864–1945) taught and wrote at Rostock University, Germany (where he also served as rector), specializing in medieval German history and law. He edited the *Historical Sources of the Frankish Period* (2 vols.; 1891–1893), and an encyclopedia of historical theory and methodology, *Historik*, originated by J. G. Droysen.

MAXIME MAXIMOVICH KOVALEVSKY (1851–1916) was both a historian and an anthropologist who studied in Germany and France as well as in Russia. He has written on the evolution of rights concerning the family and land in Russia, the Caucasus, England, and Switzerland among others. His chief works include *Communal Landholding, Causes, Course of Its Decline* (1879), *Historico-Comparative Method in Jurisprudence* (1880), *Law and Custom in the Caucasus* (1887), *Evolution of the Family and of Property* (1890), and *Modern Custom and Ancient Law in Russia* (1890).

FREDERIC WILLIAM MAITLAND (1850–1906) combined a mastery of both law and history in his teaching and publications. He taught English Law at Cambridge University from 1884, holding a chair in that subject, and was offered, but refused, a chair in History (the Regius Professorship) in 1902. His most important writings are *The History of English Law* (written in collaboration with Frederick Pollock, 1889), *Domesday Book and Beyond, Three Essays in the Early History of England* (Cambridge University Press, 1910; reprinted 1960), and the *Collected Papers,* H. A. L. Fisher, ed. (3 vols.; Cambridge University Press, 1911). Maitland unfortunately suffered from ill health in his later years, which cut down his productivity and shortened his life.

FREDERICK POLLOCK (1845–1937) was educated at Cambridge University and after a brief period as a practicing barrister gave himself wholly to writing and teaching of law. He was

Professor of Jurisprudence first at the University of London, then at Oxford, where he succeeded to Sir Henry Maine's chair. His interests were exceedingly wide and his industry prodigious, for he published textbooks for students on Contract, Possession, Methods of Jurisprudence, etc.; he wrote a *Life of Spinoza;* he edited the *Law Quarterly Review* and *Law Reports* for many years. His *History of the Science of Politics* (1890) is far from outdated. He published on other questions ranging from *The League of Nations* (1920) to Natural Law.

FREDERIC SEEBOHM (1833–1912) was primarily a historian, having turned to that field from legal practice and banking. His early works dealt with *The Oxford Reformers* (1867) and *The Era of the Protestant Revolution* (1874). His later works dealt with the history of land right and the law: *The English Village Community* (1883), *The Tribal System in Wales* (1895), *Tribal Custom in Anglo-Saxon Law* (1902), the posthumous *Customary Acres* (1914).

PAUL GAVRILOVICH VINOGRADOFF (1854–1925) came under the influence of Vasily Kliuchevsky and Theodor Mommsen in his formative period. He lectured in history at the University of Moscow, where his earliest publications were on feudal Italy and England. He maintained a liberal policy in tsarist Russia, both at the University and in politics, which caused him to leave and establish himself in England, in close association with Maitland. His major works include *Villeinage in England* (1892), *The Growth of the Manor* (1905), *English Society in the Eleventh Century* (1908), *Outlines of Historical Jurisprudence* (2 vols.; 1920–1922). His *Collected Papers* (3 vols.; 1928) were issued by Oxford University.

INDEX

Abbots and abbeys, 316–317, 320–321
Accruer by survivorship, 179
Adoption, 239–240
Æthelbert, quoted, 312
Æthelric, 186 n.
Æthelstan, King, 176
Alfred, King, 186
Alien law, corporation theory of, 291
  doctrine of, 294–296
Ancestor worship, 149
Ancestors, 186 n., 219, 227–228
Anglo-Saxon laws, 68–69, 99, 184–185, 197
Anglo-Saxon society, 176
Anthropology, early law and, 9
  law and, 10–12
  in historical jurisprudence, 3–5
Antiquities of family law, 173–193
Aristotle, quoted, 59
Associations, without bond of vicinage, 274–278
  convivial, religious, and scientific, 275–277
  industrial, 274–275
  political, 277–278
  classification of, 250–253
  corporate and proper, 285–289
  German law of, 285–299
  mark- (see Mark-associations)
  neighborhood, 264–267
  agricultural, 264–266
  developed under law of water and mining, 266
  transportation, 266–267
  significance of, 249–250
Austrian Civil Code, 248
Azo, 307, 309

Bachofen, J. J., 14–15
Balliol, John, 218–219 n., 221
Balzer, O., Professor, 127
Baptism, 241–242
Bastards, inheritance by, 228–229
Beaulieu, Anatole Leroy, quoted, 167–168
Beaumanoir, Philippe de, 24–25
Bell, H. E., 16
Beowulf, 54–55, 82, 100–112
Bereford, J., quoted, 210 n.
Berwick, Sir John, 24
Beseler, H., 297
Betrothal, 141–142, 145, 149, 153
Betrothal contract, 141–145, 153
Birth, 239
  proof of, 240–241
  registry of, 242
Birth-rights, 181–182, 188
Bishops, 317–319, 329
Blackstone, William, 50, 217, 222 n., 327
Blood-feud group, 175
Blood-feuds, 66–67, 82–83, 90, 100–112, 174–175, 191
  gold compensation in place of, 68–70
Blood fines (see Galanas)
Blood relationship, 223–227
  (See also Half-blood; Kinship)
Bogišić, V., 125, 150, 159
  quoted, 149
Bondsmen, 48–49
Boniface VIII, 22
Book-land, 33–37, 41–42, 186–187
Borough English, 212
Bracton, Henry, 24, 29, 178 n., 202, 207, 210, 212, 218 n., 221 n., 223–224, 227–228, 246, 307, 309–311, 322, 326, 336
  quoted, 320 n., 327

Britton, 210, 218 n., 221 n., 224
Bruce, A., 198, 218 n.–219 n., 325

Caesar, quoted, 254
Canon Law, 21–24, 245, 293–294, 330
Canonists, 22–24, 307–308, 315, 321
Carlisle, Statute of, 321
Catholic Church, 21
Celts, relationship among, 62–63
Ceolfrith, Abbot, 185 n.
Charters, 333
Chayes, Abram, 235
Chieftains, 76–77
    payment of food-rents to, 84–90
    and succession, 109, 112
Children, dependence of, 157
    marriageable, protection of, 151
Christianity, 159, 176, 190, 310
Chronicle of Nestor, 158
Church, the, 309
    Catholic, 21
    marriage and, 151–152
    State and, 294–295
    (See also Churches)
Church lands, 310–313, 316–319
    hereditary, 329–330
Churches, corporations and, 300–322
    as persons, 313–314
Clans, 63–66, 74, 176–177
Cnut, 194 n.
Code Civil, 242–244, 248
Co-heirs and co-heiresses, 179, 187, 197–198, 206–209, 282–284
Coke, Edward, 321
    quoted, 335
"Collective hand," communities of, 278–285, 289–290
Commercial law, medieval, 27
"Common appendant," theory of, 45
Common land, 34, 43–46
Common law, 24–25, 27, 29, 211, 214 n.
Compurgation, 74
Communities, family, 117
    formation of, 40
    in Germanic law, 253–285
    of "collective hand," 278–285
    house, 160–161, 165

of knights, 282–284
land, 322
village, 160
Constantine, 20–22
Co-parcenary, 179, 185
Copyholds and copyholders, 47, 49–51, 212 n., 214 n.
Coquille, Guy, 170
Corporation aggregate, 315, 319
Corporation sole, 315
    king as, 323
Corporations, 232–235
    churches and, 300–322
    heads of, 305–306
    liability of, 306–307
    person and, 300–336
    personality of, 302–304, 315
Corporations, Davis, 235
Craft guilds, corporate character of, 271–272
    origin of, 267–271
Crafts, decline and disappearance of, 272–274
Custom, law and, 8–9, 11, 17–30
Customary laws, old English, 31–52
Cymric Codes, 72, 75, 78–79, 84–87, 92–96
Cymric evidence, the, 75–99
Cymric tribal society, unit of, 75–77

Davis, J. P., 235
Death, civil, 244
    claustral, 244–245
    presumptive, 246–249
De Lacy, Henry, 88
Denbigh Extent, 65, 76 n., 84, 86–87, 89, 93
Denbigh Survey, 80–81
Descendants, 193, 218–220
    (See also Heirs)
Descent, 171
    law of, 193–229
Dimetian Code, 79, 94–95
Division of Labor in Society, Durkheim, 10
Domesday Book, 66, 194–195 n., 197, 204 n., 311–313, 316–317, 319 n.
Domesday Survey and surveyors, 89, 203–204
Dominium, 324–325

Dooms, 176 *n.*, 184, 186
Dracon, law of, 61
Durkheim, Emile, 10–11

Earle, J., 100 *n.*–101
Edward I, 198, 203, 205–206, 224, 320, 327, 332
  quoted, 205–206, 325
Edward II, 224, 332, 335
Edward III, 331
Edward IV, 304, 306
Efimenko, Aleksandra, 152
Egbert, King, 185 *n.*
Eike von Repgow, 24, 237
England, common land in, 43–46
  custom and law in, 17–18, 24, 29–30
  land tenure in, 32–36, 46–52
  study of historical jurisprudence in, 3
English law, 301
  ancient, 173–193
  Anglo-Saxon, 68–69, 99, 184–185, 197
  of descent, 193–229
  of impartable succession, 210
  of inheritance (*see* Inheritance)
  of intestate succession, 182–184, 188
  old English customary, 31–52
Enslavement, 245–246
  (*See also* Slaves)

Family, 63
  agnatic, 223
  point, 117–128, 181
  law of (*see* Law, family)
  membership of, 131–132
  modern Russian, 148–170
  patriarchal (*see* Patriarchy)
  undivided, 162, 181
Father-right, 176
Fathers, land partition and, 181–182
Feoffment, 184, 195 *n.*, 202
Feudalism, 37–38, 195, 198
Feuds, 73–74, 223
  (*See also* Blood-feuds)
Ficker, Julius, 28–29
Fiefs, inheritance of, 195 *n.*–196, 198–200, 208 *n.*, 215
Fischer, H. A. L., 8
Fitz Peter, Geoffrey, 208 *n.*

Fleta, 218 *n.*, 221 *n.*, 224
Folk-land, 32, 34–35, 42
Food-rents, 84–90
Forests, 45
Fortes, Meyer, 232
France, 207 *n.*
  Code Pénal, 244
  customs and law in, 25, 29–30
  feudalism in, 195, 198–199
  inheritance in, by half-blood, 225 *n.*
  land partition in, 199–200
Frazer, James, 7, 54
Freemen, 38–39, 49
Friedrich, Paul, 114
Fustel de Coulanges, Numa Denis, 13, 16, 63

Galanas (blood fine), 82, 90–95, 98–100
  amount of, 92–95
  list of, 99
  payment of, between kindreds, 90–92
  by non-tribesmen, 98–99
Gau-marks, 256
Gautamo, 58
Cavelkind of Kent, 194, 203–206
Generations, 227
Gentes, 176, 178
  organization of, 158–159
German Civil Code, 253, 274, 298–299
Germanic law, 231, 237–299
  associational organizations in, 249–253
  of associations, alien, reception of, 291–299
  general principles of, 285–299
  legal development of, 285–299
  native, renascence of, 296–299
  communities in, 253–285
  family, 129–147
  of intestate succession, 183, 190, 192
  of marriage, 137–139
  modern, 284
  renascence of, 291–299
Germanic peoples, joint families among, 127
  mother-right among, 174
  partition of realms among, 196

Germany, blood relationship in, 227
  custom and law in, 25–26, 28,
    193
  inheritance in, 215
    by half-blood, 225 n.
    by women, 225 n.
  land distribution in, 180 n.–182,
    199 n., 215
Gierke, Otto, 9, 16, 24, 178 n., 232–
  233, 249 n., 253, 297, 315 n.
Giraldus Cambrensis, 84
Glanvill, Joseph, 29, 202, 205–
  206 n., 209 n., 221 n., 226,
  328
  quoted, 187, 200, 228–229, 325
Golden Bough, The, Frazer, 7, 54
Gratian, 22
Greece, ancient, relationship in,
  59–63
Gregory IX, 22
Guardianship, 74, 164, 177–178
Gwely (kindred group), 75–77
  constitution and working of, 77–
    82
Gwentian Code, 87, 93

Hale, M., 217, 222 n.
Half-blood, law of descent and,
  222–225
Hart, H. L. A., 15–16
Hastings, 198, 218 n., 325
Heir-land, 33–36
Heirs, 185, 187, 190–193
  expectant, 185–188
  (See also Co-heirs)
Henry II, 29, 200, 206–207 n.
Henry III, 198, 203, 207 n., 308,
  325–328, 332–333
Henry VIII, 179 n.
Henry the Pilgrim, 246
Herital fraternities, 283
Heusler, A., 178 n., 181 n.
History of English Law, Maitland,
  12–13
History of German Law, Huebner,
  12
Hoebel, E. A., 15–16
Hohfeld, W. N., 12
Homicide, liability for, under
  Cymric Codes, 82–83
House-elder, 162–164
Household, 63

law of, 113–115
  patriarchal, 143
  undivided, 158–159, 162, 165,
    169–170
Hubert de Burgh, 333
Huebner, Rudolf, 3, 11–12, 114,
  231–232, 234
  quoted, 129–147, 237–299
Hugh of Lincoln, St., 328–330

Iceland, kinship organization in,
  70–72, 74
Impartible succession, law of, 210
India, joint families in, 118–123
  kinship in, 74
Individual, land ownership by, 178–
  180
  rights of, 115
Indo-Europeans, study of legal institutions of, 5–8
Inheritance, 28, 117, 171, 174
  half-blood, 222–225
  kinship and, 215–225
  of land, 179–229
  law of, 27, 174, 182–193, **200,**
    206, 209–210, 216
  nature of, 188–189
  royal, 325
Innocent IV, 307, 314
  quoted, 308 n.
Interregnums, 332
Intestate, succession, law of, 182–
  184, 188
Ireland, 170, 209

Jaroslav, 151, 159–160
Jeaffreson, John Cordy, quoted,
  214 n.
John, King, 203, 205 n., 325, 331
John of Cobham, 205–206
Judges, 25
Juries, 24–25, 27
Jurisprudence, comparative, 14
  historical, 3–5

Kantorowicz, Ernest, 232
Kenulf, King, 194 n.
Kindred, 61–63, 70–74, 171
  feuds and, 112
  liability of, in homicide, 82–83
  marriage and, 112

payment of galanas between, 90–92
renunciation of, 73
(*See also* Kinship; Kinsmen)
Kindred group (*see* Gwely)
Kingdoms, 331
Kings, allegiance to, 335
  charters granted by, 333
  as corporation sole, 323
  crown and, 322–336
  homage to, 209
  land held by, 330
  language of, 323
  and the law, 326–328, 334
  rights of, 324–326
King's Two Bodies, The, Kantorowicz, 232
Kingship, hereditary, 196, 218, 220–221
Kinship, 28–29
  agnatic, 58–64, 70, 72, 149, 175, 221, 223
  cognatic, 58, 63
  inheritance and, 215–225
  law and, 53–55
  organization of, 57–74
  reasons for, 58
  proximity of, 215
  traced through women, 175–177
Kinsmen, blood, 220
  maternal, 175, 177
  paternal, 175
  (*See also* Kindred)
Kluchevsky (Kliuchevsky), V. O., 159
Knights, 210
  co-heir communities of, 282–284
Knight's fee, 195 *n.,* 199–202 *n.*
Kohl, J. G., 67
Kohler, Joseph, 6
Kovalevsky, Maxime, 3, 9, 12, 114–115
  quoted, 148–170
Krader, Lawrence, 232, 235 *n.*

Laen-land, 36–37
Lammas lands, 42–43
Land, 31–37, 42, 171
  church, 310–313, 316–319, 329–330
  cooperative tilling of, 176

co-ownership of, 178–179, 183, 185
  freehold, 222
  gifts of, 184–188
  grants of, 35–37
  inherited, 46–47, 49–51, 77–81, 179–229
  king's, 330
  occupation of, in parage, 197, 206, 209
  in Wales, 77
  ownership of, 33, 42, 178–180
  corporate, 178
  family, 178–184, 186, 188
  partition of, 179–182, 196–206
  purchase of, 220, 222
  and tenancy, 36–39, 46–47
Land-books, 184–185, 187 *n.*
Lanfranc, Archbishop, 333
Law, canon, 21–24, 245, 293–294, 330
  commercial, 27
  common, 24–25, 27, 29, 211, 214 *n.*
  common denominators on, 5
  custom and, 8–9, 11, 17–30
  early, anthropology and, 9
  English (*see* English law)
  family, 29, 113–115, 328
    antiquities of, 173–193
    Germanic, 129–147
  of inheritance (*see* Inheritance)
  kings and, 326–328
  kinship and, 53–55
    Anglo-Saxon, 68–69, 99
    Icelandic, 70–72
  of nature, 23, 238
  Norman, 196–197, 225 *n.*
  Roman, 17, 19–22, 247, 249, 252, 291–297
  and society, 12
Law merchant, 27
"Lawspeakers," 26–27
Legal action, capacity for, 238–239
Legal institutions of Indo-Europeans, study of, 5–8
Leges Henrici, 175, 194 *n.,* 200
Leges Willelmi, 194 *n.,* 200
Legislation, 19
Legists, 22
Leontovitch, Professor, 159
Lex Salica, 184, 192–193

Libri Feudorum, 226 *n.*
Linton, Ralph, 231
Llewellyn, K. N., 16
Lodge, Mr., 184 *n.*–185 *n.*
Louchitzky (Lushitsky), Professor, 160
Lowie, Robert H., 232

McLennan, J. F., 14
Mægð, 176–178, 184
Maid of Norway, 218, 220, 325
Maine, Sir Henry, 3, 7–9, 12–13, 148, 158, 170, 180 *n.*
    quoted, 196 *n.*
Maitland, Frederic W., 3–4, 7–9, 11–13, 29, 63, 171–172, 231–232, 234
    quoted, 173–229, 300–336
Malinowski, Bronislaw, 231
Man as holder of rights, 237–239
Manors, 46–47, 96, 232
    ancient demesne, 213
Manu, Laws of, 109, 122
Mark-associations, dissolution of, 263–264
    free, mixed, and manorial, 260–261
    legal nature of, 257–259
    old, transformation of, 261–263
    organization of, 259–260
    origin of, 255–257
Marriage, 83, 110–111, 132–136
    contracting of, 136–140, 150–155
    requisites for, 140–147
    Germanic law of, 137–139
    patriarchal, 133, 148–151
    among Prussian peasants, 150–157
Marshall, William, 227, 333
Matriarchy, 123, 148
Maurer, Georg Ludwig von, 13, 16
Miklosich, F., 67
Military tenure, 228
Minors, guardianship of, 74
Mitteis, L., 20, 291 *n.*–292 *n.*
Money rent, 204
Montfort, Simon de, 207 *n.*, 214
Morality, social, 234
Möser, Justus, 273
Mother-right, 174–176

Mothers, legal position of, 133–134
Moujik, 166–167

Nobility and knighthood, 37–40, 46–47, 50, 211–212, 214
    (*See also* Knights)
Non-tribesmen, 90
    payment of galanas by, 98–99
    treatment of, 95–99
Normandy, 198–200
    laws of, 196–197, 225 *n.*

Oath-help, renunciation of, 73
Opet, 194 *n.*
Ouspensky (Uspensky), G. I., 166–167
Outlawry, social, 243–244
Ovens, common, 89

Parage, law of, 210
    occupation of land in, 197, 206, 209
Parceners, 207, 209 *n.*–210 *n.*, 226–227
Parish lands, 44
Paterna paternis materna maternis rule, 189, 220–221
Patriarchy, 58–60, 129–131, 148, 157
    and marriage, 133, 148–151
Peasants, 213
    dependent, inheritance by, 215
    Russian, marriage among, 150–157
Person, 231–233
    church as, 313–314
    corporation and, 300–336
    definition of, 233
    juristic, 249–253
    law of, 237
    "natural," 301
Personality, 329
    of corporation, 302–304, 315
Pollock, Frederick, 3, 11–13, 18, 171
    quoted, 31–52, 173–229, 300–336
Popes and the papacy, 21–22
    (*See also* names of popes, as Innocent IV)
Post, A. H., 6
Pound, Roscoe, 12
Pravda of Jaroslav, 151, 159–160

Primogeniture, 198–201, 205–211, 213 n.–215, 229
spread of, 228
Property, public, 35
self-acquired, 122–123
Provender rents, 204
Prussian *Allgemeines Landrecht*, 248
Purchaser, definition of, 220

Radcliffe-Brown, A. R., 11, 16
Relationship, 58–63
Rent, 204
(*See also* Food-rents)
Richard Coeur de Lion, quoted, 196 n.
Rig Veda, 118
Rights, capacity for, 237–238
beginning of, 239–242
loss of, 243
of individual, 115
of kings, 324–326
man as holder of, 237–239
Roger of York, Archbishop, 329–330
Roman Empire, 19–20
Roman law, 17, 19–22, 247, 249, 252, 291–297
Rome, ancient, relationship in, 59, 63
Russia, 114–115
Christianity introduced into, 159
family organization in, 131
joint families in, 126–127
modern family in, 148–170
Russian novelists, 166–167

Saints, 329–330
as landowners, 313
Salvius Julianus, 20
Samokvosov, D. Ya., 161
Savigny, F. C. von, 8
Saxon Code, 248
Scandinavia, custom and law in, 26, 29
Scotland, crown of, 218, 220–221
law of, 226
Scott, Sir Walter, 64
Seebohm, Frederic, 3, 7, 9, 12–13, 54
quoted, 75–115

Seisin, 223, 320 n., 324 n.
Serfs and serfdom, 39–40, 46, 48–49, 95–98
(*See also* Slaves)
Servian law code, 160
Sib (*Sippe*), associational character of, 253–254
disintegration of, 254–255
origin of, 253
Slatovraczky (Zlatovratsky), Mr., 166–167
Slaves, 95, 98, 246, 250
(*See also* Serfs)
Slavs, blood-feuds among, 67
family organization among, 131
joint families among, 123–127
marriage customs of, 149
undivided households of, 158
Smith, Robertson W., quoted, 57
Socage, 203, 211
free, 228
partible, 229
Social outlawry, 243
Society, Cymric tribal, 75–99
law and, 12
and the State, 58, 64, 66
Sokemen, free, 201–203
infant, 178 n.
State, the, 250–251, 294–295, 301
modern, 238
society and, 58, 64, 66
Stephen, King, 328
Stobbe, O., 215 n.
Strangers, treatment of, 95–99
Succession, of chieftains, 109, 112
impartible, law of, 210
of kings, 218
(*See also* Kingship, hereditary)
Sutras, the, 118, 122
Swiss Civil Code, 248
new, 280, 298

Tacitus, 183, 265
Tenancy, 36–39, 46–47, 51
in common, 179
and co-parcenary, 179
by entireties, 179
joint, 179
Tenants, 204
joint, 179
women, 194, 211, 213

Tenements, freehold, 212–213
  peasant, 213, 215
  villein, 210–213
Teutons, relationships among, 59–60
Thomas Aquinas, 23
Tourgenieff (Turgenev), I. S., 166
Tref (group), 85–86
Trefgordd, 86–90
Trespass, 306
Tribes, 75–99
Trusteeship, 331

Ultimogeniture, 211–212, 214–215
Universitas, 302–303, 307, 309, 314, 322

Viability, 241–242
Villein tenements, 210–212
Villeins, 47–49, 214
Venedotian Code, 72, 78, 85, 93–94
Verrentrapp, 255 n.
Vialla, 67
Village greens, 44–45

Vinogradoff, Paul, 3–4, 7–8, 11–14, 17–18, 53–54, 113–114, 231–232
  quoted, 19–30, 57–74, 117–128

Wales, kinship organization in, 65–66, 72
  land distribution in, 180 n.
  tribal customs in, 100–112
  tribal systems in, 75–99
Walter, Archbishop Hubert, 205
Watkins, C., 212 n.
Wergeld, 177, 191, 204 n., 227 n.
Wife-abduction, 136–137
Wife-purchase, 138
William the Conqueror, 331, 333
Women, land inheritance by, 193–195, 206 n.–209, 213, 226
  (See also Co-heirs and co-heiresses; Matriarchy; Mothers)

Zlatovratsky, N. N., 166–167